WILLIAM & KATE
THE LOVE STORY

WILLIAM & KATE

THE LOVE STORY

A CELEBRATION OF THE
WEDDING OF THE CENTURY

WITH EXCLUSIVE PICTURES BY NIRAJ TANNA

ROBERT JOBSON

JOHN BLAKE

Published by John Blake Publishing Ltd
3 Bramber Court, 2 Bramber Road
London W14 9PB, England

www.johnblakepublishing.co.uk

First published in hardback in 2010
ISBN: 9781844547364

British Library Cataloguing-in-Publication Data:

A catalogue record for this book is available from the British Library.

Design by www.envydesign.co.uk

Printed and bound in the UK by CPI Mackays, Chatham, ME5 8TD

1 3 5 7 9 10 8 6 4 2

Papers used by John Blake Publishing are natural, recyclable products
made from wood grown in sustainable forests. The manufacturing processes
conform to the environmental regulations of the country of origin.

CONTENTS

ACKNOWLEDGEMENTS

My goal in writing this book was to present a serious examination of Prince William and Kate Middleton – two people whose journey together will fundamentally shape our 21st-century monarchy. I wanted to explore what makes our future King and Queen Consort tick and examine the backgrounds of these two young people and discover what cemented their love. From my research I hope to also explore what we the paying public can expect from this new royal double act. Members of the Royal Family understandably guard their privacy jealously. Therefore, telling their story has not always been straightforward. However, I believe the completed work will both enlighten and entertain you.

Of course, this book would not have been possible without the vision of my publisher John Blake – this being our third book together. Thanks too to Rosie Virgo and my editor Lucian Randall and the rest of the first-class editorial team at John Blake Publishing Ltd for producing this book at rapid speed. Editor Andy Armitage worked hard and fast to pull everything together. Special thanks too to my agent Humfrey Hunter and to photographer Niraj Tanna of Ikon Pictures for his exclusive photographs.

I am also indebted to many people without whom this book

would have been impossible to write. To preserve their privacy, some of them have asked that I keep their contribution anonymous. But they know who they are and how much I appreciate their help.

However, I am glad to acknowledge the support of the following: Miguel Head, Paddy Harverson, Colleen Harris MVO, Ailsa Anderson LVO, Lt Ed Perkins, Felicity Murdo-Smith CVO, Ryan Sabey, Dominic Herbert, Arthur Edwards MBE, Robin Nunn, HP, Ingrid Seward, Mo Davies, Elena Nachmanoff, Sigi DeVos, Ken Wharfe MVO, Laura Squire, Deborah Hinton, Jessica Hay, Richard Kay, Harry Arnold, Camilla Hitchcock of First Steps Academy, Fulham, Alexandra Hambrook for her brilliant ICT skills, Ian Walker, Mark Stewart, Jean Figg, Michael Dunlea, Kent Gavin, Lord Janvrin, Geoff Crawford, Stuart Robertson, Mark Bolland, Patrick Jephson, Dave Ofield, Jamie Lowther-Pinkerton, Stuart MacLean, James Weatherup, Tim Ewart, Tom Bradby, Neil Wallis and David Mannion and the rest of my colleagues at ITN. I would also like to thank Ian Edmondson for the original concept and for his friendship and of course my editor at the *News of the World* Colin Myler.

Last, but by no means least, I would like to thank my family, particularly my mother and late father for their love and guidance. I would also like to thank my wife for her unbelieveable patience and love and for putting up with me while I tried to finish this book at rapid speed.

For Camilla, Charles and Alexandra

'A princely marriage is the brilliant edition of a universal fact, and, as such, it rivets mankind.'
WALTER BAGEHOT (1826 – 77),
AUTHOR OF THE ENGLISH CONSTITUTION

CHAPTER 1

THE PRINCESS BRIDE

'A multitude of rulers is not a good thing.
Let there be one ruler, one king.'
HOMER, *THE ILIAD*

16 NOVEMBER 2010, ST JAMES'S PALACE, LONDON

Tightly holding the arm of the only man she had ever truly loved, Catherine Elizabeth Middleton tried her best to maintain her poise. With a beaming smile and gently leaning on her royal prince – Royal Air Force Flight Lieutenant William Wales – they looked a couple deeply in love, completely at ease with each other. He had given countless interviews in the past, usually with his younger brother Prince Harry, a natural performer in front of camera, stealing the show with one-liners and derogatory quips about his older, more considered brother.

Giving 'the boys' that experience had been part of palace strategy, to help both princes, second and third in line to the British throne, to learn the ropes of royal life as well as how to cope with the ever more demanding modern media. In the past, royals didn't do interviews – Queen Elizabeth II still hasn't after nearly 60 years on the throne – but this new generation has no choice but to do them unless it wants to seem completely out of touch.

This time William took the lead, gently guiding his bride-to-be through the minefield of her first outing before the unforgiving British press. After all, this was a new experience for Kate, but it was one that she would have to get used to. She knew her every

1

move and nuance was being scrutinised, her every word reported around the globe to millions of television viewers, who until now had seen her image only in glossy magazines and newspapers; but they were now at last hearing her voice for the first time. She was clearly nervous; who wouldn't be? But she was not about to show it. After all Miss Middleton was honed from sterner stuff.

That morning William's father, the Prince of Wales, had released a press statement that had made headlines on the 24-hour news channels around the globe. It began, 'His Royal Highness Prince William of Wales and Miss Catherine Middleton are engaged to be married.' It continued, 'The Prince of Wales is delighted to announce the engagement of Prince William to Miss Catherine Middleton.

'The wedding will take place in the spring or summer of 2011, in London. Further details about the wedding day will be announced in due course.

'Prince William and Miss Middleton became engaged in October during a private holiday in Kenya. Prince William has informed The Queen and other close members of his family. Prince William has also sought the permission of Miss Middleton's father.

'Following the marriage, the couple will live in North Wales, where Prince William will continue to serve with the Royal Air Force.'

At last the marathon courtship of the second in line to the throne, more than eight years in all, was over. Life for this handsome young couple, both 28, would never be the same again.

Prince Harry, who had been in flying training at Middle Wallop that day – the young man with whom he had suffered so many of the slings and arrows of outrageous fortune in life, not least their mother Princess Diana's death in 1997 – was the first to comment on his big brother's happy news: 'I'm delighted that my brother has popped the question! It means I get a sister, which I've always wanted.'

Back in London Kate was taking her first tentative steps in public life. 'It's obviously nerve-racking,' she admitted in a cut-class, English, public-school accent when asked whether she was excited or nervous about marrying into the Royal Family. She said the Queen had been 'welcoming', as too was her new father-in-law Prince Charles. Now, with Princess Diana's 18-carat, oval, sapphire ring on her finger, she had realised her destiny. Containing 14 small diamonds surrounding the blue stone, in a cluster setting from the royal jewellers Garrard, the engagement ring had cost Prince Charles £28,000 thirty years earlier, when he had placed it on the finger of the shy Lady Diana Spencer, a young woman not long out of her teens. In today's money it would have cost £100,000, so perhaps in this age of austerity giving his fiancée a recycled ring wasn't a bad PR move. But that had not been William's motivation.

'It was my mother's engagement ring, so I thought it was quite nice because obviously she's not going to be around to share any of the fun and excitement of it all – this was my way of keeping her close to it all,' he said. It was a touching gesture that some commented on: after all, hadn't it been an ill-fated ring that marked an ill-fated marriage and doomed match? It took Kate's breath away when William produced it from his rucksack out of the blue while they holidayed together in Kenya. 'It's beautiful. I just hope I look after it. It's very, very special.' In a single deeply significant gesture, William had brought his iconic mother right back into the public consciousness and onto the newspaper front pages that she had graced during the latter part of the 20th century, when she ranked as one of the most famous people in the world.

But this soon-to-be-royal princess was no innocent girl like Diana. Nor was she a shy aristocrat caught up in a fairytale whirlwind. When Diana had second thoughts before the ceremony, she could not escape because her face was already on the commemorative tea towels, as her sister Lady Sarah McCorquodale reminded her. Kate's image was already imprinted on a special £5 commemorative coin with her husband-to-be, produced by the Royal Mint. It has started. But, unlike Diana, Kate is already a woman, and somebody who had already endured the trials and tribulations of a modern long-term relationship. With William she had experienced the pain of perceived betrayal, she had suffered the stress and self-doubt caused by splits and long periods of separation too. 'We did split up for a bit,' William said. 'We were both very young. It was at university. We were both finding ourselves as such and being different characters and stuff.

It was very much trying to find our own way and we were growing up. It was a bit of space and a bit of things like that, and it worked out for the better.'

He was of course not quite on the money. They *had* split at university, but the split people remember was later than that one – just three years, in fact, before their engagement was announced to the world. She, however, was more specific. 'I, at the time, wasn't very happy about it, but actually it made me a stronger person. You find out things about yourself that maybe you hadn't realised. I think you can get quite consumed by a relationship when you're younger, and I really valued that time for me, although I didn't think it at the time.'

Of course, there had been great highs and joys of real love, too, and this moment, when this intensely private couple declared their love to each other in front of the world, ranked among the highlights so far. There would be many more to come.

During the bitterness and recriminations of divorce from William's father, Diana later described herself as 'a lamb to the slaughter'. That troubled princess always felt her much older Prince Charming – Charles – had betrayed her with his refusal to abandon his extramarital affair with his married lover Camilla Parker Bowles. Diana never truly forgave, although, thankfully, she had mellowed towards the father of her boys by the time of her sudden, tragic death in a car crash in 1997. Kate was different. She was older, wiser. She was going into this marriage with her eyes wide open. She wouldn't, if she could help it, make the same mistakes. She would be a traditional wife and mother. She would, as one senior palace adviser told me, 'walk one step behind her husband'. She would not take on solo engagements and instead would team up with her husband at the outset at royal engagements to present a united front. She had had a long time to think about what sort of princess she would be, had studied what had happened to Diana, and had taken it on board. The monarchy is after all a fiercely traditional organisation. Prince Philip, the Duke of Edinburgh, walks one step behind the Queen and nobody says it makes him less of a man. It is just his royal duty.

Kate had already suffered the heartache and public ignominy of a very public split with her prince in 2007. They had split up a couple of times before that too, but every time the power of their love, like a magnet, had pulled them back to each other during their roller-coaster eight-year courtship. This English lady was a new breed of outsider who dared to marry into the Royal Family. She may be compared to the 'people's princess' throughout her royal career as she tries to carve out her own role and reputation, but in truth she is a true 'Princess of the People'. A middle-class girl born and raised in the country from loving, solid, hard-working parents with high aspirations who had worked tirelessly to earn the money to do the very best for their three children. Catherine, the eldest, had simply met and fallen in love with a prince when they were both undergraduates at the ancient Scottish seat of learning, St Andrew's University. Now she is on the cusp of becoming our new 21st-century princess and in line to be our future Queen Consort. With luck, if fate smiles on her, she will be mother and grandmother to future sovereigns, too.

Kate and William's first public appearance as a newly engaged couple was all but outshone by a shocking blaze of camera flashes from the battery of handpicked photographers invited from the world's media outlets to meet them in a state room at St James's Palace for their first official joint engagement. They had tried their best to answer the quick-fire questions but they were almost drained by the frenzied clicking cameras shutters. A little earlier, sitting in a quiet side room at Clarence House, his father's London home, it had been a calmer atmosphere, although the questioning, while soft, was still testing. William and Kate gave the first glimpses of the intimacy of their relationship. Seated side by side in their first interview together, the happy couple spent more than 15 minutes chatting informally to ITV News's political editor Tom Bradby, a newsman the prince liked and had chosen as the conduit of his good news, much to the chagrin of the BBC. Relaxed and often sharing a joke together, William and his bride-to-be talked about their happy news and revealed that they wanted to start a family. That, of course, was a foregone conclusion for a prince entrusted with securing the line of succession of one of the oldest and most celebrated monarchies in the world with a thousand-year history. Now, at his side, looking stunning in a beautiful peacock-blue dress by her favourite designer label Issa, was the woman with whom he would start that family.

When they were asked if they wanted lots of children, William was the first to speak: 'I think we'll take one step at a time. We'll sort of get over the marriage first and then maybe look at kids. But obviously we want a family so we'll have to start thinking about that.' In truth, his number-one priority, securing the line of succession, is one of the prerequisites of the job as an heir to the throne. But these children would be special: they would be princes and princesses born from the people. For an accident of birth had meant Catherine's ancestors had toiled underground for generations to earn slave wages in coal mines in County Durham in the North of England. In a twist of fate, they were the mines owned by the family of Prince William's great-grandmother, Queen Elizabeth the Queen Mother, who was Lady Elizabeth Bowes-Lyon before she too became one of the first 'commoners' (albeit a landed aristocrat) to marry into the British Royal Family. Lady Elizabeth became the darling of the nation as Queen Consort to George VI during World War Two and in later life as the beloved 'Queen Mum'. She enjoyed a wonderful life that spanned just over a century (born in 1900, she died in 2002), but it had not been all plain sailing. She had played a key role in guiding her stuttering, tempestuous husband through the tears and tempers of the Abdication crisis of 1936, a crisis that nearly rocked the monarchy to its foundations.

In the media frenzy that followed William and Kate's royal engagement announcement, comparisons between William's fiancée and his iconic mother Diana were inevitably splashed across the press. If Catherine could emulate any royal career, that of Lady Elizabeth Bowes-Lyon would be, perhaps, a better role model. King George V, the father of her husband, Albert, Duke of York (later George VI), had made that union possible. He had decreed in 1917, to secure the interests and survival of his newly christened Windsor dynasty, that the usual custom of marriages with German princesses was outmoded. His children, he said, could wed British commoners if they wished, a politic move given that German Gotha bombers were launching the first ever bombing raids on London from the air in the so-called war to end all wars, World War One. At the time, old royal houses across Europe were being toppled amid clamour by the masses for enfranchisement. The House of Saxe-Coburg-Gotha was killed off so that the newly christened, English-sounding House of Windsor could survive. George, a canny king with his finger on the nation's pulse, feared the worst. The wild spread of socialism had cost his lookalike cousin, the bumbling but ruthless Russian tyrant Emperor Nicholas II, his life. George was not about to follow, not if he could help it. He knew that, if his royal dynasty was to avoid the same bloody fate, he had to get the newly enfranchised working man on his side.

Kate's working-class forebears had helped make the Bowes-Lyons family and fellow colliery owners just that little bit richer. As they sweated their lives away deep underground, scraping a desperate and dangerous living, her ancestor James Harrison, a miner at the Hetton Lyons colliery in 1821, would never have believed his great-great-great-great granddaughter would one day be Queen. (More on James Harrison later.) But these are changing times for us all, and for the British monarchy too.

Like his great-great-grandfather, George V, William is a man with his finger on the pulse of his people too, mainly because his mother had impressed upon him from an early age that, while he was special, he had to be himself, to make his own choices. Like so many of the people he will one day serve as King, he lived with his girlfriend before he wed, something that in George V's day would not have been accepted. During the engagement interview William explained why he took so long to pop the question, saying he wanted to give Kate a chance to 'back out' if she felt she couldn't cope with life as the future Queen Consort. 'When did you first set eyes on each other?' Bradby probed. 'It's a long time ago now, Tom,' the Prince replied. 'I'm trying to rack my brain. We obviously met at university – at St Andrews. We were friends for over a year first and it just sort of blossomed. We just spent more time with each other, had a good giggle, lots of fun, and realised we shared the same interests and had a really good time. She's got a really naughty sense of humour, which kind of helps me because I've got a really dry sense of humour, so it was good fun.'

Kate was less polished, speaking more slowly and in a more considered way as she turned to her husband to be, as if for reassurance, and said, 'Well I actually think I went bright red when I met you and sort of scuttled off, feeling very shy.'

The proposal has been truly romantic. Exactly out of the textbook for princes on white chargers sweeping their chosen damsels off their feet. His mother, whose step-grandmother Dame Barbara Cartland made a fortune peddling such stories in slushy romantic novels, would have been proud. William revealed in his engagement interview, 'It was about three weeks ago on holiday in Kenya. We had been talking about marriage for a while, so it wasn't a massively big surprise. I took her up somewhere nice in Kenya and I proposed.' Kate added, 'It was very romantic. There's a true romantic in there. I really didn't expect it. It was a total shock ... and very exciting.'

Bradby asked, 'And he produced a ring there and then?' She replied with a beaming smile, 'Yes.' William explained, 'I'd been carrying it around with me in my rucksack for about three weeks before that and I literally would not let it go. Everywhere I went I was keeping hold of it because I knew this thing, if it disappeared, I would be in a lot of trouble; and, because I'd planned it, it went fine. You hear a lot of horror stories about proposing and things going horribly wrong. It went really, really well and I was really pleased she said "yes."'

But why had he waited so long to propose? 'I wanted to give her a chance to see in and to back out if she needed to before it all got too much. I'm trying to learn from lessons done in the past and I just wanted to give her the best chance to settle in and to see what happens on the other side,' he said.

In fact, his proposal plan had been truly adventurous and wildly romantic. He had selected a remote spot beside a shimmering African lake in Kenya to ask the most important question of his life. Just five miles from the equator and 11,500 feet above sea level, Kenya's peaceful Lake Alice is so far from civilisation that only a handful of sightseers witness its astounding beauty each year. The lake has stunning turquoise waters and is surrounded by lush green hills against the backdrop of a snowy Mount Kenya. It is not difficult to see why the prince had selected this destination to propose to his future wife.

Helicopters usually land on a rough shingle beach at Lake Alice's southern tip. Once the rotor blades have stopped spinning, passengers are treated to the kind of silence that can almost be heard. With no other humans for several miles in any direction, the only sounds that are made are those of nature – a rare passing bird or the splash of a fish or frog. Meanwhile, the lake's waters bob with unusual floating rocks – lightweight black stones serving as a reminder of its volcanic origins. With a blazing blue sky and a brisk mountain breeze, William and Kate used borrowed rods for fly fishing from the pebbly beach before the prince plucked up the courage to ask for her hand in marriage.

Most who go to Lake Alice fall in love with the place on sight. The peace is breathtaking. It is a unique place where one feels as if nobody else had ever been there. It takes so much effort to reach the place it feels virtually untouched by man. It is a hundred per cent seclusion and a hundred per cent romantic. William had spent weeks planning his trip to Kenya, where the couple stayed in a romantic log cabin. Without air transport, Lake Alice is at least a four-hour journey from the nearest tarmac road – 20 miles on slimy dirt roads accessible only by four-wheel-drive cars, before a gruelling two-hour uphill trek.

But the prince decided instead to arrive in style and flew in a chartered helicopter, carrying his mother Princess Diana's sapphire engagement ring in his rucksack. It was, as Kate said, truly romantic.

Lying in the top of a long-extinct volcano, Lake Alice is now surrounded on all four sides by a ring of ridges, which protect it from the icy high-altitude winds. Poking out from behind one of the nearby peaks is Mount Kenya – the second-highest mountain in Africa – whose snowy summits are famously difficult to reach. Lake Alice was formally discovered in 1935 by British explorer Kenneth Gander-Dower. William enlisted the help of family friend Ian Craig, who owns the nearby Lea game reserve where the couple spent most of their holiday and who arranged for their helicopter ride. Details of William's romantic proposal came as the staff at a secluded Kenyan lodge where the couple stayed revealed how they spent their final romantic day before the prince popped the question.

Stunned staff at the isolated Rotunda lodge said they had no idea they were hosting the heir to throne when William arrived last month with his future bride – just hours before he asked Kate to marry him. The peaceful hotel consists of just two simple wooden cottages nestled high in the Mount Kenya range, around three miles from Lake Alice, and is permanently staffed by three local workers, who live on site to greet the guests and tend to their every need.

But the royal couple were undemanding. William and Kate asked for virtually nothing as they enjoyed a back-to-basics stay during which they tucked into a simple supper home-cooked by the future King. Jackson Kimutai, 28, one of the members of staff, said the pair's only request was to be taken fishing for trout from the back of a rickety rowing boat. And he added that the team believed William and Kate were just another ordinary young couple when they arrived at around 3 p.m. on 20 October in a rented Toyota Landcruiser. The prince was dressed in a casual shirt and chinos, while Kate wore a summer dress. Kimutai recalled, 'They came by road and jumped out of the car. The man introduced himself and said, "Hi, I'm Willy." She was very smiley and happy and said her name was Kate. We took their luggage to the cottage for them – it is transported over a gorge on a special rope runway. Then we showed them the place. We had no idea who they were and they gave us no reason to believe they were anyone special.'

He added, 'We only get supplies here once a month, so all of our guests must bring food and drink with them. William and Kate had a box of things which they put in the kitchen.' The staff said the royal couple first spent a few minutes relaxing in Rutundu Lodge's rustic wooden surroundings. The couple's cosy chalet is fitted in a comfortable but basic fashion. Bare polished wooden floors in the living room and bedroom are covered with warming fluffy rugs, while the bathroom includes a large bath and a toilet, which seeps into a septic tank. Guests book in on a strictly self-catering basis and have use of a basic kitchen attached to the cottage. Most meals are cooked on two simple gas ring burners, while essentials are chilled in a traditional 'fridge' – several wooden shelves in an external cupboard.

The cottage overlooks the stunning Lake Rutundu, another mountain pond stocked with trout and surrounded by rolling hills. Rutundu worker Cosmos Kiecan, 30, said cheerful William and Kate later went to the water for a fishing trip. And they abandoned any idea of grandeur as they cast their rods from the back of a decades-old wooden rowing boat.

He said, 'When they arrived they said straightaway that they wanted to fish, so after they had settled in we took them down to the lake. It is a big lake and well stocked with trout. Some of them are up to four pounds and most of the guests want to try and catch some for their supper. We allow two to be taken and eaten every day and the rest are thrown back.

'Some people fish from the jetty or the banks, but William was keen to go out in the boat, so Jackson and I rowed them out to the middle of the lake. It is a small boat but it works very well.

'They sat at the back facing the water so they could flick their rods for fly fishing. We were at the front and rowing for them. They were having a great time. It is only fly fishing which is allowed and he spent some time showing her how to do it. Sometimes she was flicking her rod wrong and he helped her to do it better. You could tell they were very close and happy to be together. She kept looking at him and smiling and he was happy too,' he added.

The couple spent around an hour on the water before eventually heading back to shore empty-handed. Kimutai went on, 'Sadly, they didn't manage to catch anything. We went back after an hour and they hadn't had a single bite, but some days it is like that. We told them it is hard to catch a fish in Lake Rutundu and they laughed. After that they went back to their cottage to relax.'

The peaceful lodge's staff are well versed in their evening procedures to keep guests warm despite the biting mountain breeze and lack of electricity. At sunset each day they leap into action – lighting a fire underneath an external water tank for hot water and burning lamps to flood the cottage with romantic light.

'We always get hot water for the guests and light two fires inside

– one in the main room and one in the bedroom,' Kimutai added. 'The only light is by paraffin hurricane lamps but people seem to like them. Although we are not cooks we always offer to help the guests with their meals.'

As darkness fell William and Kate ran themselves a hot bath and snuggled up beside the front room's roaring fire. The prince cooked them up a simple meal they tucked into using the cottage's off-white plates and tarnished well-used cutlery. Meanwhile, the staff said the couple didn't even have any wine – choosing instead to sup mugs of tea made from hot water left for them by the workers in a battered vacuum flask.

'He was very happy to cook,' Jackson Kimutai said. 'They had brought their own supplies, although we did not see what. We usually ask people to leave their dirty plates and things in the sink so we can wash up for them, but they hardly left any mess. Sometimes there are also lots of empty bottles of wine or beer but we didn't see any sign of any alcohol from these guys. We think they just drank the tea we left them and enjoyed themselves by the fire.'

Later, the couple retired to the bedroom, where a rustic wooden four-poster stands alongside a set of bunk beds for families with children. At night the cottage is enveloped by total silence, broken occasionally only by the flapping of nocturnal birds or the occasional wandering buffalo or antelope. Lying at the heart of the Mount Kenya National Park, Rutundu is protected by three permanent rangers, who watch for intruders or poachers and use a radio link to summon armed colleagues when required. The site's blissful tranquillity is ensured, as the nearest mobile signal is receivable from a rocky outcrop about a 30-minute walk away through the bush. But by night the presence of deadly animals means guests are warned not to attempt the journey and advised instead to stay tucked up inside their cottage.

The next morning William and Kate emerged blinking into the African sunlight before enjoying a simple breakfast on the terrace prepared by the prince. The staff said they took the couple for a second, shorter, fishing trip before they left – in time for the 10 a.m. checkout.

Cosmos Kiecan, the other staff member, said, 'They had

obviously had a really lovely time and had burned a lot of wood for the fire. We took them down to the lake again and then they left. Willy was joking that they had heard a tapping on their window when they woke up. He pulled back the curtains to see who it was and it was a weaver bird banging at the glass. They are bright yellow and often come up to meet the guests. Willy said after that it went around to all the other windows and tapped on the glass there too. The whole time the couple were here they were really chatty with us and very friendly. He was joking about the weather because he said he had been here before and got cold. Although it's usually sunny it's very high here so it does get cold – especially at night. This time he said he had brought two jumpers and she also had some clothes for the evening with her.'

The staff only found out later who the special guests were and were amazed. The trip to Rutundu was one of several excursions planned by the prince during their holiday at the nearby Lewa wildlife park, where William had spent a month working during a gap year before he met Kate at university. The reserve is owned by Ian Craig – the father of William's ex-girlfriend friend Jessica (or Jecca, as she is known). He is believed to have put the royal couple up for part of the time in his personal house on the 55,000-acre site, which is home to dozens of animal species, including lions, giraffes, zebra and antelope. William and Kate also spent several nights at the spectacular Sirikoi game lodge, where they shared a romantic tented room in the wilderness. Happy locals have told of their joy that the prince chose Kenya to confirm his commitment to the future princess. David Kamau, 23, works at a craft stall in the Lewa reserve and said he was delighted when William came into buy hand-crafted local decorations for the couple's Christmas tree.

He said, 'Everyone is so pleased that they came to Kenya to get engaged. To have a prince and princess staying was wonderful. I met William when he came to my shop. He chatted to us for ages and then bought a pack of ten wire angels and a pack of ten beaded Christmas trees. It is great that we know they got engaged in our place – and even better to know our work will be decorating their Christmas tree.'

Both wrote in a visitors' book after their romantic trip to the log-cabin hideaway. Kate wrote, 'I had a wonderful 24 hours. Sadly no fish to be found but we had great fun trying. I love the warm fires and candle lights – so romantic! Hope to be back again soon.' William's note, dated 20–21 October 2010, said, 'Such fun to be back! Brought more clothes this time! Looked after so well. Thank you guys! Look forward to the next time, soon I hope.' He signed it William; she signed hers Catherine Middleton. Soon she will have a different name and title as she joins the House of Windsor.

What followed was an extraordinary attempt by the couple to keep their engagement a closely guarded secret. Even the Queen was kept in the dark for over two weeks. 'We're like sort of ducks,' said William, 'very calm on the surface with little feet going under the water. It's been really exciting because we've been talking about it for a long time, so for us it's a real relief and it's really nice to be able to tell everybody. Especially for the last two or three weeks – it's been quite difficult not telling anyone, keeping it to ourselves. I was torn between asking Kate's dad first and then the realisation that he might actually say no dawned upon me. So I thought if I ask Kate first, then he can't really say no.'

William even kept his big news a secret from the Queen as he and Kate excitedly made their plans for a future together. He was determined to do it his way, and protocol went out of the window. It also gives us an insight into how the new-look House of Windsor will be led from the front by William when he becomes King. One senior member of the Royal Household told me, 'He did not tell his family until the last minute because he knows once it was official there was a danger he would lose control of it all. William is determined his wedding to Catherine is going to be their day as well as one of public celebration.

'He knows it is a public event but it is also going to be their special private moment, too, and they don't want that to be forgotten by the courtiers charged with the organisation.'

The timeline of the run-up to the engagement announcement started when William and Kate flew to Kenya; he asked her to marry him on 20 October; then followed an extraordinary royal roller-coaster ride of happiness and treading carefully, as the couple desperately tried to keep their big news secret. They were all smiles for the cameras when they arrived for their pal Harry Meade's wedding. They were already secretly engaged as they boldly strolled through the front of the church before a battery of waiting photographers. But Kate, of course, did not have on Princess Diana's sapphire engagement ring.

A week later, on 30 October, William invited Kate's parents to Birkhall on the Queen's Balmoral estate in the Scottish Highlands. It was there, in the Queen Mother's favourite old royal retreat, that William – knowing his bride-to-be had accepted his proposal – asked her father Michael for his daughter's hand in marriage. They were preparing to announce the news on Wednesday, 3 November, once he had told the rest of his family. Just four days later, on 7 November 2010, I penned an article in the *News of the World* breaking the story. The headline read, WE WILLS WED NEXT SUMMER, with a strapline deck below that read, 'Royal engagement to be announced Xmas'. The opening line of the story could not have been clearer. It read: 'Prince William and his patient girlfriend Kate Middleton will announce their engagement before Christmas, the *News of the World* can reveal.' Nine days later I was to be proved right. In the past the dates and venues are announced simultaneously. But in typical William style he wanted it his way.

Palace officials – who still had not been told of the arrangements – refused to confirm the story. The otherwise happy story was not without tragedy, however, with the death of Kate's paternal grandfather, Peter, on 2 November, aged 90, in his home in the village of Vernham Dean, Hampshire. Kate and the rest of her family were devastated by his loss and all focus was switched from her big day to the preparations for the funeral on 12 November. A close source said, 'It's not clear at this point if [Kate's father] Mike had actually told [her mother] Carole, because William and Kate had asked them not to say anything.' Kate even admitted that there was an awkward period when she was not even sure if her mother even knew. 'We had quite an awkward situation because I knew that William had asked my father but I didn't know if my mother knew.' So she came back from Scotland, where they had been photographed on the royal Balmoral estate on a shoot. Carole did not make it clear to her daughter whether she knew or not.

Then, on his last solo engagement before the big news broke, William flew to Afghanistan along with the Defence Secretary Dr Liam Fox. In a surprise visit to Camp Bastion in Helmand Province, he joined about 2,500 servicemen in the remembrance ceremony, laying a wreath to remember his own friends and others who had lost their lives. He returned on Monday, 15 November, and that night he telephoned the Queen to tell her the good news. She was delighted. His father, too, was happy, although the Prince of Wales's comment that his son and future daughter-in-law had 'practised long enough' was a classic illustration of his emotional limitations. That, coupled with the timing of his comment that he did expect his wife the Duchess of Cornwall to be Queen when he is King raised eyebrows, and suggested possible future tensions between his and his son's rival courts.

On 23 November 2010, I attended a St James's Palace press briefing where they announced that the marriage would take place on Friday 29 April 2011 at Westminster Abbey. They were keen to stress that the Royal Family would pay for the wedding, with the Middletons chipping in too. It was, they said, a precedent set by the marriages of the Prince and Princess of Wales in 1981 and Princess Elizabeth and Prince Philip in 1947. Jamie Lowther-Pinkerton, the sharp former SAS officer turned courtier revealed it would be a 'classic' royal wedding with all the pomp and pageantry the world expected of the British. He said the couple, who were 'over the moon' were very much in charge of the arrangement. They wanted it to be their wedding and even though it would take place at Westminster Abbey, the Royal Family's Church, in the high altar it had the feel of an English Parish Church. They wanted everyone to enjoy the day and welcomed Prime Minister David Cameron's suggestion that it should be a public holiday, allowing everyone to celebrate. 'This is their day,' Jamie said. 'They are calling the shots.'

William and Harry's Household at St James's Palace would take the lead on making the arrangements, backed by the Lord Chamberlain Office at Buckingham Palace – who know exactly how to put on a royal extravaganza. 'It will be a classic example of what Britain does best,' added Jamie. The Archbishop of

Canterbury Dr. Rowan Williams would conduct the service, but the couple were keen that they would have an input on the vows and the all important question of whether she would vow to 'obey' her husband. Although who would attend the wedding had not been announced before this book went to press, the courtiers did reveal that heads of state, probably including the Sarkozys of France and the Obamas from the US, would be on the list. 'It certainly won't be an empty church,' one courtier said, meaning that thousands would witness their historic union.

This was William's first victory. He had wanted it to be a spring wedding and he got his way. But it was also William's decision to place Diana's ring on his fiancee's finger, thus thrusting the late princess back into the spotlight, just when some were beginning to believe she could now rest in peace. Would Kate, the new princess of a new generation, find that intimidating? 'Obviously, I would have loved to have met her and she's obviously an inspirational woman to look up to.'

But there would be pressure?

'There's no pressure, though,' William said. 'Like Kate said, it's about carving your own future. No one's trying to fill my mother's shoes. What she did was fantastic. It's about making your own future and your own destiny and Kate will do a very good job of that. We are hugely excited and we are looking forward to spending the rest of our lives together and seeing what the future holds.'

But make no mistake, as I wrote in the concluding line of my first book about the couple, *William's Princess*, published in 2006, 'Kate's days as William's "princess in waiting" are drawing to a close. Her time as his princess and, one day, Queen is about to begin.'

And with that public role, whether the couple welcome it or not, there will be both public and private pressures that will test them to the limit. Only time will tell how this new royal double act will cope.

CHAPTER 2

MOST NOBLE ORDER

'The couple are completely over the moon, I have
never seen two happier people, they are on Cloud 9.'
JAMIE LOWTHER-PINKERTON, PRIVATE SECRETARY TO
PRINCE WILLIAM, 23 NOVEMBER 2010

Prince William's embarrassment was palpable. He suddenly came into view wearing a floppy hat with white ostrich and heron feathers and flowing, velvet, dark-blue robes looking as if he had stepped straight from the Middle Ages. As he paraded before the public and press in this anachronistic garb, he appeared awkward and a little uneasy. Nevertheless, he knew he *had* to do it. Like it or not, maintaining the traditions of a hereditary monarchy that stretched back more than a thousand years to his distant ancestor the Anglo-Saxon Egbert, King of Wessex, was at the core of his duties. It simply went with the territory.

William is a modern prince, a man of his time, happiest in jeans, trainers and a T-shirt. The sight of him dressed in such ancient finery seemed to overwhelm the immaculately dressed young brunette wearing a tailored dark suit with little white polka dots and a charming black-and-white headpiece, sitting next to his brother Prince Harry, watching on as the ceremony unfold. She gasped loudly enough for those close by to hear, 'Oh my God!' Then she and the irrepressible Harry proceeded to have an uncontrollable giggling fit. It was perhaps unseemly, but very natural. William, who had caught their eye, did his best to pretend he had not noticed, but of course he had.

19

The unforgiving British press could easily have exaggerated the inappropriate behaviour had it not been for the fact that the presence of the woman in question, Catherine Elizabeth Middleton, at the ceremony of the Most Noble Order of the Garter on 16 June 2008, was clearly far more significant to the unfolding royal story than a bit of juvenile silliness. Thankfully, Kate, as the media had now dubbed her, regained her composure quite quickly, although it took William's flame-haired younger brother Harry a little longer. As Kate watched the investiture of her boyfriend as 1,000th Knight of the Order of Chivalry, founded by King Edward III in 1348, at St George's Chapel in the shadow of Windsor Castle it was obvious that we were witnessing a highly significant moment in the shaping of our modern monarchy.

William's romance with the alluring middle-class girl he had met at St Andrews University, and had since been dating on and off, had been the subject of relentless media debate. Now it seemed the speculation would soon be over. Her attendance at such an important and public royal engagement, one presided over by the Queen and attended by fellow Garter Knights such as William's father Prince Charles and aunt Princess Anne the Princess Royal, was a defining moment in the relationship and her importance. It meant that the royal 'Firm' had now officially embraced her. The day when she would walk down the aisle as William's bride – perhaps at the royal chapel where this royal ceremony was taking place – was now, surely, only a matter of time. It seemed it was now a case of *when*, not *if*.

Moments earlier the gaggle of about 30 royal photographers, accredited by the ever-expanding communications department at Buckingham Palace to record the event, had waited patiently for more than an hour behind steel barriers in the specially erected press pen positioned to capture the shot of William, then 26, outside the chapel. The lens men, some who had been covering the royal beat for many years, were taking it all in their stride, chatting among themselves with the usual banter reliving past glories, or at least perceived ones. Then, suddenly, in scenes reminiscent of the excitement caused by any appearance by William's mother, the iconic Diana, Princess of Wales, they went into frenzy, pushing and shoving to get the best position to get the best shot. A car containing Prince Harry had drawn up to a side entrance. For once Harry, the so-called 'playboy prince' and third in line to the throne, was not their focus. Climbing out of the car with him, Kate followed the prince to the Galilee Porch of the chapel. She and Harry joined a number of royals, including Prince Charles's second wife, the Duchess of Cornwall Camilla Parker Bowles), and Prince Edward's wife, the Countess of Wessex (Sophie Rhys-Jones), who like Camilla, had wed her prince, Edward, at St George's Chapel inside the wall of Windsor Castle.

As far as the assembled media were concerned, the rest of the royal group might as well not have turned up. Even the Queen was now less important in their eyes. The day was now all about Kate, the lithe, five-foot-nine woman six months her royal boyfriend's senior. This was the first time she had attended an official royal engagement in public. By inviting her and asking his brother to act as her chaperone, William had sent out a clear message. He was effectively saying, 'This lady is the most important person in my life, and you can read what you like into that.' The notoriously media-cautious William knew exactly how the media would react. He knew too that, although on paper this was his day and he was centre stage, Kate would steal the show that day. Now, not for the first time and certainly not the last, all eyes were on her. If it fazed her, she certainly did not let it show.

In all her years at his side as his girlfriend, Kate had quite simply never put a foot wrong. Without any training, she had ticked all the right boxes. She and her family had braved and endured appalling snobbish insults from people who, despite her flawless style, inexplicably decreed the monarchy needed to avoid marrying outside its circle. The daughter of former pilot Michael and attractive former flight attendant Carole, wealthy owners of a mail-order and online party-paraphernalia business, Party Pieces, was seen as too common to marry a future king. Some even questioned whether Kate's poise was natural, claiming she was overly controlled and controlling. Some went further and even suggested the small number of close friends she and Prince William had in some way reflected badly on her. Nearly all were his magic circle, from either Eton or college, or family friends from his teenage years. There were rumours too that even the Queen was 'anxious' for Kate to get a job and be seen to be doing something useful instead of apparently just waiting around a little too patiently for William to pop the question and ask her to be his bride. They were cheap shots. True to form, Kate remained unflappable under pressure. After all, this was the girl who, when asked if she felt fortunate to be dating a prince, had responded with supreme self-confidence, '*He's* lucky to be going out with *me.*'

Almost exactly three years earlier, on 23 June 2005, Kate – sitting five rows in front of the prince in St Andrews University's Younger Hall, wearing and a short black skirt beneath her graduation gown – had watched her student boyfriend presented with his master-of-arts degree. She had not just been a spectator that day: Kate too had collected her scroll to denote her academic success in the history of art. Smiling broadly as she returned to her seat, she caught William's eye. He flashed back a proud smile.

That day, Dr Brian Lang, vice-chancellor of the university, got to his feet and made a prediction. 'You will have made lifelong friends. I say this every year to all new graduates: you may have met your husband or wife. Our title as "Top Matchmaking University in Britain" signifies so much that is good about St Andrews, so we can rely on you to go forth and multiply.'

In light of William and Kate's announcement, in November 2010, of their engagement, one can't help but wonder if they thought this referred to them.

CHAPTER 3
A CLASS APART

'Being a Princess isn't all it's cracked up to be.'
DIANA, PRINCESS OF WALES (1961–97)

H e is a prince with vast wealth, ancient ancestry and coveted
royal title dubbed the world's most eligible bachelor. She is
a beautiful middle-class Englishwoman of unexceptional family
background who is now catapulted into an extraordinary world of
global celebrity and royal duty. Together they will indubitably
become one of the most enduring double acts of their generation,
instantly recognised wherever they go. The marriage of Prince
William Arthur Philip Louis of Wales and Catherine Elizabeth
Middleton is therefore an enormously important moment in the
history of our *modern* monarchy.

This union bucks historic trends, with the direct heir to the
throne choosing a bride outside his social circle and class, a
commoner no less. It is a marriage born of love, not one like those
of English princes of old: forged for dynastic or diplomatic reasons.
Kate is not even an aristocrat like William's late mother Diana,
Princess of Wales, who was the last commoner to wed a direct heir
to the throne. When she arrived at St Paul's Cathedral to wed, she
was Lady Diana Spencer.

William's choice of a commoner bride signals his clear intention
to be his own man when he ascends the throne. He will reign *his*
way and has made it clear he will not be 'an ornament' but is

23

determined to get more involved with public life than his predecessors. Effectively, he wants to get his hands dirty. So will Kate. Those close to them insist this couple more than any other royal couple will become the embodiment of modern monarchy and in doing so will silence the growing band of Republicans who demand a democratic replacement of the sovereign and the end monarchical system with an elected, accountable head of state.

It is true that both William and Kate are people of their generation, albeit privileged ones. Only time will tell whether William's statement of intent that he made as a 27-year-old will be easy to live up to, especially as the demands of the formal side of his role engulfs him. Many believe as a couple William and Kate have the ability, intelligence and desire to drag the institution into the 21st century. The comparative youth, good looks and experience will, courtiers hope, make it more relevant to the people it after all exists to represent as a symbol of unity and national pride. They are the people who, after all, pay for the royals' privileged lifestyle and can expect value for that money. There will always be detractors, but, with William at the helm and Kate at his side, this ancient, hereditary institution can perhaps still justify a place in our new British society, a society where social mobility is not just a buzzword but a reality.

Like his mother Princess Diana, William has the heart and natural grace to become a beacon of national hope for a new, more demanding generation – if you like, a 'people's prince'. With that in mind, his choice of bride is perhaps both significant and crucial. If he had wed a European princess or aristocrat, inevitably people would see them and the children they produce as elitist. But, like him, Kate is a woman of her generation, possessing the perfect pedigree and lack of stuffiness to convince people that this modern monarchy is for real, an institution that has a future as well as a past

That is why this marriage is a defining moment for the British Royal Family. Together, they will be world stars, the most famous couple on the planet in historical terms, ranking alongside the likes of Charles and Diana, John F. and Jackie Kennedy and, latterly, the Obamas. Their arrival as an official couple immediately gives the Royal Family a younger, fresher more relevant feel. As King, when that day comes, William will reign with Kate as his side as Queen Consort – the country's first since Queen Elizabeth, the Queen Mother – since Camilla, if the palace spin-doctors are as good as their word, will adopt the lesser rank of Princess Consort on the Prince of Wales's accession. William and Kate's union, perhaps for the first time since Charles and Diana kissed on the balcony of Buckingham Palace on their wedding day in 1981, the British monarchy is back into the global media spotlight for the right reasons.

Only once in our history has a future British sovereign married a commoner, and then it was in very different circumstances. In what was then a religious society divided, the relationship between Catholics and Protestants was at best an uneasy one. In 1659, at Breda in Holland, James, the Duke of York, secretly wed while the Royal Family remained in exile following the English Civil War and Cromwell's Interregnum. James's brother, later King Charles II, insisted his wayward, weak-willed brother marry Anne in an English ceremony, saying that her strong character would be a positive influence. This commoner would hold a significant place in history, becoming the mother to two queens.

Much more recently, in the 20th century, the woman who later became known as the Queen Mother was technically a commoner too when, as Scottish aristocrat Lady Elizabeth Bowes-Lyon, she married the then Prince Albert, Duke of York, later King George VI, in 1921. At the time her husband's older brother the Prince of Wales, later Duke of Windsor, was heir to George V.

Placed in historic context, William and Kate's love match is therefore significant. It is a royal marriage where thankfully love and royal duty truly entwine. It is a modern marriage that started from a chance meeting and shows just how far monarchy has evolved. This clunky institution seems at last to be prepared for real change.

Gone are the days, thankfully, of forced royal marriages. Gone too are the days when it was very acceptable for princes to live with their mistress for love. The last King called William, William IV – who came the throne in 1830 – lived with the actor Dorothea

Jordan for 20 years and she bore him ten children, who took the surname FitzClarence.

The world has changed, even the royal world. William and Kate's marriage is a truly modern match – ironically, a trend started by his grandmother the Queen, who as a teenager fell for the dashing Philip Mountbatten (his real surname was the Germanic Schleswig-Holstein-Sonderburg-Glücksburg) at first sight. Almost from that moment, Princess Elizabeth was determined to marry him. It helped, of course, that he was a great-great-grandson of Queen Victoria and a nephew of the Machiavellian Lord Louis Mountbatten.

William and Kate, however, come from very different backgrounds. Kate is a woman who descends from both working-class and middle-class roots, unique for a royal bride and something William's great-great-grandfather George V would not have believed possible. Would he have condoned his great-great-grandson's marriage to a commoner? I doubt it.

Equally, if Kate and William had come from an earlier generation – and she had had a title of course – their long courtship would never have taken place, It would have been sealed in marriage years ago. In their time together, they have been relatively free to experience a loving relationship before committing to marriage.

Placed in the context of the British Royal Family's colourful and illustrious history, Kate's ascendance is quite simply extraordinary. She is destined to be one of the most famous women in the world, a British royal and one day expected to reign alongside King William V (should he decide to use that name). Kate certainly appears to possess the media savvy and natural grace needed to navigate the rough and tumble of the often brutal royal world where her every public move, and some private ones are caught on camera, her every utterance scrutinised.

As soon as it became clear that Kate's relationship, despite very public blips and splits, had the necessary staying power, genealogists began to look even deeper, tracing her family history in earnest further and further back, hoping to find contrasts to William's royal bloodline. What they discovered made interesting reading. For in the year that Prince William's illustrious ancestor, his great-great-great-great-grandmother Queen Victoria, was born at Kensington Palace in 1819, a young man named James Harrison took his first nervous steps down a coalmine in County Durham in the North of England. For the next 120 years, Harrison and his descendants served the nation diligently, facing daily jeopardy underground. His origins could not have been lowlier. He came from solid working-class stock, where life was often cheap and short – the very opposite of the glittering court life of Britain's monarchy at the time. Yet Harrison's bloodline was strong. Now, more than two centuries on from his birth, this miner's descendant is the new bride of the future King.

Kate can also trace her lineage to the literary world. She is a distant cousin of the late children's author Beatrix Potter, but is also a long-lost relative of *Swallows and Amazons* creator Arthur Ransome. Ransome's sister Joyce was married to Hugo Lupton, the cousin of Kate's great-grandmother Olive.

Though polished, sophisticated and in every way fit to accept William's proposal of marriage, Kate brings to the Royal Family a vital lineage that will qualify her to be truly titled the Princess of the People. Her family's story is an uplifting one, a story of one family and its road from obscurity and poverty all the way to the steps of the British throne.

William was christened by the Archbishop of Canterbury Dr Robert Runcie, raised in a palace and educated at top prep schools and Eton College; Kate's childhood and upbringing was obviously very different. She had a traditional middle-class family background; comfortably off and privately educated. However, when one digs a little deeper, one finds – as with most families – one or two skeletons in the ancestral cupboard. Their errors, of course, are no reflection on her. You can, after all, choose your friends but not your family. One of Kate's forebears had a prison record. Another, even closer to home, was Kate's fun-loving multimillionaire uncle Gary Goldsmith, then 49, her mother's brother, who heaped shame on the family in 2009 when exposed in a sex-and-drugs sting by the redtop *News of the World* in which he bragged of his niece's royal associations.

It is fair to say there is nothing in her ancestry and family history that would have helped predict that Kate's life would take such a remarkable course. Prince William's great-great-great-grandfather was the notorious womaniser monarch King Edward VII; Kate's was a jailbird. As Prince of Wales, William's Victorian-born ancestor had infuriated his mother Queen Victoria with his lavish, extravagant and often hedonistic lifestyle. He scandalised the monarchy, becoming the first British royal to appear, in 1891, as a court witness in a case brought by William Gordon-Cumming, a friend found cheating at baccarat, Edward's favourite, but illegal, game of chance. A decade earlier Kate's great-great-great-grandfather, according to the 1881 census, another Edward – Edward Thomas Glassborow – then 55, went one better than a court appearance, for he was doing hard labour in London's Holloway Prison.

Prison records have not survived from that era, so it is impossible to know why the father of seven, who worked as a messenger for an insurance company, had ended up behind bars. In those days, Holloway was the destination for prisoners of both sexes sentenced at the Old Bailey or Guildhall Justice Rooms. Glassborow, who lived in Hackney, east London was one of 436 inmates when the census was taken. It is unclear when Kate's ancestor was released, but by the time, his third son Frederick – Kate's great-great-grandfather – married on 1 June 1886. For by then Edward was describing himself as a 'gentleman of independent means', which was quite an extraordinary turnaround for a former felon. Glassborow died aged 72 in 1898, with Frederick at his bedside. The cause of his death was recorded as apoplexy the result of chronic rheumatism.

Frederick's eldest son, also named Frederick, conscripted to the army at the outbreak of World War One, went, like thousands of his contemporaries, to Belgium to fight the Hun on the frontline. When peace came, he returned to his job as manager of the London and Westminster Bank, where he met and married a young woman named Constance Robinson. The couple travelled across Europe due to Frederick's work. Kate's grandmother, Valerie, and her twin sister, Mary, were born in Marseille. In 1942, at the height of World War Two, the family returned to Britain, where Frederick was transferred to Leeds to become manager of the Westminster Bank. Valerie eventually married Peter Middleton, the son of a wealthy Yorkshire solicitor, who served as an RAF pilot during World War Two and worked as a commercial pilot after he demobbed. Peter had just ended his career as a commercial pilot and had taken up a job as a pilot instructor with the Air Service Training.

Kate's father, Michael Francis Middleton, was born on 23 June 1949 in Chapel Allerton Nursing Home in north Leeds. The family home, where Peter lived with his wife, the former Valerie Glassborow, was the aptly named King Lane in an affluent suburb of Leeds in West Yorkshire. He was raised within walking distance of three golf clubs – Headingley, Moortown and Sand Moor close to the Eccup reservoir – with his older brother Richard, born two years earlier. Michael Middleton, Kate's father, eventually married a glamorous air hostess, Carole Goldsmith, Kate's mother.

Carole Middleton's side of the family makes interesting reading too. Unlike her father, Carole has unmistakeably working-class roots. The daughter of a lorry driver, Ronald Goldsmith, and housewife Dorothy, formerly Harrison, she was born in Perivale maternity hospital ten miles west of central London six years after her future husband on 31 January 1955. A decade on from VE Day, with a young Queen Elizabeth II on the throne for only three years, the country was emerging from the depressing recovery post-war. There was more prosperity, and working-class people, whose aspirations had been strangled by the class divide before the war, believed they could make something of themselves. The British Empire no longer ruled the waves or the world. Many youngsters were taking their lead from America, where rock and roll was the new sensation. 'Change' was certainly the buzzword of the time.

When Carole Middleton was barely a toddler in July 1957, Prime Minister Harold Macmillan reflected the mood of the country with his famous optimistic speech in which he said, 'Our people have never had it so good.' True, as with all politicians, Macmillan was painting a rosy picture of Britain's economy while urging wage restraint and warning that inflation was the country's most important problem of the post-war era. Carole's family home was a modest property, 73a Dudley Road in Southall. Ron, as family and friends knew him, had ideas for bettering himself and had plans to become a builder even then. Certainly, given their background, Kate's maternal grandparents would not have dreamed it possible that one day their granddaughter would become the future Princess of Wales and ultimately Queen Consort, but they knew their daughter would raise Kate to be a lady.

CHAPTER 4

PARTY PIECES PRINCESS

'You may be a princess or the richest woman in the world, but you cannot be more than a lady.'
JENNIE, LADY RANDOLPH CHURCHILL, MOTHER OF SIR WINSTON

An attractive, ambitious girl, Carole Goldsmith always had a burning desire to travel and see the world. Ron and Dorothy Goldsmith's daughter was born Carole Elizabeth Goldsmith on 31 January 1955 in Ealing. She was a popular girl who set her sights on becoming a flight attendant after finishing secondary school. Determined and attractive, she was never in any doubt that she would get her dream job. Soon, the letter of acceptance arrived. It was heady days for the flight industry, as more and more people were getting the chance to experience what was once the domain of the rich and famous. It was while at BA that she met the man who was to change her life. In the 1970s, that she started dating the handsome Michael Middleton, and they married in Chiltern, Buckinghamshire, in 1980. British Airways was an exciting place to work in those days. Flying was still for the privileged few but it was just beginning to open up to a wider, socially mobile populous. Britain was on the cusp of the birth of Thatcherism, a perfect platform for the ambitious Michael and Carole to build their new world. Carole soon attracted Michael, who was a flight dispatcher at the time. The middle-class Michael was her first true love. Carole's mother Dorothy was delighted. It was, in her view, a perfect match.

Michael had followed his father Peter, a pilot instructor at British European Airlines, but the former graduate trainee changed career course, switching from pilot training to ground crew. When he met Carole, he was responsible for coordinating aircraft between arrival and departure and afforded the same status as a BA captain. They dated for a few years before moving into a modern flat in Arborfield Close, in Slough, a few miles from their base. It was not the ideal place to raise a family, so they began hunting for a country home, settling on the village of Bradfield Southend. Eight months after moving into their new home on 21 June 1980 the couple wed at the idyllic venue of the Parish Church of St James the Less in the village of Dorney by the River Thames. Carole had everything she could possibly want. Her proud mother Dorothy, then 44, looked on as 49-year-old Ron proudly walked down the aisle with Carole on her arm. Michael's parents, Peter, 59, a witness, and Valerie, 56, were on the other side of the aisle. A swanky dinner at a manor house followed.

Two years later, on 9 January 1982, the eldest of three siblings, Catherine was born – five months before Prince William was born at St Mary's Hospital, Paddington, on 21 June 1982 – at the Royal Berkshire Hospital in Reading. Those who came to visit noted her mop of dark hair. Her christening followed at the local church, St Andrew's, a flint-and-chalk construction on the banks of the River Pang that dated back to the 14th century. It was a chance for a family gathering. Carole, ever flamboyant in a Laura Ashley dress, looked a picture, but Kate, round-faced and bonny, stole the show, wearing a full-length white christening gown. The family celebrated at the manor afterwards. Her younger sister Philippa, known as Pippa, was born 20 months later on 6 September 1983 at the same hospital and baptised the following March at the same church. With two young girls, she was quick to make friends and took her daughters to the mothers-and-toddlers playgroup held every Tuesday at the local St Peter's Church Hall.

Kate's early life was worlds apart from that of her future husband. All had solid family values and an expectation of an extremely comfortable standard of living. Both little Catherine and Pippa attended St Peter's Preschool. Of course, this was before Carole launched herself into her second career, founding and running her company, Party Pieces. She had time to be a full-time mum, relying on husband Michael's British Airways salary, although she was already showing the business nous that would see her personal fortune grow, making party bags to sell to mothers.

When Kate was four, in 1986, she went to the local village school, Bradfield Church of England Primary School, adjacent to the family home. A couple of years later Pippa joined her there and both did well. Kate, always an outgoing child, loved outdoor life and had a natural affinity with sport, excelling in rounders and athletics.

Three months after Kate's fifth birthday her brother James William arrived, on 15 April 1987, again at the Royal Berkshire Hospital. Later he recalled enjoying an idyllic childhood with his family, playing with his sisters and protected by their loving parents. He later recalled in an article published in the society bible *Tatler*, 'I have great childhood memories of my mother baking cakes and I was always willing to participate, especially if it meant I could lick the bowl and revarnish the kitchen floor with treacle.'

Around this time, Carole had a germ of a business idea. She realised there was serious potential in ideas for children's parties. She wanted to inspire other mothers to create magical parties at home, and make a tidy profit, too. She rented a small unit in Yattendon, four miles from the family home, to store merchandise. Her daughters came in useful too, modelling some of the outfits they sold, including T-shirts with their ages on. They were earning their keep, but, as the business went from strength to strength, they would be the beneficiaries. Their parents wanted the very best for their children, and paying for the best private education they could was number one on their agenda. First, though, she needed to secure the cash needed; her dream depended on the success of her business.

Perhaps it was her working-class roots, or just the firm belief in social mobility, that inspired Carole. The business began to thrive, and Kate's parents agreed to pile some of the profits into school fees. They decided to send their children to a private prep school, St Andrews in Pangbourne, a few miles away from

Bradfield Southend. In today's money, the annual fees are more than £10,000.

Known to her friends and family as Kate, she loved dressing up in the sparkling dresses and mini-tiaras of a princess. Kate was taught the value of things, her mother often reminding her to be careful, as the outfits would later be packaged up and posted off to fulfil other little girls' dreams at a profit.

She was a Brownie, a junior girl scout, along with Pippa, at the 1st St Andrew's pack of 24; she loved amateur dramatics and took part in the school's public-speaking competitions. Commended for her manners, Kate did her best not to put a foot wrong. She rarely failed. In 1992, then just ten, she won the starring role as Eliza Doolittle in a production of *My Fair Lady*; she was also picked for the school's production of *The Nutcracker* and performed in a musical called *Rats*.

Despite her willingness to step out on stage, back then – according to classmates – she was rather awkward and more than a little self-conscious. Skinny and quite tall among her peer group, Kate would occasionally stay overnight at St Andrew's school, as it operated a flexi-boarding system at the time. Back home, her entrepreneurial mother was busy building her business, devoting more and more time to developing the mail-order firm. Carole was a sharp entrepreneur, spotting the possibilities the new internet offered, they quickly established a website and were in business. It was great foresight. Today, on its website, which Kate has assisted in developing, it claims to be 'The UK's leading online and catalogue party company'.

By 1995, business was going very well. There was enough in the bank for the firm to move to larger premises, a collection of farm buildings a mile further away at Ashampstead Common, Berkshire. The same year, they sold their house and moved to the outskirts of Chapel Row in the parish of Bucklebury. They had made it to 'millionaires' row', where their neighbours included football club owners and TV and rock stars.

There is, however, certain piquancy in the fact that Kate's self-made parents, had achieved wealth by packaging childish dreams for retail. It had enabled them to buy a substantial five-bedroom house, Oak Acre, ringed by towering oak trees, which backs onto the privately owned Bucklebury Estate. The house, an imposing building with its tile-hung walls graced with liberal amounts of wisteria and vine, presents a charming prospect. It may not be the kind of place royalty of old would visit, preferring instead to drop in on the grander estates, but times have definitely changed. Village life as a child for the young Kate in the narrow wooded lanes that stretch between Reading and Newbury in Berkshire was idyllic.

The immaculate shorn green is surrounded by well-groomed houses and the local post office, where cream tea is served. It is the nearest thing to the rural England of P. G. Wodehouse, genteel and unblemished by the march of time. The Middleton family are a fixture of village life and are often seen at the charity fairs that boast sheep racing, splat the rat and jugglers. For Kate, the village was a place of stability and industry and was the backdrop for her early life and development.

This little girl with a mop of brunette locks had developed into a beautiful young woman – one with no need to borrow the trappings of other girls' dreams. She was, after all, within touching distance of realising her own dreams and becoming a real-life princess. Kate had become William's passion, his soulmate; she was the companion and consort to the young man destined to be King. She was sharing his bed, helping him through his youthful angst, encouraging him in his hopes and allowing him, in some measure, to experience the sort of loving stability that she had been raised to take for granted. It was something his late mother had so desperately wanted for him, something in her short life she had never managed to attain for herself.

Yet in those miners' contribution to Kate's gene pool – and to any children she may have – are the resilience and fortitude that had enabled them to triumph over poverty, malnutrition and the cholera epidemic. The last link with that Northern heritage, Kate's grandmother Dorothy, died in July 2006 after a brave battle against cancer. She was 71, and with her went a 200-year unbroken chain back to 18th-century England. Her latter years were happily spent with her husband Ron at a little riverside cottage in the Berkshire village of Pangbourne, very different indeed from the subterranean hell of Hetton. She, more than any, must have marvelled at the long journey taken by her family from Hetton-le-Hole and its mines to the gilded palaces and ancient castles now her granddaughter's destiny.

Kate may not have the lineage, the connections or the huge wealth that in the past would have been prerequisites for her to marry a future king, but, amid her plethora of attributes, she has the one thing that William appears to value above all others: she has her prince's heart.

Back then, 15 years and close to 100 miles separated William from the one person who would in the future truly afford him the normality he craved. For as William and Harry played in the labyrinth of rooms of Kensington Palace under the watchful eye of a nanny and plain-clothes police guard, a little girl was playing at home within sight of her parents.

CHAPTER 5

SCHOOL DAYS

'Every boy in the school fancied her rotten.'
KATE MIDDLETON'S SCHOOL FRIEND GEMMA WILLIAMSON

In the months after Princess Diana's death in 1997, Prince William emerged from her shadow as a heartthrob for thousands of girls. They tore down their Leonardo DiCaprio posters and replaced them with images of the handsome, young, tragic prince. The impressionable Kate Middleton was one of those girls. Thirty miles down the road from Eton College, in the dormitory at Marlborough school that she shared with two other girls, they had a picture of Prince William on the wall. Back then, Kate was a giggly, hockey-obsessed pupil who took little interest in the poorly concealed adolescent lust of the Marlborough boys. Kate later claimed in her engagement interview that she actually had a poster of a Levi model, not William. But one of the roommates, Jessica Hay, told me after the announcement of the engagement that it was true. 'We all fancied Prince William. He was gorgeous. It's fair to say that it wasn't just Kate but his picture was on the wall.'

Kate arrived at Marlborough at the age of 14, having arrived from Downe House, an exclusive girls' boarding school a few miles away in Berkshire. It was midway through the academic year, which just added to the apprehension of joining new classmates at her fourth school in a decade. Dressed in her new uniform, a smart blue blazer and tartan skirt, the teenager arrived at the renowned public school driven by her parents. Her time at her previous school had not been a happy one and it showed in the pale, rather reedy figure she presented. There was talk of bullying and it had shattered her confidence. Carole knew she had to act, and, after devouring all the glossy brochures, thought Marlborough College offered the solution. It would not be cheap, but for the inspirational Carole she believed it would be money well spent.

Founded in 1843, and situated in one of the most attractive market towns in the country, Marlborough is a flourishing and co-educational, independent boarding school for pupils aged 13–18. It was used to educating the sons and daughters of the cream of society and old aristocratic families. Notable 'old Marlburians' included those with royal links. Lord Janvrin, the Queen's loyal former Private Secretary, Sir Anthony Blunt, the Queen's art historian and traitor communist spy, the poet laureate Sir John Betjeman and the Queen's biographer Professor Ben Pimlott. Others included her future husband's first cousin HRH Princess Eugenie of York as well as the courtier Sir Alan 'Tommy' Lascelles, private secretary to the Queen and her father George VI. Actors James Mason and James Robertson Justice and Statesman Rab Butler are also on the illustrious list of old boys. Surely, a former pupil as a future Queen caps the lot.

The school, motto, *Deus Dat Incrementum* – 'God Giveth the Increase', taken from Corinthians I – was to establish itself as the first choice of parents who are seeking for their children an excellent, modern education in a coeducational environment. It boasts a community where scholarship is cherished, creativity is celebrated, diversity is evidenced, and conversation – the means by which knowledge is elevated into wisdom – is paramount. Certainly, it came as a welcome change for Kate. At first, Kate was homesick and chose to keep her own company after dining at Norwood Hall. She was conscientious, studying hard – but it added to her sense of isolation. She lacked confidence, was perhaps a little overwhelmed.

Soon, though, she began to relax. Collecting the nickname 'Middlebum', she began to mingle and form firm friendships. A capable teenager, she played hockey for the school, was in the first pair at tennis and was an accomplished cross-country runner and netball player.

Jessica Hay, her best friend from those days, who shared a dormitory with her, recalls her as a girl with 'very high morals'. She is not alone in her opinion. Gemma Williamson, who along with Jessica and Kate made up a trio of firm friends during their schooldays, also remembers Kate as self-contained and modest in the true sense of the words. Towards the end of her schooling she may have blossomed into a fun-loving and popular member of the school but, when she first pitched up at the gates of the £21,000-a-year establishment, she bore little resemblance to the striking young woman she would become.

Gemma explained, 'Catherine arrived suddenly in the middle of the year. Apparently, she had been bullied very badly in her previous school [St Andrew's, Pangbourne] and she certainly looked thin and pale. She had very little confidence.' It can't have helped that, with typical teenage cruelty, boys from more senior years would rate new girls as they came into supper by holding up paper napkins with marks out of ten written on them; Kate scored only ones and twos. One summer later her scores would leap. By the following year her willowy figure had softened and filled out. She was still lithe and sporty but the colour was back in her cheeks. She was, her friends recall, 'totally different'.

'Every boy in the school fancied her rotten,' Gemma claimed an observation with which Jessica concurred. Nevertheless, Kate, who was put in the all-girl schoolhouse of Elmhurst, was never terribly interested in all this newfound attention. She had a couple of innocent kisses and harmless fumbles but those who knew her best knew that Kate was saving herself for someone special. As any school populated by the privileged offspring of wealthy but often absent parents, Marlborough has its fair share of wild teenage behaviour. Drink is smuggled into dormitories, cigarettes secreted in blazer pockets and teenage flirtations turn awkward youths and prim girls into sexual adventurers – but not Kate. Her school pal Jessica: 'She didn't have any serious boyfriends at school. She is very good-looking and a lot of boys liked her but it just used to go over her head. She didn't get involved in any drinking or smoking but was very sporty instead and very family-orientated.'

She went on, 'One of Catherine's best assets is that she has always been very sure of herself. She has never allowed herself to be influenced by others and there's no way that she would be involved in any of that. She still doesn't really drink and certainly doesn't smoke. You're much more likely to find her going for a long walk across the moors than going to a nightclub. We would sit around talking about all the boys at school we fancied but Catherine would always say, "I don't like any of them. They're all a bit of rough." Then, prophetically, she would joke, "There's no one quite like William." We always said that one day she would meet him and they would be together."'

Kate may have gossiped with her friends about the boys she fancied, but her attitude to sex was, by all accounts, very old-fashioned – especially at a school where, as Gemma says, 'Half the pupils were already having sex.'

Kate, however, wasn't alone in her dream of meeting and marrying William. There were tens of thousands of girls just like her. Besides, William had grown into a strapping figure of a young man. But this teenage girl believed fate was on her side. When the pair of them appeared in the same Marlborough newsletter – both pictured in back-page sports articles, she playing hockey, he polo – she believed their paths would cross. A school source said, 'She called it her "kismet" picture because she truly believed fate would bring them together. Some of the girls thought it was a dream, but who is deluded now? She's got her man, so maybe there was something in it.'

It was at this time that the young Kate had a teenage crush on the swashbuckling adventurer Willem Marx, who was 'ever so slightly' supposed to have broken her heart. The two were to remain friends as got tongues wagging many years later when he accompanied her to a nightclub without her royal boyfriend in tow.

Accusations would follow that Carole would engineer Kate's choice of university with the express purpose of seeing her daughter beguile, then ensnare, a future king, a charge that was wholly inaccurate but one that stuck. Like many well-off students, she took what the British call a 'gap year' between secondary school and college, spending three months of it in Florence learning Italian at the British Institute. While she was there, friends noticed that, though they frequently overindulged, Kate often nursed a single drink throughout the evening.

Like many teenagers on the cusp of adulthood and readying themselves for life as full-time students, William, too, decided to take a gap year. In August 2000, while he learned of his A-level results, he was already in the jungles of Belize and preparing to embark on survival exercises with the Welsh Guards ahead of his travels to Chile. His gap year, or at least a large part of it, he spent in South America as a volunteer with Raleigh International; these jungle manoeuvres were part adventure, part necessity. Kate too was preparing for her own gap experience. However, hers was a less rugged itinerary and one more in keeping with the history-of-art course at St Andrews, on which she would soon enrol. Kate was planning to spend three months in Florence – the Renaissance capital, steeped in history and promising months of relaxation and mind-broadening culture. In the corridors of the Uffizi and the cobbled streets of the city, she would see at first hand some of the treasures that, the following October, would exist for her only in the pages of her course textbooks. Her preparation focused on booking language lessons at the British Institute, organising accommodation, studying guidebooks to the city and excitedly poring over her travel plans with friends and family.

While St James's Palace was rather pompously, 'pleased to announce' the prince's A-level results (B in history of art, A in geography and a modest C in biology) the beautiful and carefree Kate was ripping open the results envelope at home in Berkshire. Secure in the knowledge that her university place was safe, she headed to Florence while William, a month after his 18th birthday, flew to those humid jungles of Belize. He mucked in with the soldiers, slept in a hammock strung between trees, swapped his jeans and baseball cap for jungle combats and floppy hat and trainers for heavy army boots, and his daily food was no more or less than the troops' British Army rations.

While Kate sent postcards home and took snaps of her travels and the friends she made *en route*, William's 'postcards' home were rather more contrived. In October, November and December he was photographed in a variety of staged PR opportunities. Using the tame Press Association, he was shown sharing a joke with ten-year-old Marcela Hernandez-Rios, while helping to teach English in the village of Tortel. There were photos, too, of him with little Alejandro Heredia, a six-year-old child who hitched a ride on William's broad shoulders at the nursery. And there were others of the future British King scrubbing toilets, carrying logs and hammering posts into the arid earth.

Kate's life was less strenuous. At this time she was enjoying an adolescent relationship with a boy called Harry. She was also, inevitably, being relentlessly pursued the Italian waiters at the fashionable Art Bar in Florence, known for its bohemian clientele and cocktails, and a place that quickly became a firm favourite for Kate and fellow romantics, drawn to the city for its art and atmosphere. Awkward teenagers and experienced Casanovas alike tried their best to chat up the stunning brunette with the dazzling smile, but it was always to no avail. 'She managed to give you the brush-off while still making you feel good about yourself,' recalled one failed suitor. Others were not always so considerate of her feelings. Harry apparently, messed her around and the two parted, leaving Kate emotionally bruised, perhaps a little heartbroken as only teenagers – heart-stung for the first time – can be.

Without Harry to distract, Kate threw herself into her studies with enthusiasm. One of her reasons for travelling to Florence was to learn the language at the British Institute in the city. There she shared a top-floor flat with four other girls – within easy reach of the Duomo and other art treasures. She and her friends could spend hours wandering through the labyrinthine streets, gazing up in wonder at buildings so perfect it seemed impossible that they had stood just so since Roman times.

Evenings were spent in the Art Bar or another similarly lively place. Unlike some students, who indulged to excess, Kate would always stop after a few glasses of wine, a sign of remarkable self-control and a moral compass already set.

While others experimented with drugs, Kate passed them by and did not partake – but she was never judgemental, never prim, and never unpopular or ridiculed as a result. Quite the opposite: she charmed all she met. One fellow student and contemporary of Kate's said, 'The Italian barmen loved Kate. In addition, because they fancied her, the rest of the girls used to get free drinks. They were charmed by her beauty and English-rose appeal.' But they would have to make do with lusting from afar. Kate never gave the slightest encouragement to her Italian suitors. Perhaps she had her sights set on higher things than the slick charms of some Latin Lothario. Whatever the source of her disinterest, it was an abiding characteristic in those days – days when, unbeknown to both, she and William's first meeting was growing ever closer.

William was expected to follow his father's example and attend Trinity College, Cambridge. A committee of advisers had made this decision for Charles, but William was given more freedom. And he grabbed it with both hands. He would not follow the Oxbridge route mapped out, however tentatively, for him. He would break with that tradition and go, instead, to St Andrews, an ancient and well-respected establishment but never before considered fit for a future King.

True to form, however, William had other ideas. He had followed his gut instinct. He plumped for the small coastal town that would, he believed, allow him a level of privacy that a Southern University might not. At the same time, Kate Middleton, was anxiously awaiting news of whether her application to her university of choice had been successful. She was every bit as set on her course as William was on his, and it was a course that would lead to a chance meeting with a prince that she had for so long only dreamed of.

CHAPTER 6

TEEN ICON

'My father always taught me to treat everybody as an equal. I have always done and I am sure that William and Harry are the same.'
DIANA, PRINCESS OF WALES, INTERVIEWED IN LE MONDE, 1997

There was no great ambition behind the trip. It was another family skiing holiday – some much-needed time for Princes William and Harry to spend with their father just seven months after the appalling loss of their mother. Before the three princes retreated to Whistler and the mountains of British Columbia to enjoy four days on the slopes, a stint of royal walkabouts had been pencilled in for the entourage on arrival in Canada.

Nobody, neither Prince Charles's closest advisers nor the following rat pack of royal journalists – including me – knew quite what the public would make of this beleaguered trio. Charles still had to contend with a great deal of blame and resentment from those among the public who ludicrously viewed him as somehow culpable for Princess Diana's death.

Meanwhile, the very mention of his grieving sons prompted outpourings of public sympathy and heavy doses of galling grief by proxy. William and Harry had been largely spared public scrutiny in the months since their mother's death. Nobody could forget their composure on the day of her funeral at Westminster Abbey on 6 September 1997, and during the very public mourning that preceded it when they had walked among weeping strangers and viewed the flowers and cards laid at the gates and along the paths and roads outside her west London home of Kensington Palace. William in particular had conducted himself resolutely in the face of almost incalculable adversity. He was much taller and seemingly much more mature than Harry, who, not yet 13, had appeared heartbreakingly young and vulnerable. It was easy to overlook the fact that William, too, was a boy who had lost his mother. Now, three months short of his 16th birthday, he was still camera-shy, by turns sullen, quick to blush and possessed of all the awkward self-awareness of teenage years.

When they touched down at Vancouver airport on 24 March 1998, the royal party did so with a great deal of apprehension and few expectations. This was, to all intents and purposes, a family holiday with a few public engagements thrown in for good measure – a sop for the devoted royalists and a scrap for the fascinated press. But within minutes of their arrival in the country's west coast capital something remarkable happened – something that would mark the trip out as a watershed for the teenage Prince William. From the instant he stepped out onto Canadian soil a new phenomenon was born: 'Wills Mania'.

Crowds of frantic teenage girls, hundreds of whom had waited for hours to see their hero, went wild as they finally caught sight of him. They jostled against police barricades and wept, screamed and waved banners offering to prove to Wills in a variety of forthright fashions just how devoted to the young royal they really were. It was an astonishing spectacle. It would have fazed the most seasoned public figure. This was the sort of adoring hysteria associated with the Beatles in their heyday, when frenzied female fans screamed themselves into fainting fits and had to be pulled unconscious from the crowds.

This was unlike anything I had seen as a royal reporter. Even the fevered adoration of Diana had stopped short of this unashamed teenage lust. There were about 30 or so of us in the press contingent that had travelled to Canada – photographers, reporters and television crews alike. If truth be told, it caught us all on the hop, but it was a dream story. The copy just flowed. My erstwhile colleagues Richard Kay and Charles Rae and I rushed around gleaning quotes and scribbling notes and filing reams of information for our newspapers back home. We knew that we were literally witnessing the making of a royal icon. Not a replacement for Diana – nothing so brash or so mired in the recent past. This was something new. After months of naval gazing and gloom, this was something so spontaneously upbeat that you could not help but get carried along with this unexpected surge of enthusiasm.

It was not an entirely uncomplicated birth for the new royal hero. As the adrenalin pumped through our reporters' veins, it was easy to forget that William – this tall, athletically handsome young man – was still just a boy, a teenager having to deal with the weight of so much expectation. It would have been all too easy to dismiss his acute embarrassment were it not for the fact that William, revealing a determined streak of character, made sure that the press and his advisers were well aware of it.

At first, he did his best to hide his discomfort at the extreme adulation with which he was met. He hated every second of it, as we were soon to find out. As he arrived at what was supposed to be a private visit to the Pacific Space Centre in the heart of the town, row upon row of screaming girls – about five thousand – greeted William. The death of his mother had turned him into a somewhat romantic, tragic hero for many a dewy-eyed teen. At first both Harry and William seemed appalled by the phenomenon. Harry's nonplussed appearance was perhaps more to do with the fact that the girl fans were not screaming for him. William was just horrified at the heaving mass of adoration.

'Look at him! I've got posters of him all over my wall,' said one.

'They should declare it a national holiday, William Day,' screamed another. The poor lad did not know which way to look. Eyes downcast, his bashful smile redolent of his late mother, William did his best and showed great resolve, rising to the occasion and spending ten minutes shaking hands with and accepting gifts from well-wishers. Not once did he allow his smile, however apologetic, to fade from his face.

One observer reported that he looked close to tears. I did not see that and I was pretty close to the action, but the young prince's discomfort was obvious. He could not wait to get inside, and when he did, and only his father and the entourage were in earshot, all hell broke loose. William had had enough. He refused to go on. The task of talking William down from the ledge fell to his anxious father, who, with a grace and diplomacy of which many believe him incapable, coaxed the petulant teen back from the brink. While his newly installed PR man Mark Bolland hovered haplessly nearby, Charles had a heart-to-heart with William. Later it fell to Bolland to try to negotiate a truce of sorts with the overheated press. There was precious little he could do to cool the ardour of a nation's teenage girls. The Royal Family, we were told, wanted our coverage to be 'calmer, cooler'.

Back in Britain, Bolland found unlikely allies in the form of various doom-mongering commentators reporting from the comfort of their desks thousands of miles away. Self-appointed guardians of the young princes' welfare did their best to dampen down the frenzy we on the ground had reported. It was not a case of our whipping it up: the reaction was natural and real. Chief among the commentators was *Daily Express* columnist Mary Kenny, who argued that the boys were being exposed far too soon after their mother's death. She wrote, 'Diana was adored all over the world. And this is a halo effect that William and Harry will carry everywhere: that they were Diana's sons. But would Princess Diana, if she were alive today, want her elder son to start carrying out royal duties at such a tender age?'

The implication was that she would not. The finger of blame pointed at Charles, not for the first time, and also at his officials for exploiting Diana's sons. As would often happen in the years following Diana's death, Charles's critics would conveniently overlook the simple fact that, despite scurrilous untrue rumours relating to Harry's paternity, the boys were both his sons too and he loved them unconditionally and would do anything to protect them. Still, it was a difficult situation. How could the princes visit the country of which, as a realm and part of the Commonwealth, William would one day be king and hide away from an adoring public? Moreover, how could they even begin to control, never mind quash, such a spontaneous outpouring of affection for William? It was too big an ask: the genie was out of the bottle and not even an accomplished media fixer like Mark Bolland could put it back and seal up the stopper. Besides, the emergence of William as the new royal star was not without its benefits for the family – once he had embraced the situation.

With his initial nerves and truculence soothed, the actor in William emerged. Maybe, just maybe, he was beginning to enjoy this. As the British media headed off in chartered helicopters for the next photo call, on the ski slopes of the Canadian Rockies, William started to perform. When the three princes were presented with bright red 'Roots' branded caps – worn by the country's Winter Olympics team – William showed his youthful credentials and a grasp of the real world that his father never possessed. The caps are worn back to front but Charles inevitably put his on the wrong way round before William, laughingly, corrected him – upstaging his father in the process. William, prince of cool, was a media triumph.

It was very different from the first time I had sought any meaningful encounter with William at another royal skiing holiday, in 1995 in Klosters, Switzerland. William was 12 when I conducted his first, brief interview. A photo call had been staged for him, along with his brother and cousins, Princesses Beatrice and Eugenie, daughters of the Duke and Duchess of York. The idea had been hurriedly conceived and executed by Commander Richard Aylard RN, who, like so many courtiers before him and since, believed he knew how to handle the media to promote his boss – even though he famously issued a memo instructing no member of the prince's household ever to talk to members of the press. Given their ages, the good commander had cleared all questions. I asked William, 'Who's the best skier?' He smiled. He was not going to admit that his little brother was better than he was.

'These two,' he said, gesturing at his cousins, 'are coming along really well.' It was a deft diplomatic touch for one so young, a mischievous batting back of my question. Yes, the whole encounter had been organised with military – or rather naval – attention to detail and William had known what questions were coming. However, one should not underestimate how nerve-racking a one-on-one encounter with the media can be. There, in that low-key interaction on the slopes, was a hint of the humour and self-possession that would unfurl in a week when he faced the press in Canada, just three years later.

In the intervening years, William would go through many shifts of character. Contrary to popular belief that has Harry painted as the tearaway – frequenting lap-dancing bars, taking swings at photographers and generally ripping up the town – William is no goody two-shoes. His character is one forged in the fires of a youth at once troubled and blessed. He would hardly be human or, frankly, particularly interesting had he not kicked against the pricks occasionally. Certainly he would not be the prince he is today were it not for a mass of often conflicting influences and a healthy dose of childish rebellion and adolescent wildness. Today, William is a young man who often confounds the predictions of those who would like simply to slot him into a convenient category. He is by turns intensely sensitive – his mother often worried that he, like her, was *too* sensitive for the life that royalty demanded – and laddishly bullish. He is the baseball-cap-wearing prince who posed for official portraits sporting a hole in the elbow of his sweater, the future king who visited amusement parks as a child, who plays football, is up to speed on contemporary culture and who enjoys a pint with his friends. But he is not, for all that, a man entirely of our time.

Home to William is still a variety of palaces and mansions where the walls are hung thick with exquisite works of art and where shooting-party weekends follow the seasons. This 'sensitive' young man loves the hunting-and-fishing lifestyle that seems a complete anachronism when set against the flipside of his character. He takes pride in bagging rabbits, grouse and stag. He plays polo and a favoured 'pub' in younger years was Club H – a bar set up by William and Harry in the cellars of their father's Gloucestershire home, Highgrove.

For many years now, William has veered between the traditional and the unexpectedly modern in many aspects of his life, including his taste in women. He has been linked – often mischievously – to pop stars, supermodels and the daughters of foreign leaders. And, with a similar degree of regularity, flirtations have been spotted, and imagined, between William and the sort of ruddy-faced, jolly-hockey-sticks daughters of aristocracy and giddy 'it' girls who fall more naturally – in some cases literally – into his royal path. He is a mass of contradictions and even more appealing to the opposite sex for it.

William is a young man on the cusp of embracing public life and, hopefully, securing private happiness. He knows that his duty makes his life a sort of sacrifice to the state. He has shown that he has not completely submerged his personal needs and desires as a result. He is starting to find a personal equilibrium that long eluded both his mother and his father in their private and public lives, perhaps partly because, in the figure of Kate, he has found a girl who can make sense of his conflicting character traits and the opposing demands of his life as a modern prince. She keeps him in touch with a lifestyle from which, by virtue of his HRH status, he will always be one step removed. And, while newspaper reports may have started to portray Kate as the 'new Diana', much of Kate's appeal lies in how she differs from Princess Diana rather than how she resembles her. Yes, she may have injected a bit of youthful glamour and a dose of romance into the Royal Family once more. More importantly, in Kate William has found a sensible and attractive girl who, in emotional terms, demands very little of him. For a boy who has lived through the heat of the War of the Waleses, that must seem like bliss – not least because his mother leaned so heavily on her elder son in her own times of need, times when William was still just a little boy.

William was a few months shy of his tenth birthday when the first hints of this became visible. On the way out of church at Sandringham, he turned to his great-grandmother, the Queen Mother, and, like a perfect little gentleman, took her arm to help her through a gateway. The photographers in the press pen opposite lapped it up. Then he popped up at his mother's side and appeared instinctively to sense her need for him to be there for her, too; unprompted he escorted her towards a waiting car.

William also had a natural knack of spotting what Princess Diana needed. Throughout the turmoil of his parents' marriage crisis in 1992 he assumed the role of supportive son. He was just ten but already, in Diana's eyes at least, he had reached that rewarding age when the child becomes a companion and friend to his parent, able to grasp, at least in part, a parent's adult troubles. Whenever Diana felt uncertain, William was there for her. He once told her he wanted to be a policeman so that he could protect her. Her heart must have ached with love at his earnest words.

The princess proudly told friends that William had become her 'soul mate'. It was a turn of phrase that left many distinctly uneasy. Some even cautioned her against confiding so unreservedly in her elder son. She insisted that her boys hear the truth from her lips – a determination that struck many as a bit rich considering the fact that Diana herself was generating much of the press speculation about her with carefully placed leaks. The princess, who felt besieged by both the media and the emissaries of her husband, claimed that she had no choice.

She chose her son as confidant at this crucial time in her life. Some psychologists claim that when a marriage is rocky the mother often turns to her older or oldest child for the sort of emotional support and advice she would normally hope to receive from her husband. This is what Diana did and sometimes she simply went too far, burdening William with problems and paranoia. Patrick Jephson, Diana's private secretary at the time, confided that the princess herself admitted to being afraid that William, like her, was too sensitive for the part he must play in the Royal Family. She continued to load him with her troubles regardless, while every embarrassing indiscretion was played out in the press.

In June 1992, Andrew Morton's groundbreaking biography, *Diana: Her True Story*, was published and with it all her grievances against William's father. Two months later portions of taped telephone calls of Diana talking to her lover, Captain James Hewitt, were made public, too. Later that same year Prince Charles suffered his own telephone scandal when details of an excruciating conversation with Camilla emerged. In it was the infamous comment in which he claimed, albeit in intimate jest, that he would 'come back' as a 'tampon'. (More romantically and significantly he also said to her, 'Your great achievement is to love me.') Even though it was never meant for public consumption it must have made William and Harry want to bury their heads in shame. But how could they? William could not escape the news of royal crisis and there was a part of him that didn't want to. Ignorance was not an option for the young prince and at times he positively sought out information. He would often slip into the room of his police bodyguard and turn on the television news and watch in silence as the story of his parents' riven love lives played out on the screen. There was hardly a day when news schedules did not include some reference to the rapidly unravelling union.

Still, when confirmation of his parents' divorce finally reached William, he was devastated. It was December 1992 and Diana drove to Ludgrove, the prep school at which both Harry and William were pupils, to tell her boys in person. In the privacy of the headmaster's study William broke down in tears. Harry just went quiet and his cheeks flushed a little red. But after his initial outburst William sensed his mother's distress. The tears ceased. He kissed his mother and said maturely that he hoped both his parents could be happier now. That night he gave his younger brother a hug. As the pair embraced they made a brothers' pact never to take sides – and they never did. It was a pity the same could not be said for their parents.

William may have assured his mother of his support that day in the headmaster's office and he would honour that vow. But the stress and emotional pain had to come out somehow and already the months of speculation and tension had taken their toll on him. Everybody deals with stress differently. Some, like Harry, retreat into their shells; for William the effect was quite the opposite: he became rebellious, he neglected his studies and his behaviour became uncharacteristically aggressive.

Two months before the then Prime Minister John Major informed Parliament that the Prince and Princess of Wales were separating, I took a phone call from a reliable contact. At the time I was starting out as a royal reporter for the *Sun* and the story my contact relayed that day was, in *Sun*-speak, an absolute corker. William, he said, had been reprimanded at school for sticking a fellow pupil's head in a school toilet and flushing it. The legendary editor Kelvin MacKenzie, desperate to splash on anything other than the collapse of the British coalmining industry that was dominating the news, loved it and plastered the sorry tale of student bullying across the front page with a giant 'Exclusive' tag. William seemed a privileged little tearaway and was dubbed the Hooligan Prince. At the time I got the story it didn't occur to me to examine it beyond the bare facts. Blissfully unsympathetic, hardened by the ignorance and ambition of youth, I saw it as a cracking story that quite rightly walked into the newspaper. It did not occur to me to consider what might have prompted William's outburst. It later transpired that William's aggression came after he heard the unfortunate pupil make a disparaging remark about his parents.

William was reprimanded by the headmaster, Gerald Barber, but the teacher was also sensitive to the growing problems his famous pupil was facing at the eye of his parents' marital storm. William was given special dispensation to telephone home more than normal so he could console his increasingly agitated mother as her world fell apart.

No doubt William empathised as, for a time, things kept getting worse for the impressionable prince as the War of the Waleses went into overdrive. Diana in particular seemed determined to outdo publicly the husband she loved to portray as an emotionally repressed, dated and out-of-touch father. Perhaps there was some truth in her claims, but however Charles may have struggled in those early days to show his love for his sons, he loved them nonetheless. In stark contrast to her depiction of the stuffy, repressed Charles, Diana wanted to be seen as exciting, fun and a thoroughly modern mother – albeit one whom marriage had placed in a gilded cage.

The boys' holidays with Charles were traditional and overtly royal, revolving around the royal residences at Sandringham and Balmoral and weekends at Highgrove. Diana whisked her boys off to the Caribbean and to Disney World in Florida. She took them go-karting and to theme parks and she made damn sure the press photographers and reporters knew about it. When the media descended on Disney World in 1993, myself among them, to witness Diana and her sons having the time of their lives it

Above: The author with Prince William in New Zealand in 2010.

Bottom: Kate Middleton in 2005.

The author's Royal exclusives included the first revelation of William and Kate's engagement.

Above: William and Kate after the Prince received his RAF wings from his father.

© *PA Photos*

Below: The author being presented with Scoop of the Year award by David Cameron for breaking the story that Charles and Camilla were to wed.

Kate in 2004. © *Rex Features*

Princess Diana with the young William.

Above: Diana and Princes Harry and William on holiday. © *PA Photos*

Below left: Kate at St Andrews University in 2005. © *Rex Features*

Below right: On a night out in 2006.

A moment alone for Kate at the Chakravarty Polo Club in Richmond in 2006.

Princes Charles and William at RAF Cranwell in Seaford, 2008.

was on a tip that came directly from the princess herself. She wanted pictures of her and the boys whooping it up on the fantastic rides and she wanted them sent back home as a very public picture postcard to her husband: 'Having a great time – glad you're not here!'

But the blows just kept coming. In June 1994, when William was just 12, his father appeared in the Jonathan Dimbleby television documentary *Charles: The Private Man, the Public Role* and admitted that he had committed adultery. He may have qualified it by claiming the betrayal happened only after the marriage had irretrievably broken down, but it did not soften the blow for his boys. A couple of months later it was reported that Diana had made a series of harassing phone calls to a married art dealer, Oliver Hoare, with whom she was having an alleged affair. Then, in October, a book was published that recounted in lurid detail her affair with her riding instructor, James Hewitt, an officer in the Household Cavalry. This particularly hurt. William and Harry had liked James as a friend and had known that he was close to their mother. The revelation that they had been lovers was a genuine shock to them both. Diana made one of her increasingly frequent dashes to Ludgrove to talk to her sons.

William knew why she had come. He had read the headlines. He had bought her a box of chocolates – a gesture that reduced Diana, now close to breaking point, to tears. Less than a fortnight later she was back again, closeted in the headmaster's study with her elder son. Jonathan Dimbleby had published his authorised book, *The Prince of Wales: A Biography*, in 1994, in which he claimed that the prince had never loved Diana but had married her out of a sense of obligation and under duress from his father, the Duke of Edinburgh. 'Is it true Daddy never loved you?' asked William. Diana sought to reassure him that it was not – that theirs had once been a love match. The thought that he and his brother were born from duty, not love, was too much for the sensitive William to bear.

As the much-maligned former butler Paul Burrell noted, this experience with his mother would have a great impact on how William would handle the future and his own dealings with girlfriends. Burrell recalled in his book, *A Royal Duty*, 'Her invaluable words of wisdom, the tips handed down over tea in bone china, will be with him for life. If he has one challenge ahead of him, it is how he handles the spotlight. He will not forget what the media spotlight – and especially the freelance paparazzi – did to his mother. It was always William who was there with a box of Kleenex when the princess became upset.'

And it was not all one-way traffic. Diana, perhaps unwittingly and a little selfishly, had given him a tough grounding at a tender age in the emotional excesses of a demanding woman. It is very unlikely that any girl he went out with would have been as difficult to deal with emotionally as his mother. But his obsessive behaviour did not put him off girls. In fact he had his first 'serious' romance at the tender age of just seven. He was so besotted with the little girl that he even proposed marriage. This first romance happened while William was holidaying in Balmoral. He first saw Anna McCart while out riding with his brother Harry. He took one look at the blue-eyed, blonde daughter of one of the Balmoral gardeners and was smitten. She said hello to him but William was dumbstruck. 'He almost fell off his pony,' one of the estate workers confided. After that the two seven-year-olds were inseparable and he spent every day of the rest of the holiday with her. Within a week, so the story goes, he plucked up enough courage, kissed her and asked her to marry him. She just laughed. But, to show his serious intent, the boy prince added, 'When I come back next year I am going to marry you.' He told her earnestly, 'My papa told me if you kiss a girl you have to marry her.' Anna took the proposal seriously and told other estate workers' children that she was going to be a princess. It was a charming story of childish love, but his comment showed that Charles was teaching his son to behave, even at a young age, with honour when it came to women.

Diana, on the other hand, was far more mischievous. Although she had grown to depend on William as an emotional crutch, they had a playful relationship, too. She enjoyed teasing her son. Like many adolescent boys with their hormones raging, William indulged in fantasies about beautiful women. He had posters of models on his bedroom wall. But, Diana being Diana, she knew how to take matters to a new high. As a youth William was no stranger to being surrounded by beautiful women. On one occasion Diana fixed it for him to share dinner with her in the presence of Cindy Crawford. Another time she ensured that William was surrounded by the world's most beautiful women, when she arranged for supermodels Naomi Campbell, Claudia Schiffer and Christy Turlington to make a surprise visit to Kensington Palace.

The following year, with William now a pupil at Eton College, the question of love was raised again. But this time it was by Diana in a television interview with Martin Bashir on *Panorama*, in which she confessed to loving James Hewitt. Diana had paid William a surprise visit at Eton the day before the programme was broadcast. She wanted to tell him about it before it was screened and, too late to stop it, she was beginning to regret her decision. The next day William was called down to his housemaster's study shortly before 8 p.m., where he watched his mother's interview in solitude. Harry had turned down the chance to join him. William watched in dismay as Diana went further than anybody had imagined she would.

William, her ever-dependable little consort, was mortified and hurt by his mother's words on *Panorama*. For a while he ignored her, not wanting to continue in his role as her confidant any more. But within a few weeks she was forgiven. His love for her was unconditional. He could never forsake her, however much her behaviour made him wince. 'My papa never embarrasses me,' he told a friend at the time. 'My mummy embarrasses me.'

Prince Charles may have been rather stuffy as far as his public image was concerned but he undoubtedly did his best to be a good father to his sons, whom he loved dearly. His own relationship with his father did not give him much of an example to draw on – theirs has always been a distant, even cold, setup. At least that's how Charles saw it.

Diana disapproved violently of the 'manly' pursuits that Charles encouraged his sons to enjoy. She tried to turn their heads with the excitement of amusement parks and thrill rides but they were devoted to their father, too, and genuinely enjoyed the outdoor activities so favoured by the Windsors. William in particular loved to shoot – something his mother could never reconcile with her image of her sensitive son. Much to Diana's disgust he bagged his first rabbit at the age of 11. Three years later, by now passionate about the pastime, he felled a stag in the Scottish Highlands with a single shot and was blooded. Diana let it pass and resigned herself to the fact that her elder son was thrilled by the chase.

When the boys were with their father they spent a great deal of time in the company of their cousins, Princess Anne's children Peter and Zara, who had also lived through the pain of a very public marriage breakdown. But Charles, perhaps stung by Diana's criticism that he was emotionally unavailable, worried that he was not providing enough of the homeliness his sons needed. He realised that whenever his sons spent a weekend or holiday with him in the country, much as they loved the riding, fishing and shooting, something was lacking. His solution was to infuriate Diana in a way he could not have imagined. He hired a nanny. It must have seemed perfectly natural to a man whose own childhood saw him spend more time in the care of his nanny and servants than his own mother and father.

Thirty-year-old Tiggy Legge-Bourke (later to become Tiggy Pettifer) seemed an ideal 'surrogate mother', just the sort to inject a bit of zest into the lives of Charles's sons when they stayed with him. She certainly enlivened proceedings for the boys. They adored her and thought nothing of telling their increasingly jealous mother of the fact. She enjoyed shooting, hunting and fishing and energised the boys' stays with their father. She became more of a surrogate sister than mother to them. Worse still for Diana, she became someone else in whom they could confide. There were none of the tit-for-tat tensions surrounding their mother and father. With Tiggy, what you saw was what you got. They loved her to bits. Perhaps a more confident woman than Diana might have seen this addition to her children's life as just that – an addition, a bonus, a positive influence that in no way diminished her own role in their development.

William's spirits were notably raised by Tiggy and as a result he took greater strides in school. During the disintegration of his parents' marriage he had begun to lag behind. Now, rejuvenated by

Tiggy, he improved dramatically, and not before time. Diana was unimpressed. She sent furious letters to her ex-husband demanding the nanny's role be defined – in other words, limited. Charles's response was to change nothing but simply instruct Tiggy to keep a lower profile in public when out with the boys. But Diana became convinced that Tiggy's inclusion in their lives was part of a ploy to brief her sons against her. Understandably, she was irritated by the idea of another woman being involved in her sons' upbringing and became convinced, unjustifiably, that Tiggy was having an affair with Charles.

Her paranoia boiled over in June 1997. Diana had decided to stay away from the traditional parents' picnic day at Eton College. She had not wanted to steal the spotlight and spoil everyone's fun. Hers was a sacrifice willingly made – until, that is, she discovered that Tiggy had taken her place. More than that, she had laid on booze, bringing bottles of champagne and offering them to everybody she knew. It was a kind, fun gesture. She was there on William and Harry's invitation. They were happy, they were having fun, and when Diana found out she simply screamed, 'That bitch!'

Her criticism was unfair and her reaction extreme. But, in the five years since her split from Charles, Diana's life was spiralling increasingly out of control. She had turned more and more to William for advice on the decisions she was facing. She spoke to him about her desire to retreat from public life. He told her to do whatever made her happy. But neither life in the spotlight nor a life of seclusion seemed to do that. She shared her fears and her loneliness with him. Diana's endlessly needy attention seeking was offputting enough for some of her adult friends, but William remained constant. His advice was always the same: she should do whatever made her happy. Who would blame William if, as he went through all the predictable changes and upheavals of adolescence, he sometimes longed for his mother's happiness if only to ensure a certain peace in his own life?

In July 1997, a month after her explosion at Tiggy's role in her son's life, Diana and the boys enjoyed what was to be their last holiday together. They spent it in the South of France. Both Harry and William had learned to live with their mother's eclectic taste in men. They didn't have much choice. In spite of berating Charles's infidelities, she had notched up a fair tally of lovers herself, both during and after their marriage. Among them were Hewitt, James Gilbey and art dealer Oliver Hoare – and there were even allegations, strongly denied, that she had a fling with married former England rugby captain Will Carling. But, perhaps with the exception of Hewitt, it was her affair with the handsome cardiac surgeon Dr Hasnat Khan that had the greatest impact. She fell so heavily for him that towards the end of 1996 there was speculation that they might marry. That always seemed a fantasy to me – but it may well have been one to which Diana aspired. (I was later told by a senior source that she wanted her personal assistant Victoria Mendham and her butler Paul Burrell to officiate at a ceremony. Bizarrely, it seems, Khan was not aware of these details.) But Hasnat Khan, a practising Muslim who has since wed in an arranged ceremony, would not be snared. Despite his passion for the princess he could not cope with the frenzied attention around Diana. It must have been a novel and entirely unpleasant experience for Diana to encounter a man who was hard to get. She wanted to make him jealous, she wanted him to know what he was missing, and it was this that led her to accept a longstanding offer of an all-expenses-paid luxury holiday courtesy of Harrods owner Mohamed Al Fayed. Of course, she wanted to give her boys a good holiday, too. William and Harry would, she thought, enjoy themselves with the four young Fayed children – Karim, Jasmine, Camilla and Omar – while Al Fayed's millions, she thought, would ensure their privacy, protection and comfort.

They stayed at the villa Castel Ste Therese, set high on the cliffs above Saint-Tropez, in a ten-acre estate complete with its own private beach and the *Jonikal*, £20,000,000 yacht, at their constant disposal. William and Harry spent their days swimming off the *Jonikal*, jet-skiing, scuba-diving or simply lounging by the pool. Never one to miss a trick, Al Fayed instructed his charming son Dodi to join the happy throng. He hoped a holiday romance might follow and his ambitions were fulfilled. Diana and Dodi Fayed had rubbed shoulders a few times before, first meeting at a polo match in July 1986. But this time, in the relaxed surroundings of the Cote d'Azur, something clicked between them. Who knows if it was a relationship that could have gone on to provide Diana with the sort of commitment and happiness she craved, or if it was only ever destined to be a holiday romance? Al Fayed certainly insists that it was very much more than that. Whatever the truth of what actually happened in those blistering South of France days, Diana and Dodi enjoyed some moments of happiness. And William, so keen to see his mother happy, witnessed it. It was, according to those close to the young prince, a source of some comfort to him in the dark days that followed.

Diana and her boys had been at Castel Ste Therese for a few days when Dodi arrived, and it wasn't long before the chemistry kicked in. One evening at supper it spilled over as some light-hearted banter and the teasing escalated into a full-blown food fight. It was hysterical: Diana was laughing again and having fun. On 20 July Diana and the boys flew back to London in a Harrods private jet. That evening, William and Harry went on to continue their summer holidays in Balmoral. Mother and sons hugged and kissed goodbye. It was the last time they would see each other.

With her boys gone Diana faced a lonely summer. So, when a smitten Dodi began lavishing her with attention, gifts and flowers, she lapped it up. An invitation to return to the luxury of the *Jonikal* followed as Dodi asked Diana to join him on a cruise to Corsica and Sardinia on 31 July. This time they would be the yacht's only passengers; this was a love cruise.

Photographs of the lovers kissing on deck predictably appeared in the newspapers back home. Diana had taken the precaution of telephoning William to warn him. She remembered the hurt the Hewitt revelation had caused him and was not going to take any chances. Besides, she knew that pictures of her and Dodi kissing would appear in print eventually – not least because her new lover had engineered the 'snatched' shots. Again, Diana confided in William, talking over the differences between Dodi and Khan, after whom she still hankered. It was an extraordinary topic of conversation for a mother to be having with her 15-year-old son, but he was well used to it. If it was William's blessing for her relationship with Dodi that she wanted, then she got it. Dodi made his mother laugh; he seemed to make her genuinely happy. At last Diana had found happiness in her private life and everybody – including her ex-husband – was pleased and relieved for her. Diana called William from the Imperial Suite of the Fayed-owned Ritz Hotel in Paris on 30 August 1997. They chatted for about 20 minutes, with her telling him how she could not wait to see him the next day after a month apart.

William and Harry were asleep when the first reports came through that something was wrong. At around 1 a.m. Prince Charles was woken and told by telephone that there had been a crash in the Alma tunnel in Paris. Dodi, he was informed, was dead. His ex-wife was injured. The prince woke the Queen. Then moments later came the call with the terrible news that Diana was dead. The poor man, racked with guilt and grief, broke down and wept.

It must have been sheer agony. The Queen wisely advised against waking the boys. Let them sleep now, she counselled, knowing that sleep would not come easily over the following days and weeks, when they would long for its oblivion and nourishment. Instead, Charles paced the corridors as they slept. Overcome with fear at the prospect of telling his sons such devastating news, he went for a lonely walk on the moors. When he returned at 7 a.m., William was already awake. Charles, his eyes swollen and red from tears, walked into William's room and broke the awful news. They hugged each other like never before. Brave and sensitive at the worst moment of William's life, he directed his thoughts to his younger brother, who was still asleep in the bedroom next door. The task of telling Harry was one that both Charles and William undertook together. Gently they explained that Diana had been injured and that the medical team had struggled and failed to save her. Now, embracing each other protectively, they wept uncontrollably as the sounds of raw pain echoed around the old house. Nothing would ever be the same for any of them.

In the sombre moments that followed his mother's death William, who had lost so much, would show in the depths of his grief a strength of character and dignity that was quite simply regal. Charles would show warmth of which his critics never believed him capable. Diana's brother, Earl Spencer, was certainly no fan. At her funeral in Westminster Abbey he delivered a eulogy to his sister riddled with both covert and blatant criticisms of the Royal Family. He insisted that the boys would continue to be influenced by his sister Diana's 'blood family', and seemed to imply that it was her kin who stood the best chance of offering them a rounded upbringing, saving them from the grim clutches of an unadulterated and traditionally royal background.

The words irked and hurt Charles, maybe in part because they struck a chord. Had a traditional royal upbringing been such a success for him? Diana's visits to homeless centres, theme parks and fast-food restaurants seemed gimmicky and had made him cringe in the past. But Charles could see that her devotion and unconventional methods had paid off. William and Harry were well-rounded little chaps with a fresh and confident outlook – in spite of the turbulence of their parents' love lives and divorce.

It was up to Charles, he recognised, to ensure that they did not become weighed down with the responsibility and duty of their birthright. He cancelled all his immediate engagements. Diana's past accusations of his being an absent father echoed in his mind. If he had been a poor husband then, now that she was gone he was not going to fail her again as guardian to the sons they both cherished. Charles threw himself into the role of devoted single dad. He took Harry with him on an official royal tour to South Africa, listened to more to their views and began, tentatively, to embrace modern life. One minute he was posing with the Spice Girls, the next he was embracing children infected with AIDS. Out of adversity, Charles triumphed – and so did his sons.

Given William's uniquely close bond with his mother, those in her inner circle were astonished at how rapidly he seemed to recover. But, then, William had shown his strength before, back when his mother needed him and used him as an emotional crutch. Now he showed that same generosity of spirit as he recognised that Harry and his father needed him. Harry was more of a worry. The gregarious, impish little boy all but disappeared;

he retreated into himself, as he had done in the wake of his parents' divorce. But with time, with William and Charles and 'big sister' Tiggy, he gradually re-emerged. The tears still flowed in private moments but Diana was never coming back and life had to carry on.

The fact that the media could not do the same did upset them. Every time there was another instalment in the Diana saga and another front page of their mother was published, the seething grief with which they were learning to live surged forward with renewed intensity. They grew protective of their surviving parent and were genuinely hurt by what they saw as unfair criticism of him. A year after Diana's death they decided to do something about it. They issued a touching personal statement calling for an end to the public mourning and what had been called the 'Diana Industry' – the commercial exploitation of the Princess of Wales. William in particular was angered by what he saw as blatant profiteering on his mother's name, such as her own Memorial Fund using her name on margarine tubs.

The two princes insisted that their mother 'would want people to now move on – because she would have known that constant reminders of her death can create nothing but pain to those she left behind'. They were distressed by the continual references to their mother's death and the endless speculation and conspiracy theories this generated, many of which emanated from Mohamed Al Fayed. There was a tart response from Al Fayed's spokesman, saying he could not rest until he knew the full truth about how his son had died.

The boys issued their statement on the day that William returned to Eton and that his brother joined him there. It was William's idea but the appeal fell on deaf ears. They would have to live with the conspiracy theories for at least another decade. Still, William continued to flourish at Eton. His housemaster Dr Andrew Gailey, a respected constitutional historian and music lover from Northern Ireland, took the prince under his wing educationally and emotionally and exacted an important and positive influence as William sought to rebuild his life. He worked hard. He proved himself to be the fastest junior swimmer at Eton in ten years and was made joint keeper of swimming – a grand title for what is in effect the school swimming captain. He was made secretary of the Agricultural Club and he received Eton's Sword of Honour – the school's highest award for a first-year cadet. This was the young man who stepped onto the tarmac in Canada and ignited Wills Mania.

He was no longer a rebellious schoolboy, but he did not simply toe the line either. He was not afraid to buck a few trends. One courtier said, 'God help anyone who tells William what to do. He listens, but he won't be pushed around by the system.' Never was that more evident than when the issue was raised of where William would continue his education once his schooldays ended.

It had long been presumed that the prince would follow in his father's footsteps by attending Trinity College, Cambridge. A committee of advisers had made this decision for Charles, but William was given more freedom. He grabbed the opportunity with both hands. He would not follow the Oxbridge route mapped out for him. He would break with tradition and go, instead, to St Andrews.

CHAPTER 7

BEST DAYS OF OUR LIVES

'I do all my own shopping. I go out, get takeaways, rent videos,
go to the cinema, just basically anything I want to really.'
PRINCE WILLIAM ON HIS UNIVERSITY LIFE

Around 3,000 onlookers lined the streets of the small, east-coast town of St Andrews, a place that revolves around the 'town and gown' divide in much the same way as Durham, Oxford and Cambridge. On the morning of 24 September 2001, all focus fell on the dark-green Vauxhall Omega with Prince Charles at the wheel as he attempted to negotiate the narrow, cobbled entrance to St Salvador's College.

A sharp wind blew across the famous Ancient and Royal golf course as Charles nosed the car in under the gothic clock tower. A group of curious students had gathered inside the ancient quadrangle, quietly holding antiwar placards aloft and shivering slightly in the crisp autumn morning. Their presence was predictable but peaceful, an opportunistic bid to piggyback on the publicity generated by the main attraction that day: the arrival of Prince William as he embarked on undergraduate life.

Dressed in jeans, trainers and a pastel sweater, the standard uniform for the modern student, 19-year-old William looked a little shaken by the size of the welcoming committee that had pitched up to mark the occasion. William composed himself quickly and fixed his trademark toothy grin. Stepping smartly from the car and adopting a suitably fixed smile, he strode, hand outstretched, towards the university principal, Dr Brian Lang. Lang stood ever so slightly in front of a host of other academic dignitaries, smiling rather too eagerly and keen to meet the VIP student who, despite his princely status, would be treated no differently from any other fresher.

This place of ancient learning would be William's academic home for the next four years. If he was nervous about what lay ahead of him, he did his best not to show it.

In the weeks prior to the prince's arrival Lang had sounded a note of caution. He implored the media to respect the wishes of the prince and other students and allow them to get on with their respective courses without constant intrusion and pestering. However, behind closed, oak-panelled doors, Lang must have quietly rejoiced at how good for business William's choice of alma mater was.

St Andrews was hardly an unknown backwater to start with. It is Scotland's oldest university. Steeped in history and myth, it dominates the small town and overlooks a sweep of sandy beach and world-famous, wind-buffeted golf courses. Applications for courses had risen by 44 per cent in the wake of William's decision to attend, and some fanciful reports claimed that female students had been ordering wedding dresses in anticipation of his arrival.

William looked every inch the student prince – a far cry from his father's own arrival at university 34 years earlier. Charles, too, had arrived by car but that's where the similarities began and ended. He turned up at Trinity College, Cambridge, in 1967, the so-called Summer of Love, when psychedelia was at its peak. Flower power was the buzz phrase and hippie types wafted around trailing the cloying perfumes of patchouli and incense in their wakes. Not that that made any inroads into Charles's sensibilities and style. He arrived at Cambridge, an 18-year-old going on 40, stiff as a board and immaculately turned out in a beautifully tailored suit. He could have been arriving for a job in the City.

But Charles never really aspired to anything that could be described as normality in the way that his sons did. He knew he was different and just never got it. In contrast, William craved the very privileged version of the ordinary life that he had occasionally dipped into during his childhood. As a student, he was determined not to stand out. It was a desire that partly lay behind his decision to study at St Andrews.

It meant that the young prince was particularly irritated by reports that his choice of St Andrews, where he was to study the history of art, geography and anthropology in his first year, had been opposed within the Royal Family. William instructed palace aides to deny rumours that the senior royals had really wanted him to attend one of the colleges at Oxford or Cambridge. The family, the officials insisted, were 'thrilled' by William's departure from tradition, not least because his choice underpinned the monarchy's firm ties with Scotland.

William took the time to explain his choice in an interview published the day before he matriculated. He had, he said, dismissed studying at the University of Edinburgh because the city was too big and busy. He maintained, 'I do love Scotland. There is plenty of space. I love the hills and the mountains and I thought St Andrews had a real community feel to it. I've never lived near the sea, so it will be very different. I just hope I can meet people I get on with. I don't care about their background.'

I am confident that the egalitarian-minded royal meant what he said, even though he had chosen a university with the highest percentage of privately educated undergraduates in the country.

However much William longed to slip quietly into student life, concessions were always going to be made for his status. He arrived a week late for a start, having decided to skip Freshers' Week, the notoriously hedonistic seven days traditionally set aside before term officially starts when new arrivals launch themselves into student life minus the inconvenience of study. William missed out on the raucous behaviour associated with drunken fresher parties. It had the potential for media frenzy, he said. 'And that's not fair on the other students. Plus, I thought I would probably end up in a gutter completely wrecked and the people I met that week wouldn't end up being my friends anyway. It also meant having another week's holiday.'

It was a well-rehearsed script, cleared by the palace PR men, upbeat and positive. William made all the right noises but he touched too on the underlying and inevitable tension that would be a feature of his student life. For most students the fun of Freshers' Week is offset by the sort of indignities best forgotten. If a few compromising pictures are taken or a few ill-advised liaisons forged, then the worst the fledgling intellectual might face is some common-room ribbing or the wrath of the dean. But how could the future King, however normal he wants to be, fall out of student bars and into student beds without generating the sort of moral outrage and public debate reserved for wayward cabinet ministers? Where other students worried what their peers might think, or sweated over whether or not college authorities might notify their parents, William had to concern himself seriously with what the nation might make of him should student high jinks get out of hand. He would have to be discreet and he would have to choose friends wisely.

With this in mind Prince Charles had sagely given Prince William a fatherly pep talk. The ground rules, he said, were very simple: no drugs, no getting caught in compromising positions with girls, no kissing in public, no excessive drinking and no giving his bodyguards the slip. Charles warned his son in solemn tones about the dangers of falling in with the wrong girls and of the excruciating consequences of being caught on the wrong end of a kiss-and-tell sting. His time at Eton had taught William all about the birds and the bees. Now it was down to Charles to give an extracurricular tutorial on the honey trap. However steeped in history and the noble pursuit of knowledge the young prince's surroundings might be, they would present no deterrent to a particular type of female on the make. William would have to be on his guard.

William had already stated in his pre-university interview that he was confident in his own ability to gauge the sincerity of strangers. 'People who try to take advantage of me and get a piece of me I spot it quickly and soon go off them. I'm not stupid,' he said. No doubt he felt the same certainty when it came to women. Besides, it must have been a bit hard for William to swallow his father's advice on his conduct when it came to the opposite sex. Like any teenage boy on the cusp of manhood, he would have felt pretty certain that his father, by virtue of his comparatively advanced years, couldn't possibly know what he was talking about. William would not be the first teenager to listen earnestly and silently to some well-intentioned parental advice while inwardly dismissing it with the thoughts, It's my life I'll do what I like, or, Poor old duffer doesn't know what he's talking about.

Prince Charles may have had a sneaking suspicion that his own track record placed him in a rather weak position when it came to doling out behavioural advice. Certainly he knew that his elder son was no stranger to the opposite sex. At that time, the shyness that many commentators and royal observers detected in him was, according to some of William's school friends, a winning trait when it came to attracting girls. In many ways 'William the bashful' was a persona he invented – a very effective cover for a boy who was growing in confidence daily. He later insisted he was never shy at all, but that he just did not like being photographed and felt that if he kept his head down people would not recognise him. In an interview to mark his 21st birthday William revealed, 'But, it's very funny. I was called shy because I put my head down so much when I was in public. It was never because I was shy. It was a really naïve thing that I hadn't picked up on. I know it's silly and that everyone will laugh at it. But I thought that, when I was in public, if I kept my head down, then I wouldn't be photographed so much.

'Therefore, I thought, people wouldn't know what I looked like so I could go about doing my own thing, which, of course, frankly was never going to work. It was so that people wouldn't recognise me and I could still go out with friends and things like that. So they just saw the top of my head. But usually I was photographed with my eyes looking up through a big blond fringe. It was very silly. I wouldn't say I prefer to be unnoticed because that's never going to happen. But I'm someone who doesn't particularly like being the centre of attention.'

Unfortunately for William, being centre of attention goes with the territory. In truth, his background and training have more than prepared him for what lies ahead. An education at Eton is not designed to instil anything other than confidence, bordering on what some might consider arrogance, and the future King was no exception.

One aristocratic lady, herself once wrongly linked romantically to William by the media, confided to me that during his teens the prince was known for his roving eye. He could give the impression that he was absorbed by a girl's conversation while checking the room for the available 'talent'. Among a circle of fun-loving, often feckless, teens who wanted for nothing and sought stimulation and excitement in an endless stream of partying, the teenage William was known for joining in with gusto. He knew he had considerable pulling power when it came to the opposite sex and it was, she said, not uncommon for him to approach and chat to the best-looking girl in the room on any given occasion. While a pupil at Eton, he could often be found in the kitchens at parties, bottle of beer in hand, encircled by a gaggle of stunning girls all clearly in awe of him. They couldn't get enough of him and he loved it.

Before he met Kate the girls in question tended to fall into a particular and predictable type: tall, slim, leggy, blue-eyed blondes with trust funds more substantial than their frames and double-barrelled, sometimes triple-barrelled, surnames. They may not have presented him with any profound connection but they were fun, they were of his circle, they had the 'right' sort of background and they were there.

In 1999 he was joined on a cruise of the Greek Isles by what was described as a positive harem of girls fitting this description. Among those invited were society girl Emilia D'Erlanger, who prompted gossip when she coincidentally enrolled on the same St Andrews course as William; Arabella Musgrave, whose father manages Cirencester Park Polo Club; Davina Duckworth-Chad, whose brother James was equerry to the queen and whose father is a former High Sheriff of Norfolk, where he owns a 2,000-acre estate; and Lady Katherine Howard, daughter of the Earl of Suffolk. Other girls who were supposed to have caught William's eye are Emma Parker Bowles, Camilla's niece; former politician Jonathan Aitken's daughter, Victoria; and Alexandra Knatchbull.

It is no coincidence that Alexandra is the great-great-granddaughter of the Earl Mountbatten and great-niece to Amanda Knatchbull, whom Mountbatten once hoped to marry off to Charles. The family have been associated with royalty for generations and Princess Diana was Alexandra's godmother. Little surprise, then, that she should find herself in the wide, if shallow, pool of William's early prospective girlfriends. Naturally, some speculation was patently nonsense. When he was 18 it was reported that William had been carrying out a flirtatious email relationship with American pop princess Britney Spears. Publicly, the suggestion was ridiculed; privately, William found it both hilarious and flattering.

By the time William was embarking on student life and preparing to embrace his increased freedom (however qualified it might remain) he was well aware of his powers over the female of the species. But equally, as another titled lady also once linked to him informed me, he was tiring of the girls who were conventionally considered his type. She said, 'He was drawn to the riskier girls and he likes a challenge. But a lot of the aristocratic girls he has been linked with are too much trouble for him. It is interesting that he's settled for an ordinary middle-class girl. It's because she does not have the baggage some of these titled girls do: problems such as anorexia, drugs, drinking. He doesn't want all those problems.' Still, William would have to negotiate some problems of his own before, as this source so succinctly put it, he would 'settle' for Kate.

In spite of the numerous girls to whom William had been linked before his arrival in St Andrews, none was deemed truly special. In his 21st-birthday interview, William insisted that he did not have a steady girlfriend but said that if the right girl came along he would make his move. Echoing his father, William seemed to agonise over the impact dating a prince would have on these girls. 'There's been a lot of speculation about every single girl I'm with and it actually does quite irritate me after a while, more so because it's a complete pain for the girls,' he said. 'These poor girls, you know, who I've either just met and get photographed with, or they're friends of mine, suddenly get thrown into the limelight and their parents get rung up and so on. I think it's a little unfair on them really. I'm used to it because it happens quite a lot now. But it's very difficult for them and I don't like that at all.'

He was, as ever, careful not to be drawn on media speculation about specific girls: 'I don't have a steady girlfriend. If I fancy a girl and I really like her and she fancies me back, which is rare, I ask her out. But, at the same time, I don't want to put them in an awkward situation because a lot of people don't quite understand what comes with knowing me, for one; and, secondly, if they were my girlfriend, the excitement it would probably cause.'

His comments showed William's natural distrust of strangers, something his mother had drummed into him. In that respect at least Charles's pep talk before delivering his son to St Andrews was probably surplus to requirements. Yet one can never be too careful and in his first term at St Andrews William's lifestyle was the epitome of royal reserve and discretion. It was not a combination that conspired to allow the young prince much fun.

University life was undoubtedly a shock to the system. However much William had claimed to be looking forward to managing his own time 'in a relaxed atmosphere', it must have been daunting. Despite his egalitarian protestations and the levelling experience of his gap year, when staying at one of the royal houses William enjoyed all the princely comforts. When in residence at Balmoral, Highgrove, Buckingham Palace, Windsor Castle, Sandringham or Clarence House, William is surrounded by order and opulence. He usually wakes at 7.30 a.m., when a footman comes into his room carrying what is known as a calling tray, bearing a pot of coffee and a few biscuits. This is placed on a table next to William's bed. He drinks the coffee black with no sugar. The footman then switches on the radio, which is usually tuned to BBC Radio 4 so that he can listen to the breaking news. Then the servant, not William, pulls back the curtains to let in the morning sun.

William then gets up straightaway, has a shave and a shower and does his Canadian Air Force exercises – a strict 11-minute regime of stomach crunches, press-ups, stretches and running on the spot inherited from his father and grandfather Prince Philip and favoured by the young prince because it is easy to do in his own room. By this stage one of his valets would have laid out his smart clothes for the day but, instead of changing into them, he would pull on a jumper and jeans and head for a breakfast of cereal with cold milk and fresh fruit. As a rule he eschews the full English breakfast which will always be on offer.

Despite having had a taste of a less privileged existence at boarding school, nevertheless his accommodation must have seemed sparse to William when he arrived at his student room in St Andrews. He carried with him his own duvet, pillows, a television and a stereo as well as a trunk full of clothing, personal belongings and selected items from the formidable-looking recommended-reading list sent to students during the summer. The following day he would collect his student identity card and get down to business with his first lecture, on Renaissance art.

William set about making his minimal room more homely, putting up pictures and unpacking books and files. Along the corridor his Scotland Yard personal protection officer, a constant reminder of the privilege and threat of his status, was going through a similar routine. On another floor of the same halls of residence – mixed but split into male floors and female floors – a certain Kate Middleton had already said her goodbyes to her family and was going through the same angst and excitement as William as she started a new phase in her life. For William the excitement was tempered by his awareness that his life was being scrutinised and governed by his family. While he may have looked forward to sowing a few wild oats, the Queen and Prince Philip and courtiers at the palace had long since kept files on the right kind of girls that might one day make a suitable bride for the future King. While the Queen and Philip were keen that William have fun and enjoy his bachelor student life, it is no secret that they favour his settling down sooner rather than later.

St Andrews, like many British universities, has a student support network designed to help first-year students settle in. Older students can volunteer to be 'parents' to first-year undergraduates, passing on the sorts of tips faculty members never acquire in their university lifetime and answering the sorts of questions students would never dream of asking them anyway. In keeping with the family feel St Andrews tries to create, these students are called mothers and fathers. In William's case his student 'mother' was Alice Drummond-Hay from Connecticut, USA, the granddaughter of the Earl of Crawford and Balcarres, a former senior member of the Queen Mother's household. His 'father' was an old Etonian, Gus McMyn.

The university and palace alike insisted that they not apply any special qualifying conditions for those wishing to become William's student parents. Equally, the palace claimed not to have made any preferences known. But, given Miss Drummond-Hay's and Mr McMyn's antecedents, it hardly seems likely that they were not checked out first. If William was to use them as sounding boards they would have to be totally trustworthy and a cut above some of the twittering 'Yahs' drawn to William's side in the early months of his student life.

Fellow students described the posh elements of the university as Yahs after their tendency to use the expression 'OK, yah' instead of 'yes'. It is a nickname that encompasses the genuinely aristocratic and the wannabes alike. And there were plenty of wannabes – most of them girls. Lecture attendance in William's chosen subjects had never been so high, or so glamorous. With their fake pashminas, artfully tousled hair, too much perfume and carefully applied makeup, girls would hang around outside his lecture halls, affecting insouciance and fervently hoping to catch his eye. Some, in more strident attempts to infiltrate the in-crowd of which he was the linchpin, would brush up against him at the student bar. One girl went a step further, boldly pinching his bottom, only to be rewarded with a thunderous glare for her efforts. Others disgraced themselves in the attempt to impress, indulging in too much Dutch courage and bitterly regretting the error. One stunning blonde had the misfortune to meet William shortly after being sick through excessive drinking. He shook her hand to put her at her ease. 'All I could think,' she said, 'was, Oh my God, I met Prince William and I had sick in my hair and sick on my hand, and I shook his hand.'

There were the real Yahs of course, those, like William, individuals with healthy trust funds, expensive hair and the glowing skin of the wealthy and young. They had good manners and cashmere sweaters, part of the uniform of jeans, shirt with turned-up collar and sweater that they, along with William, wore to pretty much everything, with the exception of black-tie events.

Kate didn't quite fit the bill on this score. She was financially comfortable but did not have the moneyed background to be one of the trust-fund elite. But nor did she have the air of desperation that would have placed her in the wannabe camp. She was different. But William is not a conformist. He may be a super-Yah but he is always capable of the unexpected. At first he declined to join the most elite and well-established social clubs in the university, including the male-only Kate Kennedy Club, of which everybody had simply assumed he would become part. He signed up only for the Water Polo Club, a sport in which he excelled from his school days (like both his mother and father, William is an excellent and regular swimmer).

From his very first term at St Andrews, Kate, hardly a true social match, was becoming part of a circle of friends tentatively established by William. Like William, Kate had taken a gap year and spent part of it abroad in Chile. From the outset they found common ground. Like William, she was touched by shyness but found it no barrier to being popular. Like William, she loved sports. In addition to skiing and riding, she was an accomplished hockey and netball player at school and adored sailing. They had a fair number of things in common and they were both young, attractive people who, over a drink or coffee or the occasional bacon butty, would chat with increasing candour and intimacy about their respective lives.

William's greatest hope in those fragile early days of student life was that he would be allowed to enjoy it without the intrusion of the press. To that end a deal had been made, an agreement between Prince Charles's office and the British media, whereby, in return for the occasional arranged photocall, in which the prince would sometimes answer a few questions too, William would be left alone to work and play.

To a large extent it was a deal that worked. Yes, there were paparazzi in St Andrews and, yes, the odd picture had been taken, but for the most part newspaper editors were not publishing them.

It was a brittle truce, however, and one that the university rector, former *Sunday Times* editor Andrew Neil (the man who during his tenure at the respected broadsheet newspaper had serialised Andrew Morton's brilliant biography of Diana), always knew would be broken. Still, nobody could have dreamt who would break it when that moment came.

Within days of William's arrival came a bombshell that was as hilarious as it was ridiculous. It led to a public row at the heart of the Royal Family. For William's privacy was indeed invaded, not by tabloid reporters but by his own uncle, when camera crews from Ardent Productions, owned by Prince Edward, descended on the university. Ardent pitched up in St Andrews looking for the shots that the rest of the press had been specifically warned were well and truly off-limits. They were in the town filming part of a programme called *An A-to-Z of Royalty*, for a California-based entertainment network. The programme was understood to be keeping Ardent afloat. Desperate times seem to have called for desperate measures on Edward's part.

When the story emerged Prince Charles understandably went ballistic. He berated his youngest sibling, furiously demanding from the Queen that Edward be made to choose once and for all between his public duties and his television production company, itself many believed little more than a vanity project dependent on Edward's title for what little success it had. Relations between the brothers plummeted to an all-time low as St James's Palace publicly criticised Edward for his idiocy and the behaviour of his production company. In unusually blunt terms a spokeswoman for Prince Charles said that he was 'disappointed, very much so'. Other officials more believably told me that Charles was in a rage about it. The word 'incandescent' was used and I learned that Prince Charles tore into his brother in a telephone conversation.

Even before the incident Edward's television programme had had little support from senior members of the Royal Family. Only the Duke of Edinburgh, who dotes on his youngest child, had agreed to be interviewed on camera as a personal favour. But not even he could condone it now. William was furious, too. He felt his uncle's company's actions had threatened to undermine the carefully nurtured relationship between St James's Palace and the media, and in turn that it would threaten the *entente cordiale* between him and the press. After all, it was a bit rich for Fleet Street editors, journalists and photographers to be cooling their heels and turning away pictures and stories that just begged to be printed while a member of the Royal Family was himself busily trying to scoop up the goods for profit.

It was acutely embarrassing for the family. Andrew Neil, perhaps showing just a little glee as a journalistic veteran, said, 'We knew when we were [making the agreement] that somebody would break it at some stage. But for it to be broken by a company owned by his uncle – well, you just couldn't make it up.' An apology came from Edward in the form of a telephone call to Sir Stephen Lamport, Charles's private secretary, rather than a direct address to Charles himself. Edward's attempt at reconciliation was not helped by the way Ardent tried to ride out the storm. Malcolm Cockren, chairman of Ardent, said, 'For the record, the filming in St Andrews by Ardent Productions was arranged with the full knowledge and cooperation of the university press office three weeks ago. Ardent Productions fully supports the restrictions on filming Prince William at St Andrews University and at no time did the crew attempt to film Prince William, gain unauthorised access or shoot on the campus.' It was a futile defence. Eventually, belatedly, the company apologised and the whole hilarious episode was over.

Despite this hiccup, William's first few months were perceived to have gone relatively smoothly. The press deal was honoured and this meant that William was able to integrate into student life and let his hair down. He was still keen to establish a core group of trusted friends, people he could trust and who, once part of his clique, he would keep close to the point of exclusivity. He was still finding his way. One of the friends who helped him to do that was one Kate Middleton, who lived just a staircase away from his own modest room.

They lived in such close proximity in the halls of residence, known colloquially as St Sallies, that it was easy for Kate and William to see each other often and without having to make any elaborate arrangements. Their lives fell naturally into each other's rhythm. They would meet in the same bars and even played tennis together. Kate was an accomplished player and had represented her school in the sport. William would occasionally invite friends back to his room for a drink and Kate would invariably be among them. During his first term of university, William had a good reason not to notice Kate, at least romantically.

Within weeks of arriving, he met and struck up an intimate relationship with another beautiful brunette, Carly Massey-Birch. There was an instant mutual attraction. Her natural aloofness and charm intrigued the prince. He pestered her and they dated for around two months. The couple agreed to cool things and split in the first term in October 2001. When he first arrived as a fresher William was enthusiastically pursued by a string of beautiful young women, girls happily impressed by his chat-up line of, 'I'm going to be King one day, how about it?' Shortly after they split, the prince fell for Kate, which led to an apparent rivalry between the two girls. In 2008, Carly's parents confirmed that their daughter and William had been 'an item', going out for a nearly two months when they were new undergraduates. According to Mimi and Hugh Massy-Birch, there is no rift between Carly and Kate. The pair – along with the prince – they said were still friends. After their relationship emerged publicly Mimi Massy-Birch said, 'Carly will be really upset that this has come out. She went out with William for six or seven weeks when they first arrived at St Andrews. However, there is absolutely no fallout between her and Kate. In fact, all three of them are best friends. Carly has her own partner, with whom she is very much in love. She really wants Kate to marry Wills so that she can be sure of going to the wedding. If he falls for someone else, she's worried that she might miss out.'

The Massy-Birches, who ran a farm and camping park near Axminster, Devon, kept their actress daughter's relationship with the prince a closely guarded secret. Soon after the relationship ended, William escorted Kate to parties at university. According to one account by the accomplished *Daily Telegraph* journalist Celia Walden, Carly felt a 'simmering resentment' towards Kate. Apparently, the aspiring actress gave William a pointed lesson in fidelity, leaving her audience stunned during a production of *Othello*, delivering the line, 'This is some minx's token, and I must take out the work? There, give it your hobby horse . . .' (referring to Othello's infidelity) while glaring directly at William, who had arrived at the production with Kate.

However, Carly's mother said, 'That really is rubbish. Carly's always been very close to Kate and William, and that's never changed. She's tried so hard to keep her friendship with him quiet – we all have – and so she'll be upset by this. It was something that happened and everybody's moved on. She just wants to get on with her acting. She's based in London and has appeared in a few plays, including some on Radio 4.'

However, contemporary sources at St Andrews claimed that the real reason William's first undergraduate relationship failed is that Carly repeatedly refused his princely charms and imposed a strict sex ban. It did not bother the ladylike Carly that her suitor was a future king. Carly even went public about the split (although she tactfully kept William's name out of it). She referred to her royal relationship in a dating column for her student newspaper *The Saint* in a column entitled 'Looking for Love'. When asked why she was single, she revealed, 'No sex before marriage.' When asked how long since she last slept with someone, she explained, 'See above.' Carly had been taking part in the 'Sad, Lonely and Desperate' column in *The Saint* after she split from William, claiming her ideal date was actor Hugh Grant.

For all the normality, after he and Carly parted it added to William's feelings of insecurity. He was increasingly unhappy and unsettled. Perhaps uncertainty and a touch of homesickness and disenchantment were the flipside of normal student life, which he had failed to anticipate. In April 2002 the first reports began to emerge that all was not well with the prince. He was apparently dissatisfied with his course and bored by his environs. He was seriously considering a change of scene. Perhaps Edinburgh University, with its city attractions and bustle, might have been a better move after all. The Scottish coastal town of St Andrews, with little to offer but a couple of pubs, a bit of charm and wind-buffeted headlands, was not, it seemed, all he had hoped it might be.

The prince was miserable. Given the crisis that once surrounded his uncle Prince Edward when he decided to quit Royal Marines training after practically completing the gruelling course to make a point to his domineering father, this was a potential scandal the palace was anxious to head off at the pass. The press pounced on Edward's failure to make the grade. With unforgiving ferocity they called into question everything from his merit as a royal to his sexuality. Nobody wanted William exposed to that sort of mauling. Besides, princes – particularly ones destined to be king – don't quit. Not any more.

Doubts about William's decision to opt for St Andrews had surfaced in the press when he went home at Christmas after just one term. He was depressed, uneasy and felt he had made the wrong choice of college. He discussed the matter with his father, spelling out his desire to abandon the four-year course altogether. Charles was sympathetic at first but understandably alarmed. Palace officials revealed that Charles felt such concern for his son's unhappy start to student life that he asked his private office to devise a strategy that would enable William to withdraw from the university should it prove necessary.

The prince's two most senior members of staff at the time, Sir Stephen Lamport and Mark Bolland, were horrified at the prospect. 'It would have been a personal disaster for William – he would have been seen as a quitter – and it would have been an even bigger disaster for the monarchy, particularly in Scotland,' a royal aide confided. Eventually, Charles took a different tack and got tough. He strongly advised his son that most students take a while to settle in and urged him to 'stick with it'. Prince Philip was predictably rather more gruff and forthright. He told him in no uncertain terms, with one of his trademark phrases, just to 'get on with it'.

William's wobble and contemplation about quitting university life was also pinned on his association with a 'beautiful PR girl'. It emerged that he had enjoyed a four-month relationship with 21-year-old Arabella Musgrave before starting university and, although they had agreed to 'cool it' before he headed for university, he still held a candle for her. Moreover, while his friendship with Kate may have been deepening, after his brief intimacy with Carly had ended, it was still just that: friendship. Claims that William was still pining for Arabella were probably unfounded, but it is true that he did increase the number of weekend returns to Highgrove, hundreds of miles away from university.

It has been suggested that Arabella was in fact his first 'serious' girlfriend and that he really missed her. They attempted to rekindle their romance in spring 2002 but William knew in his heart it was a long-distance affair that would not work. Their romance had started in June 2001. They had known each other for several years as Arabella's family, including her mother Clare and sister Laetitia, lived in a beautiful home near Stroud, not far from Prince Charles's Highgrove estate. Her father, Nicholas, is the manager of Cirencester Park Polo Club in Gloucestershire, and she was at the time a well-known member of the game's younger set. In William and Arabella's brief time together they enjoyed quiet weekends in the Cotswolds and were often seen drinking at the Tunnel House pub in the village of Coates, two miles from Cirencester.

Arabella, who has remained good friends with William to this day, had a new boyfriend by the time the *Sunday Mirror* tracked her down and reported that she was the reason for William's homesickness. She was not amused and wanted to kill off the story once and for all. She said in an interview at the time, 'I hated being famous for going out with William. I have a new boyfriend who is in property.'

But William had no choice. When he explained first-hand how he wrestled with the idea of quitting university, he said, 'I think the rumour that I was unhappy got slightly out of control. I don't think I was homesick. I was more daunted.' He conceded there had been a problem and that his father had been a big help. 'We chatted a lot and in the end we both realised – I definitely realised – that I had to come back,' he added. But being told to belt up and knuckle down is not likely to solve any deep-seated concerns. William did go back, but he was still toying with the idea of making his excuses and leaving.

Coincidentally, another first-year student was having wobbles and doubts, too. Kate was struggling with the transition from school to university. She had her tearful moments, telephone calls home and anxieties over work. It was something she and William shared as she became his confidante and he hers. Something was beginning to shift between the two. It was Kate who suggested that perhaps what William needed was not a change of scene but a change of course. It was Kate who really averted the crisis of his flunking-out of his first year at university, translating it instead into a perfectly acceptable decision to change from history of art to geography – a subject he had always expressed a particular interest in.

William had admitted before going to St Andrews that he was 'much more interested in doing something with the environment'. It was something his father had drummed into him at an early age and the connection was made. He switched courses and he immediately felt happier, as if a huge weight had been lifted from his shoulders. His social life began looking up, too. The reticent prince, who had held back from joining the societies everybody thought he would, became a member of the Kate Kennedy all-male dining club. Kate became, in turn, a founding member of the female equivalent, the Lumsden Society. As part of a group of friends they went for meals in the local pizza restaurants and trips to Ma Belles, a favourite student bar in town, where they enjoyed a few drinks but nothing excessive. William liked beer and wine, but his favourite tipple was a pint or two of cider. He rarely drank during the day, sticking to spring water, having ditched fizzy drinks such as Coke in his early teens. Life was fun and Kate was, it seemed, a more central fixture in it.

Kate was also by now known in public and linked by friendship to the future King. In April 2002 pictures of Kate entered the public consciousness as the lithe brunette was seen strutting down a student catwalk for a charity fashion show watched by a clearly mesmerised William. She wore a black lace dress over a bandeau bra and black bikini bottoms. William had paid £200 for a front-row seat and he was not going to miss Kate's sexy-model show for the world. A fellow student tipped-off the *Mail on Sunday* and on 7 April 2002 the story ran under the headline William and his undiegraduate friend Kate to share a student flat. Earlier that month he had been on the cusp of quitting university; now, after a heart-to-heart with Kate, he was not only staying but he had begun looking for a flat with Kate and two friends.

The student mole revealed, 'Kate was the real reason behind William's decision to go [to the fashion show]. She's one of a group of good mates he has who all hang out together and have helped him through the past few months. She's a nice girl and good fun. However, they're strictly friends; there's nothing more in it than that. Four of them are going to share a flat for the second year.' The *Daily Mail*, who referred to Kate and the prince as 'firm friends', picked up the story. They had only scratched the surface. Until then Kate had been an anonymous friend. Now she was well and truly on the public radar. So-called 'friends' were quick to contact the press in the hope of making a fast buck and pass on the details of Kate and William's friendship.

It was exactly what William had been hoping to avoid, but there was no stemming the flow of information. The press had promised to leave William alone; that meant they would not publish anything unless it was arguably in the public interest and too good to pass up. Information about Kate was also, some argued, genuinely within the bounds of public interest. Besides, there was nothing negative in the reports. 'They get on really well. She's a very lovely girl but very unassuming. She's very bubbly but also discreet and loyal to William,' confided one friend. 'She treats him just like any other student. Many girls, especially the Americans, follow him round like sheep and he hates that. He just wants to live with people knowing he can be himself,' said another. He just wanted to live with Kate.

When William began looking to move from the university halls of residence into off-campus accommodation observers were surprised that he and Kate, along with their pal Fergus Boyd, were considering properties in the town itself. For reasons of privacy, it had been assumed that William would look further afield – and when it came to it the student quartet did eventually move to a more remote residence, Balgove House, close to St Andrews golf course. It was still close enough to the town for the elite 'community' surrounding William to socialise but, significantly, it was far enough out of town to be away from prying eyes. There were a number of properties on the farm known as Strathtyrum estate just off the A91 three-quarters of a mile from the outskirts of the town. The property was owned by the cousin of Kate's closest university friend, Alice Warrender, a fellow history-of-art student, and daughter of the well-known artist Jonathan Warrender, descended on his father's side from an early-18th-century Lord Provost of Edinburgh. She was somebody Kate could always count on, and, along with her circle of pals, Bryony Daniels and Ginny Fraser, she had a good support network. She would soon need them.

The move to the farm marked a sea change in William's approach to life, which some ascribe simply to growing up but others put down to Kate's influence. However, while all seemed to be going swimmingly well for William and Kate there was one small problem: Kate already had a boyfriend. While William stuck to his father's advice and was careful not to become involved romantically in the early days of his student life, Kate had fallen for a good-looking chap called Rupert Finch. He was her second serious boyfriend after she had split from Ian Henry. Rupert was darkly handsome, sharing the same patina of privilege and sporting good health with which Kate herself is blessed. He excelled at many sports, but cricket was his main game and he even led the university cricket team on a tour. He wanted to become a lawyer and had the brains and the charm to suggest that, if he did, he would be a successful one. He was, in many respects, a very good catch for Kate. More her speed, some might say, than the future King.

But, as her friendship with William blossomed, Kate must surely have felt torn. All those chats, those shared confidences, all that opening up to each other was bound to turn her head, and it did. Set against royalty, the future solicitor Finch did not stand a chance, especially as William had apparently been Kate's secret passion, albeit in the form of an adolescent crush, for years. As William and Kate began to be bolder towards each other, what had passed for friendship became obviously something more. Kate's youthful passion for Rupert began to dwindle. It might well have done anyway. After all, this relationship mushroomed in the early days of student life. It certainly could not, and did not, survive her moving into a house with William, however much they continued to insist that there was nothing going on between them. Finch confirmed his courteous credentials when questioned about his relationship with Kate by the respected *Mail on Sunday* journalist Laura Collins. He told her bluntly that his relationship with Kate and the circumstances under which it ended was not a subject he would discuss, saying, 'It's not something I'll ever talk about. It's between Kate and me and was a long time ago.'

Only Kate and William will truly know the moment when friendship turned to passion and the platonic sham ended in favour of a more honest intimacy. Kate and William began cohabiting in their second year, living a normal student existence. 'I do all my own shopping. I go out, get takeaways, rent videos, go to the cinema, just basically anything I want to really,' William said, acknowledging that the deal struck with the media was working. Some evenings he would stay in and cook. Discussing his prowess in the kitchen he said later, 'I've done a bit at university when I had to feed my flatmates, which was quite hard work because a couple of them ate quite a lot.'

The fact that William and Kate were living such a cosy existence inevitably led to increased speculation that they were intimate and not just good friends. One university contemporary told me, 'There was a bit of a buzz about them living together. But they were so careful in public you would never have guessed they were an item in the early days. They had the whole thing off pat. Obviously Fergus Boyd [their flatmate] knew, but at first they were seen as just mates.'

And perhaps they were, at least at the outset. In May 2003, Kate's father felt moved to make a good-natured rebuttal of a report that Kate was William's girlfriend. 'I spoke to Kate just a few days ago and can categorically confirm they are no more than just good friends. There are two boys and two girls sharing the flat at university. They are together all the time because they are the best of pals and, yes, cameramen are going to get photos of them together. But there's nothing more to it than that. We're very amused at the thought of being in-laws to Prince William, but I don't think it's going to happen.' Nevertheless, in spite of her father's denials there was no mistaking just how integral a part of William's set Kate had become.

Whether Kate kept her father in the dark or whether it was just another smokescreen is unclear. Despite her father's strong denial, the media were convinced that they had the right girl. Barely a month after Michael Middleton's light-hearted statement, Kate turned 21 and her parents threw a party in the grounds of the family home. Old school friends turned out in force as well as her crowd from St Andrews. There was champagne and a sit-down dinner in a marquee with everybody dressed, on Kate's request, in 1920s fashions. In addition, there, slipping unannounced into the marquee was William. He and Kate exchanged knowing looks. William told her she looked stunning. She smiled her acknowledgement and they began talking and relaxing into each other's company. William left soon after dinner with the party still in full swing. Discretion has always been crucial to William and Kate's relationship.

However, perhaps Michael Middleton was telling the truth, because in the autumn of 2003 William was not behaving like a young man in a full-time relationship. When back in London he became a regular at the hedonistic Purple nightclub based in the grounds of Chelsea Football Club, a favourite with the local Sloanes and owned by Fulham businessman Brian Mason. The club, now closed, had been a haunt of Prince Harry, too. They were heady times. Buoyed by his newfound freedom and not restricted emotionally, William was enjoying spreading his wings.

His exuberance, however, got him into trouble that summer and back onto the front pages. In June 2003 Prince Charles was forced to apologise on behalf of his elder son to an aristocrat who condemned William for 'driving like some yob in a beat-up car' during a weekend break from university. The 76-year-old Lord Bathurst prompted a security scare in a road-rage incident when he chased the prince, who had overtaken him on a private road on the earl's estate in Gloucestershire. It was an extraordinary drama, occurring just a month shy of William's 21st birthday, which again showed his readiness to take risks. It came after William had played a polo match at Cirencester with his father. Ignoring the unofficial speed limit on the estate, William was pursued by a furious Lord Bathurst in his Land Rover, blasting his horn and flashing his lights at the prince's vehicle. William's police bodyguards intervened. Despite the apology, the aristocrat blasted William's behaviour. He said, 'I don't care who it is, royalty or not – speeding is not allowed on my estate. The limit is twenty miles an hour. If I were to drive like that in Windsor Park, I'd end up in the Tower. I thought he was some young yob in a beat-up car.' When he was unable to give the speeding prince a telling-off, the earl turned on the prince's bodyguards, whom he described as 'looking like a pair of yobs'. Charles's officials played down the encounter as, 'a very minor incident in which no one was injured'. However, it did demonstrate William's more reckless side.

In September 2003 all Prince Charles's warnings about being careful with the opposite sex also came back to haunt William. It was not the most lurid kiss-and-tell. In fact, it was just that: a kiss and nothing more. When an Australian model William met at Purple told her mother back home about a 'snog' she'd had with the future King the story quickly found its way onto the front pages of the world's newspapers. The mother of 19-year-old Elouise Blair could not wait to tell anyone who would listen about her daughter's encounter with William and soon found herself on television relating the incident. 'Elouise rang me,' she recounted, 'to say that she had been invited to a private function for Prince Harry and Prince William at a nightclub, the Purple nightclub in Chelsea, and she [was] all excited about going and having fun and hoping to see them in the crowd. Then I got another call a few hours later from her, and she said, "Guess what, Mum. I've spent the night with Prince William, dancing and laughing and having fun with him." And she was really excited about it.'

The model was dancing on the balcony in the nightclub, her mother said, when William came up to her and said, 'Hi, I'm Will and, err, would you like to dance?'

Harry approached and said, 'You're being a bit public.'

The model's mother continued, 'William said, "It's great; we're having a great time dancing and being together – come on, we'll go down to the public area downstairs," and grabbed her hand and they went down there and stayed there for the rest of the night.'

Ms Blair said the couple kissed during the four hours they spent together. Asked if William was a prince charming, Ms Blair said, 'He is. Oh yeah, she said he was so sweet, so normal, just like any friend. They were talking about music . . . and travel . . . he asked her about Perth. So she said he was a really normal, sweet guy and she really liked his company.' Blair said that her daughter's evening with the prince came to an end when his minders took him away. 'She would like to [see him again] because she really, really enjoyed his company . . . and if it happens, well, we'll just see,' she said.

After this sort of publicity, it was the prince and Elouise's first and last night out and was a salutary reminder that Kate, in all the time she had shared with William, had never been anything other than utterly discreet. William went off into that particular night with his minders, a little the worse for wear. By Christmas of that year it was clear to those who knew them that things had changed. He and Kate were now more than just good friends: they were an item, no matter how much they continued to publicly deny it. That Christmas, at a water-polo ball held at St Andrew's Sea Life Centre, William was seen in a corner, kissing a 'mystery brunette'. She was curvaceous, locked in his embrace and totally at ease with the prince. She looked, eyewitnesses say, remarkably similar to Kate.

But William was still the target of opportunists. One night at Purple, William, dressed casually, paid the £15 entrance fee and was shown with his police bodyguard and three friends to the club's roped-off VIP area to enjoy the 'Dirty Disco' theme night that was taking place. It should have been a night of fun but William showed the strain on his face as he glumly sat drinking bottles of beer at a table furthest from the dance floor. He looked as if he was about to leave when long-legged blonde Essex girl Solange Jacobs made her move. Solange – who turned out to be a 29-year-old single mum from Chigwell – flirted outrageously with William and ended up spending three hours in his company, and they eventually swapped mobile-telephone numbers.

Typically, the girl's 'friends' went to a Sunday newspaper to tell how the two had flirted all night. They claimed that William was definitely interested in taking it further. The friends cleverly kept her name out of the newspaper, and just told the story of the 'Prince and the Essex girl'. The following week, after it emerged that William was serious about Kate, Jacobs, perhaps a little aggrieved, went on the record about her three-hour flirtation with the prince. Speaking with the confidence of somebody who had known William for years instead of hours, her message to Kate was unequivocal: 'Wills has too much of a roving eye to settle down.' She then went on to tell her story the Sunday tabloid the *People*.

'The way he was acting with me,' she said, 'he didn't seem to be in love with anyone else. He also chatted with a dancer and eyed up a girl in the VIP area. You would not have guessed he was seeing Kate. Wills looked very much on the prowl, so Kate had better watch out if she doesn't want to be made a fool of.'

The former glamour model and single mother claimed that William had charmed her by telling her she was good-looking and joked that he was going to invite her to Buckingham Palace for a party. Jacobs added, 'Wills made no mention of a girlfriend. I don't think Kate will be too pleased that he chatted me up. He was a gentleman but it seems odd that he took my number. Anyway, I wish Kate the best of luck. She might need it.'

It was a blunt warning for the girl he had supposedly been dating for four months. Perhaps it was a necessary warning, too. When William returned to the same club the following August, Kate – perhaps taking no chances with his roving eye – was this time at his side.

By then Kate and William's romance had become well and truly public. Four months after the Christmas ball, in April 2004, the *Sun* published pictures of William and Kate on holiday in Klosters, the ski resort in the Swiss Alps. The paper had already speculated about the nature of the relationship, reporting that it had flourished thanks to a series of trips to the Balmoral bolthole cottage, Alltcailleach, a getaway given by the Queen to William and Harry.

The Royal Family's officials reacted furiously to the newspaper's decision to publish the pictures from the slopes. 'We are very unhappy with what the *Sun* has done,' said a Buckingham Palace aide. In due course, Clarence House banned the *Sun* from upcoming official photoshoots of Princes William and Harry. Freelance photographer Jason Fraser, a man who had made such a success of photographing William's mother, sold the pictures of Kate and William to the *Sun*. His scoops included the infamous final staged kiss between Diana and Dodi Fayed on their love-boat holiday. The Klosters images of William and Kate had nothing to do with legendary *Sun* royal photographer Arthur Edwards, a recipient of the MBE for his services to journalism. It was simply a decision made by *Sun* editor Rebekah Wade (now Rebekah Brooks and chief executive of News International) in the belief that, if Kate was a serious contender for the title of princess, then this was both too good a story and too much in the public interest to pass up. It was bold and brilliant: publish and be damned. The knee-jerk reaction from Clarence House's Paddy Harverson, effectively publish and be banned, was a public-relations disaster. Worse from the palace's point of view was that the *Sun* did not take its punishment lying down. The newspaper issued a blunt and defiant statement, insisting, 'Now that [William] is a mature adult, there is public interest in knowing what romantic interests might be developing in the prince's life. One of William's girlfriends could become queen one day. Her subjects will be entitled to know all about her.' It added pointedly, 'Our story about Prince William and his girlfriend Kate Middleton is 100 per cent true. Therefore, there is a strong public interest in publishing these delightful pictures.'

Brooks had a valid point and she was right to stick to her guns. Harverson later privately admitted that he misjudged the situation, particularly with regard to slapping down the much-admired and warmly regarded Arthur Edwards for something that had nothing to do with him. Later, when the *Sun* hosted a party to honour his service and to mark his 65th birthday at the RAC Club in Pall Mall in 2005, Harverson and his press team from Clarence

House, as well as Lord Janvrin, the Queen's private secretary, and the communications team of Buckingham Palace all attended. The Queen and Prince Philip as well as Charles and Camilla, and Edwards's republican supreme boss Rupert Murdoch, sent personal messages of goodwill.

Edwards, not for the first time in his royal career, was in the firing line. Another UK tabloid, the *Mirror*, believed that Kate and William were an item, too. It claimed that they had been romantically involved for at least four months and only close friends of the couple knew about the relationship. The newspaper also claimed that flatmate Fergus Boyd was one of the few sworn to secrecy and that William and Kate had gone to great lengths to ensure that their true feelings for each other remained private. They never held hands or showed affection in public. Every time they left their cottage home, they made a concerted effort to give the appearance of being nothing more than housemates. In the immediate aftermath of the *Sun* story, written by royal reporter Paul Thompson, people close to William, who liked to think of themselves as well informed, seemed confused and caught on the hop.

Predictably, Clarence House issued a po-faced statement in which they tried to muddy the waters. They pointed out that William and Kate 'don't live together', at least not as a couple. They had shared a student house for 18 months. They also claimed that they did not share a bed. I have no doubt that they did not have to, in the sense that Kate had her own bedroom complete no doubt with her own bed. The fact was that William and Kate were sharing a bed in the sense in which the *Mirror* clearly meant to imply – that their relationship was physical as well as emotional.

Privately, William, a young man now just shy of his 22nd birthday, had been proudly showing off Kate and introducing the stunning, dark-haired girl to various friends. Just over a week before the April trip to Klosters he and Kate had travelled from St Andrews to join a group of his friends riding with the coincidentally named Middleton Hunt in North Yorkshire. Even there they were at pains not to show the extent of their attachment to each other. One observer noted, 'They were not touchy-feely.

They were really so very careful, and afterwards, when everyone else went for a meal, they'd disappeared.' It was no bad thing for Kate to be publicly associated with William. With her by his side, the sometimes irritable prince was notably more at ease.

During that holiday in Klosters Kate was one of the royal ski party of seven who had flown from Heathrow to Zurich airport. The group included Harry Legge-Bourke (younger brother to William's unofficial nanny, Tiggy), Guy Pelly, William van Cutsem, son of Charles's old Norfolk landowning friend Hugh, and van Cutsem's girlfriend, Katie James.

Kate had already been a guest at Highgrove at least three times, as well as at Sandringham, the Queen's Norfolk estate. William had taken her for weekends to a Highlands bolthole, the cottage of Tom-Na-Gaidh, Birkhall, Ballater, on the eastern edge of the Balmoral estate, by the River Muick, given to him and Harry by the Queen and renovated at a cost of £150,000. It was inconceivable that she would escape notice. She was, after all, his first publicly acknowledged serious girlfriend. In Klosters she was part of a lively, wealthy bunch that, every night after an energetic day on the slopes, set out to enjoy the après-ski. One evening the now remarkably carefree William, with his girl by his side, took to the microphone for a rousing shot at the karaoke bar. Kate sat at a table with Charles, there with his old pals Charlie and Patty Palmer-Tomkinson. Laughing at William's attempts, totally at ease in such elevated company, Kate was a picture.

William did not attempt to deny that Kate was his girlfriend after the pictures appeared in the *Sun*. He did not, as he had done with Jecca Craig months earlier, issue a statement denying that they were anything more than just friends. Then, the prince had been unequivocal: 'St James's Palace denies there is, or ever has been, any romantic liaison between Prince William and Jessica Craig.' Now, however, there was only silence and the pictures of happiness. Finally, after speculation that began simmering two years earlier with those catwalk images of the shapely Kate, there was no doubt that she was William's girlfriend. The issue now, one on which royal observers including myself were divided, was: just how important was Kate?

CHAPTER 8

TOO YOUNG TO WED

'Look, I'm only 22, for God's sake. I'm too young to marry at my age. I don't want to get married until I'm at least 28 or maybe 30.'
PRINCE WILLIAM'S COMMENT TO A REPORTER

As the older of the boys and the one more physically resembling his late mother, Princess Diana, William was the *de facto* spokesperson for the royal brothers. His blessing, perhaps as far as the wider public were concerned, was the one that mattered most. The official line was that both William and his younger brother Prince Harry were 'delighted' that their father Prince Charles had at last found happiness and was finally ready to marry his long-term mistress, Camilla Parker Bowles. Experience had taught me to be wary of official lines. Sure enough, once the surface had been scratched it soon clear that, privately at least, the princes' mood was more one of 'acceptance' rather than undiluted joy at the prospect of having Camilla as their stepmother. She had, after all, been their mother's principal enemy throughout her troubled life, and no son, no matter how loyal to his father, could dismiss that overnight.

It was not until the end of March 2005, several weeks after I had broken the story in the London *Evening Standard* that Charles and Camilla were to wed, that I had my first chance to judge the princes' true reaction for myself. At an official press call in Klosters, where William and Harry were holidaying with their father, a reporter asked William how he felt about the wedding. He paused for a second or two, before he replied to the assembled press pack in his soft upper-class accent, 'Very happy, very pleased. It will be a good day.' Asked about his role as a witness at the ceremony, he added, 'As long as I don't lose the rings it'll be all right. But with the responsibility I'm bound to do something wrong.'

He looked relaxed as he made his remarks to the 50 or so press, myself among them, who had flown to the Swiss Alps for the especially for the occasion. Charles, in sharp contrast, looked decidedly uncomfortable, bad-tempered even. Harry did his best to lighten the mood and get his father to see the funny side, turning to Charles and saying sarcastically, 'This is so much fun.' Harry then revealed the boys had thrown an impromptu stag party and delighted in the fact that the hordes of media people had missed it. He added mischievously, 'It was good fun.' When another reporter asked if Charles had ended up chained to anything the heir to the throne looked very baffled, until Prince Harry explained that it was what sometimes happened at stag parties.

The press call, arranged by the prince's communication secretary Paddy Harverson, became infamous due to Charles's ill humour and the curmudgeonly aside in which he attacked the press. Unfairly the prince even singled out the unfortunate BBC correspondent Nicholas Witchell for personal criticism when Witchell asked a perfectly legitimate question of how the princes were feeling about the wedding. As only Prince William had answered, the seasoned TV journalist repeated his question. Charles, clearly not amused, answered, 'Well it's a nice thought. I'm very glad you have heard of it anyway.' He then famously muttered under his breath, but picked on the TV microphones, 'These bloody people. I cannot bear that man. I mean, he's so awful, he really is.'

There could be no real excuse. Charles may have been gloriously unaware that the remote microphones placed in the snow at his feet by his own press team had recorded his sneering remarks, but he was informed what the questions would be before the press call. Inevitably, it led to a spat with the BBC, who rightly defended their man. In reply, the BBC issued a statement saying, 'Nicholas Witchell was in Klosters at the invitation of Clarence House. He has been our royal correspondent for seven years, has worked for the BBC for nearly 30 years and is one of our finest. His question was perfectly reasonable under the circumstances.' It was a gaffe more befitting of his father Prince Philip and it overshadowed everything else about the day – well, almost.

News never stands still and, even on the eve of Charles and Camilla's marriage, Prince William for the first time found himself asked by a television journalist in the pack whether another royal wedding was on the cards – his own perhaps. William's upbeat mood changed in an instant. He almost visibly stiffened. His face flushed a little redder. Now *his* private life was the focus of attention and he did not like it one little bit.

'No, I don't think so,' he said after a short pause. 'I'm just gagging to get back on the slopes.'

The press call was over. The issue of William's relationship with girlfriend of two years Kate Middleton sidestepped. Nevertheless, a new agenda was flickering into life that would not be easily extinguished. The press hounds had the scent of a royal story and they were not about to give it up.

It had been a long night in Casa Antica, a nightclub in the Swiss Alps and a popular venue for the Klosters après-ski crowd. It is one of Prince William's favourite hangouts. On the evening in question, 30 March 2005, it was no surprise that he could be found amid the smoke and throbbing music, holding court at a table in a dimly lit and sectioned-off room at the back of the club.

Sitting next to a flushed Prince Harry, who was a little the worse for wear himself, Prince William did something completely out of character. He spotted a tabloid reporter in conversation with his Scotland Yard bodyguards and spontaneously invited him over for an impromptu chat. Duncan Larcombe, a new royal reporter for the *Sun* and just a few years his senior in age, had arrived at the club just after midnight on a hunch that the princes and their friends were there. He had wisely made himself known to the protection team, some of whom he had met while covering Harry's earlier holidays to Africa with then girlfriend Chelsy Davy, offering to leave if they felt that his presence was a problem.

Fortuitously for the tabloid reporter, at that precise moment Guy

Pelly, William's eccentric but often hilarious friend, seen by many as his court jester, burst out of a side room wearing nothing but a pair of brown, silk boxer shorts. Inexplicably, he sat on the reporter's lap; perhaps assuming the journalist was a new royal protection officer (although quite why that would justify his behaviour is another matter) and began talking to the officers. Much to William's amusement, Pelly disappeared almost as quickly as he had arrived when one of the officers introduced the chap on whose lap he was sitting as 'the *Sun*'s new royal reporter'.

Perhaps sensing an embarrassing headline in the newspaper the next day, William indicated to the bodyguards that he would like a chat with the hack. Emboldened by drink, William decided to give him an interview. Apparently, at no stage did the prince say his comments were off the record – although the next morning a flustered Paddy Harverson, Prince Charles's communication director and media minder for the boys on the ski trip, insisted that the conversation was private and not meant for publication. The editor of the *Sun*, Rebekah Wade, by now reading the copy back in the newspaper's headquarters in Wapping, east London, rightly stood her ground.

They discussed the latest picture taken of the prince and Kate on the slopes. The previous year, the *Sun* was banned for reproducing such paparazzi pictures. This year, however, William was relaxed about the photographs, although he appeared genuinely surprised as to why there was such frenzied interest in them. The reporter suggested it was because there had been speculation that this relationship could lead to marriage and that an engagement could happen soon. Perhaps, gaining in confidence, the journalist did not expect a response but it was certainly worth a punt. He had thrown the talk of marriage into the conversation, almost in jest, never seriously anticipating that William would take it on. The prince's forthright remark gave him quite a story: 'Look, I'm only 22, for God's sake. I'm too young to marry at my age. I don't want to get married until I'm at least 28 or maybe 30.'

With those few words William had given the *Sun* a notable exclusive. The next morning, over five pages and in what was billed as a world exclusive, the paper ran the details of the extraordinary moment in which the young prince 'opened his heart' to one of its reporters.

Kate Middleton had been in the same room as he had chatted informally to the reporter, but at no stage had William thought of making an introduction. If Kate had serious feelings and hopes for her relationship with William at that point, such a public dismissal of the prospect of a proposal any time soon might naturally have upset her. After all, she was standing close to William when he uttered his surprisingly frank words.

William's candour did little to dampen Kate's spirits. Far from appearing subdued, she joined wholeheartedly in the drunken rough and tumble of the evening. Good-natured horseplay ensued, resulting in the beaded bracelet that Prince Harry was wearing, a gift from girlfriend Chelsy, being grabbed and broken. As he scrabbled around the club floor trying to retrieve the beads, his whooping sibling, Kate and friends swooped on the intoxicated royal, threatening to pull down his trousers and underwear. Lost in peals of laughter, glowing and hot with the night's excesses, Kate was hardly the image of a girl who had just witnessed the man she loved inform a relative stranger that, romantically speaking, he was still up for grabs.

William is media-savvy. There were many in his circle of friends who suspected that the world exclusive, the denial of any serious thoughts of marriage blurted out so apparently carelessly, was, in fact, a smokescreen designed to cool the media frenzy about William's steady girlfriend.

Despite the sensational coverage given to the chat, this statement surprised no one among the royal press corps. He was simply trying to have it both ways. He saw what happened to his mother and what happened to his father. His father made a catastrophic mistake in letting the woman he loved, Camilla, slip through his fingers 30 years ago and was miserable for years. On the other hand, his mother married far too young, and he had not wanted to make the same mistake.

Whatever William's reason for uttering them, those few off-the-cuff remarks have now been marked down for posterity. When he *does* marry in 2011, William is bound to find his comments revived and repeated – as either a foolhardy statement or a sage moment of prescience. There are many, myself included, who believe William may have been disingenuous that night.

The prince, echoing his father's view, often jokes with friends that the press 'never let the truth get in the way of a good story'. But William and his advisers know very well that in recent years the band of royal writers of which I was a part, known with a mixture of irritation and affection as 'the royal rat pack', got it right far too often for the Royal Family's liking. Fleet Street legends, such as James Whitaker and Richard Kay, have been working the royal beat and breaking stories with relentless accuracy for many years. This is no mean feat when their enquiries are often met with a stream of lies, half-truths and denials from palace officials and even from the mouths of members of the Royal Family themselves. Like his late mother, Princess Diana, and in spite of his relative youth, William knows how to play the media. Would it really be so surprising if, in an attempt to put the press off the scent and give his relationship with Kate time to develop, William had embarked on a little late-night subterfuge in the Swiss Alps when he poured scorn on talk of marriage?

One senior official on that same skiing holiday left me in no doubt about what the future held for the prince and his girl. He revealed, 'The prince knew exactly what he was doing; he would not open his heart about his private life to a reporter he barely knows, no matter how much drink had been taken, without thinking about it first. It was for show, a way of dampening down speculation about him and Kate, a way of protecting her from the press.'

Kate's obvious lack of concern as she partied with her boyfriend showed just how close the couple had become. She, like others who know William intimately, knew that whatever he said was with Kate's best interests – rather than the next morning's headlines – in mind. William has a protective instinct towards all of his friends when it comes to the press. He has inherited a style from his supremely loyal father. It is understandable, given his position and past. Emotionally scarred by the death of his beloved mother, he still believes, like Diana's embittered brother Earl

Spencer, that the paparazzi had hounded the princess to her death.

He may now accept that the real fault lies with Henri Paul, the driver who was way over the legal drink limit when he took the wheel of Diana's Mercedes on 31 August 1997 and drove both her and her lover, Dodi Fayed, to their deaths in the Alma tunnel, Paris. There are many who are still quick to remind the young prince that none of the events that led to his mother's end would have occurred were it not for the pursuit of an insatiable press. There would have been no frenzy, no last-minute changing of plans, no desperate high-speed chase, no decoy car – in short, none of the aggressive and fatally misjudged attempts to evade the paparazzi who, in reality, presented less of a threat to Diana's safety than the men entrusted with her care.

Little wonder, then, that, with such a sobering example to draw upon, William wants to ensure that Kate remains as safe from the ruthless excesses of some elements of the press as is humanly possible. If that means the occasional misleading remark, then so be it. In fact, William later regretted the bold statement, fuelled in part by a healthy intake of alcohol that night. One senior palace source later told me that the prince looked back on his words with a degree of embarrassment, laughing but admitting shame-facedly that he had been somewhat 'rash' to speak out.

From that night on, Paddy Harverson placed himself in charge of William's press during his Klosters holiday. He took it upon himself to be William's chaperone, inhabiting a sort of awkward no-man's-land between laddish companion and maiden aunt on all the princes' subsequent visits to nightclubs. As is so often the case, though, the spin doctor was resolutely slamming the stable door shut long after the horse had bolted.

Unbeknown to Harverson, undercover reporters had been working in the resort for more than a week, observing the young royals' drunken antics in all their glory, including Harry's bid to turn the tables on some members of the press by snatching up a camera and pursuing them as he snapped pictures and howled with laughter. The royals' relationship with the press – especially the tabloids – has always been a protracted game of cat-and-mouse. In addition, on that particular royal 'stag' trip, as it was dubbed, it was the last holiday Charles and his sons would enjoy before his wedding to Camilla in April 2005.

Within days, I heard a markedly different story from a reliable – perhaps in this instance *more* reliable – source than the prince himself did. A senior royal courtier let slip during conversation that the relationship between William and Kate was very serious and developing at a fast pace. It rang true.

'The relationship is very much ongoing. Just because the two of them choose to keep things private and play their cards close to their chest does not mean it is waning. Far from it: in fact it is quite the opposite,' a senior contact told me.

Given the seniority of the source, I did not hesitate to rush this story into print. The following morning the *Evening Standard* splash (newspaper jargon for a front-page story) carried the banner headline, Seriously in Love. Beneath were the words, 'Wills and Kate romance moving at a rapid pace, say royal sources'. A photograph of a smiling William looking lovingly into his girlfriend's eyes accompanied the report. The look of love certainly seemed to me to betray something of the besotted prince's true emotions, even if his own words had not.

When I returned to London a couple of days later I heard from an insider that Kate had been given professional guidance on how to deal with the press and the intrusion of the paparazzi. Her master classes had come from the press officers of Clarence House – Prince Charles's staff. Mindful perhaps of how disastrously ill prepared Diana was for public life, Charles had already asked this same personnel to school Camilla in the minutiae of making the transition from private individual to fully fledged member of the Royal Family. That a similar exercise should now have been undertaken by Kate was clearly a significant move and a sign that she was being groomed to step, however softly, into William's official life as well as his private domain.

It was not the last time that the prince would enlist the help of his father's office in his anxiety to offer guidance and protection to Kate. Nor was it the only occasion on which both father and son would attempt to erect boundaries around the young woman with whom William is passionately in love and on whom Charles dotes.

Above: Princes Harry, William and Charles and Camilla, Laura and Tom Parker Bowles n their 2005 Christmas card.

© *PA Photos*

Below: William and Harry take to the stage at Wembley in the concert dedicated to Princess Diana.

© *PA Photos*

Left: William and Kate out in St James.

Right: Kate in party mode in 2008.

ate at the wedding of Captain Nicholas van Cutsem and Alice Hadden-Paton in August
09. William and Harry were ushers.

Kate's father, Michael Middleton.

Kate with her mother Carole.

Holiday lunch at a restaurant in Zermatt, Switzerland.

© *Rex Features*

bove: Training with the Sisterhood on the Thames for an attempt on the Channel.

elow: Out with friends in 2008.

Above: At the Potting Shed pub in Crudwell, Malmesbury, in July 2009.

Below: Kate's sister Pippa graduates from Edinburgh University with Michael and Caro[le] in attendance.

Together they have effectively mounted a sort of pre-emptive campaign to defend Kate's privacy. Both know all too well that the interest will only intensify over time and as Kate's role in William's life grows. If the course of Diana's life has taught the Royal Family anything, it is this: when it comes to establishing the ground rules for a royal partner's privacy it is impossible to act too swiftly or too aggressively.

In October 2005, just seven months after William's rash denial of any serious plans, one photograph and the reaction it generated demonstrated the truth of this lesson learned. The infamous and astute paparazzi team of Brendan Beirne and Anthony Jones captured the image. Years earlier, they had worked together in pursuit of William's late mother. On this particular autumn day, the target was once again somebody well loved by the prince. Beautiful and oblivious of the lenses trained on her wistful gaze, Kate was captured daydreaming, staring from the window of a red double-decker bus in west London. She could have been any one of thousands of attractive young women working in the British capital, fresh from studying at university and embarking on their working lives. That, in part, was her charm and, as Jones and Beirne knew very well, that was the charm of the picture. Here was the woman courted by the future King of the UK and the Commonwealth, travelling not in splendour and privacy but on a rattling, noisy and diesel-guzzling public bus.

Thanks to digital technology, the pictures were shot, sent and sold before Kate had even roused herself from her reverie and stepped off the bus at her destination. The respected picture editor of the London *Evening Standard*, Dave Ofield, was not the first to see the photographs that day. They had appeared on computer screens of the big-spending picture editors across what is known more out of nostalgia than accuracy as Fleet Street. Both photographers knew that the London *Evening Standard* was a great shop window for their goods across the world. Besides, despite the fact that no rules or press codes had been breached in taking the photographs – Kate had been in a public place, as had the photographers – some picture editors were beginning to get cold feet. The pictures were certainly different and interesting: candid shots of the woman who had been dating the second in line to the throne for well over two years, travelling with neither protection nor retinue nor, it seemed, much in the way of funds. Defending a charge lodged with the Press Complaints Commission is something many newspaper executives would rather avoid – but not *Evening Standard* editor Veronica Wadley in this instance. She had a reputation for making tough decisions decisively. She liked the pictures and published then in a blurb strap across the front page and in colour inside.

In years to come, the images may very well become iconic in the way that the pictures of 19-year-old nursery assistant Lady Diana Spencer did when she was photographed while smilingly unaware that her skirt had become transparent against the sun. Back then, Diana was an unknown and the rumours of her relationship with Charles were circulating. With this in mind a pack of freelance paparazzi descended on the nursery school in which she worked, pressed their cameras up against the windows and began taking pictures. The infants inside began to cry, so Diana, in a bid to calm her young charges and to quell the snappers' hunger for an image, stepped out into that sunlit afternoon. Unlike Kate on her morning commute, Diana knew she was in the photographers' sights. However, her naïveté was such that the pictures appeared no less candid for it. The result on both occasions was the sort of natural moment that becomes impossible to capture once the palace publicity machine is set in motion.

When the picture of 23-year-old Catherine Middleton appeared in the *Standard*, the royal response was heavy-handed. Royal lawyers Harbottle and Lewis, acting for Kate but on the payroll of Prince Charles, claimed that the prince's girlfriend was subjected to an unjustified intrusion of her privacy. The message was blunt and clear: leave her alone. No other newspapers carried the picture the following day but the legal tactics were not entirely successful. Nobody likes a rap on the knuckles, especially when the so-called offence is out of proportion to the punishment inflicted. Even the quality press felt that Kate and her young prince had gone too far. They had been too defensive and had taken the situation too seriously. Typically, the *Daily Mail* had a dig. Under the headline SO YOU WANT TO BE ALONE, KATE?, middle England's newspaper of choice ran a report chronicling another occasion when Kate seemed perfectly at ease with the presence of photographers.

'Prince William's 23-year-old girlfriend made it clear,' it said, 'that she was happy to be photographed as she and her mother, Carole, did some early Christmas shopping.' An onlooker quoted described good-natured scenes as three photographers pursued a high-spirited Kate, saying, 'On one occasion she almost bumped into one of the photographers as she came around the corner. She burst out laughing.'

One of the photographers who occasionally took photographs of Kate told me at the time, 'There is more than a bit of hypocrisy going on here. Kate is a stunning girl and she knows exactly what the camera wants. Obviously, she has to play by the palace rules and is careful not to cooperate. To portray her as a frightened rabbit caught in the headlights is just absurd. She is an astute woman who knows how to handle herself with the media. She laughs, flirts even, with the people. Of course, she cannot appear to be cooperating. If she did that she would blow her chances with the prince – it is all a game to her at the moment.'

If it was a game it is fair to say she was winning hands down. She was getting the press attention *and* the protection of the palace. Bodyguards were on hand when she was with William and lawyers were ready to do her bidding. Some might describe it as a win–win situation.

There was nothing new in Kate's 'Greta Garbo' moment. In the early days of Diana's marriage to Charles the Queen felt compelled to step in on behalf of her daughter-in-law, who felt overwhelmed by the attention of the paparazzi. The Queen's press secretary, Michael Shea, was instructed to convene a meeting between the monarch and Fleet Street editors and television and radio executives. Before the Queen arrived Shea informed the assembled executives that Diana's treatment was the subject for discussion and that the palace was making a formal request for her to be left alone. The Queen then made her entrance for this rare royal audience with the press. It did not go well.

The then *News of the World* editor, Barry Askew, recalled a complaint that Shea had made prior to the sovereign's arrival, in which Diana had been followed by the press as she bought sweets from the local shop in Tetbury, the Gloucestershire village near Charles's sanctuary of Highgrove.

Determined to show the Queen did not intimidate him, Askew, a man aptly nicknamed the 'Beast of Bouverie Street' (where the *News of the World* used to be housed), addressed Her Majesty: 'Would it not be better to send a servant to the shop for Princess Diana's wine gums.' The Queen gave him her most steely glare. She then dismissed the quip, saying, 'Mr Askew that was the most pompous remark.' A few weeks later Askew resigned from his post – not, it must be said, for insulting the Queen, but that cannot have helped.

Obviously, it would be impossible for the Queen to intervene in a similar fashion on Kate's behalf while her relationship with William remained informal. Even though she had, by then, met her on a number of occasions and liked Kate personally, such an act would be tantamount to an engagement announcement. Which is where the involvement of Charles's lawyers in their swift letter to Fleet Street's finest is so revealing. Kate may have held no greater status than that of William's girlfriend but already her protection had become a matter of importance to the Firm. Seven months earlier William had scoffed at the very thought of marriage, yet here Kate was being treated like a treasured daughter-in-law. Perhaps Charles sees in his elder son's genuine love and happiness echoes of his own early relationship with Camilla, an affair that he blew through his procrastination first time around.

William had the benefit of his father's rather chequered history to draw upon. From the outset he was determined not to make the same mistakes. As one close source told me, 'William is acutely aware of the past. He knows that his unique position brings with it real difficulties with one's personal life. He knows that his father made rather a hash of things and he's determined not to do the same. He and Harry think it's good that their father has found contentment in later life; but knowing the heartache their mother suffered they don't want to suffer in the same way. Both of them are determined to marry for the right reason, for love and love alone.'

Perhaps that is why William in particular was so stubborn and resolutely private. Unlike his father, and contrary to the general perception of Charles, William is fortunate to have a parent who is prepared to listen and bend with the times. Charles admitted that he never took Prince Philip's advice until he was in his teens, but one does not get the same impression of the relationship between Charles and William. For years Charles was unfairly perceived to be a distant father, probably due to Diana's desire to rubbish his efforts and present herself as the perfect parent to her boys and to her adoring public. He hated the long absences from his sons that duty foisted upon him. Observers recalled that he would weep with joy, literally, when he saw them after a long time away. He would be openly affectionate with them, too, hugging and kissing his boys.

When William – his 'little Wombat' as Charles called him – was born on 21 June 1982, at 9.03 p.m., in St Mary's Hospital, Paddington, Charles described it as the happiest day of his life. He wrote to his godmother Patricia Brabourne, Earl Mountbatten's daughter, describing his delight: 'The arrival of our small son has been an astonishing experience and one that has meant more to me than I could ever have imagined . . . Oh! How I wish your dear papa could have lived to have seen him, but he probably knows anyway.'

It was touching that even at his happiest moment, Charles was still thinking of the man who had perhaps more than any other guided him through the turbulent waters of his youth. As the years have passed, he has tried to follow Lord Louis Mountbatten's example when it comes to his children. Prince Charles today happily allows William and Kate to share a room at Highgrove when she stays. He has the loving and sympathetic nature of a man who has suffered.

As one palace insider put it, 'The prince is not an overbearing man with his children. He knows they have experienced immeasurable pain with the loss of their beloved mother at such a tender age and he in many ways has overcompensated. I am not saying he's let them run wild, but he certainly has not tried to run their lives for them in the way, perhaps, the Duke of Edinburgh did for him.'

For, where Charles bowed to his father's and Great-Uncle Louis's desire for him to enter the Royal Navy, a less-than-subtle strategy to separate him from the inappropriate Camilla, William has done nothing of the sort. It was strongly suggested to him by his grandfather, Prince Philip, that he ought to go into the Royal Navy. He was told it would be a fitting choice for the future King. William, showing his strength of character and determination not to be bullied from his path, has cleverly avoided this. The prospect of months at sea was not one that inspired him. Instead, he chose to train at Sandhurst, the elite military academy. Harry was already a cadet – and destined to pass out before him in April 2006 – when William enrolled in January of the same year. It was a decision that led many royal writers to point light-heartedly to the potential embarrassment of his having to salute his younger brother as his superior. It was a minimal price for William, and one well worth paying if it meant remaining on the same soil as Kate.

For a member of the Royal Navy there would be no contact for months on end. There are some, like Diana's former private secretary, ex-Royal Navy Commander Patrick Jephson, who believed that that may have been a good thing: 'That is precisely why the Duke of Edinburgh was suggesting it. He is a pragmatist. He knows that young men can grow too attached too soon and it would give them the perfect excuse to get William away, as far as possible if it was felt such a course was needed.'

But it was not a view shared by William himself. He stood his ground and won, although he did eventually enjoy a short stint as 'Sublieutenant Wales' when he was seconded to the frigate HMS *Iron Duke* during a tour of the Caribbean in summer 2008 just months before finally quitting his military career.

As a trainee officer in Sandhurst he could invite Kate to dinners and balls and, when William was allowed to leave barracks, the couple could enjoy time together. There would be nothing to prevent their relationship continuing apace. Like his father all those years ago, William is a young man in love and under pressure. Unlike his father, he seemed determined from the outset not be bullied into marrying one of his 'own'. He had fallen in love with a pretty, middle-class girl, someone to whom he is not only drawn physically but who is his intellectual equal: they both achieved upper seconds at St Andrew's, he in geography, she in history of art. They share similar interests and, perhaps most importantly and most unusually for a young man in William's rarefied world, they are able to console and confide in each other with absolute trust. Nobody, friends have noted, is allowed to berate William like Kate. Nobody, other than Kate, is capable of bolstering his spirits when they flag. Theirs is a truly modern 'marriage', a union in the 21st-century sense. Unlike any other royal couple in history they have openly lived together, first in St Andrews in a house full of friends, later in Chelsea, London, and even sharing a bed at a royal palace prior to marriage without raising an eyebrow. It was a degree of commitment, however coyly the young prince may present it, that his father failed to demonstrate to any of the women in his life.

Of course, with this more 'real' relationship, a far cry from the private teas and prearranged liaisons at friends' country houses that his father had to tolerate, come more real disputes. William and Kate's relationship has not always run smoothly. There have had their fair share of stand-up fights, uncomfortable silences, public flirtations with others and trial separations.

Kate has had a few boyfriends too. She had, as we have seen, been dating the handsome Rupert Finch, when she and William first met. It could not have been easy for Kate or Finch to come to terms with the fact that her friendship with William was blossoming into romance. Kate also had to deal with the mixed blessing of knowing about William's past life and loves. As an intelligent girl she took an interest in press reports and, truth be told, had long since had a girlish crush on William. A less confident girl might easily have been put off by the rumours and reports of what on paper looked like more suitable love rivals from around the globe.

But the only girl who ever seemed to present a clear and present danger to Kate was Jecca Craig. Jecca is a girl whom William has fiercely and protectively described as a friend and nothing more. But his protestations did little to convince observers of that fact. The prince and 24-year-old Jecca have a long history. They first met in 1998 and it was to the Kenyan wildlife conservancy at Lewa Downs owned by Jecca's parents, four hours north of Nairobi, that William went in May 2001 when he spent four months travelling in Africa. He had just finished his schooling at Eton and was embarking on what he may look back on as the most carefree year of his life: abroad, unburdened by responsibility and duty, free from schoolwork and, largely, from press intrusion.

With her long, honey-brown hair, naturally tanned skin and a sort of wild, bohemian take on fashion, Kenyan-born Jecca must have seemed a breath of fresh air to a prince used to the company of Chelsea clones and Home Counties gals. It seemed that both enjoyed the relative privacy of postcolonial Kenya. Her friends describe Jecca as 'sweet, loyal and very outdoorsy', similar attributes ascribed to Kate. In 2005, William took Kate to visit Lewa Downs, staying with her in the breathtakingly beautiful resort of Il Ngwesi, high on a hill overlooking the Ngare Ndare river. The couple slept beneath mosquito nets on a platform dragged into the night air so that they could gaze upwards at the clear, starlit Kenyan skies. If Kate wondered whether William had once shared a similar experience with Jecca, she was no doubt far too sensible to ask. Yet Kate must have been aware of the reports of William's closeness to Jecca. Who would have blamed her for questioning whether her prince, who had visited the lodges at Il Ngwesi twice before their own romantic break, had fallen in love with more than just the location's beauty and isolation?

Jecca and William were said to be so close that in 2000 they performed a mock engagement ceremony on her parents' 55,000-acre wildlife reserve at the foot of Mount Kenya. In June 2003, Jecca flew thousands of miles to be by William's side as guest of honour at his 21st-birthday party in Windsor Castle. The speculation surrounding them was intense. It continued well into Kate's relationship with the prince and could well have caused a less self-possessed girl to waver. In November 2004 Jecca was pictured slipping into the side entrance of Chester Cathedral at the marriage of Hugh van Cutsem and Lady Tamara Grosvenor (the son of close friends of Charles and daughter of the Duke of Westminster respectively). Both William and Harry were ushers at the lavish society ceremony attended by the Queen and Prince Philip. Jecca was a vision in buckaroo hat, her hair long, shining and allowed to hang loose over her shoulders. She wore knee-length boots and her turquoise coat was tied at the front with leather thongs. Kate was far more conservative in dress, wearing a white fitted jacket, adorned with black embroidered swirls and nipped in at her enviably small waist. Lace from her stylish, small hat spilled over her face; she wore a pencil skirt and high-heeled court shoes. Both girls must have known that all eyes were on them as supposed rivals for William's affections. Jecca kept a low profile. Kate maintained a smiling reserve.

But it was a set of candid pictures that revealed more than anything about the true state of William and Kate's relationship that drizzly November day. Strolling down a lane near the Duke of Westminster's Cheshire estate of Eaton, where a lavish reception was held, William and Kate were caught on film. The couple, at that time resolutely non-tactile in public, were barely touching but the image was an intimate insight into their affections. They were walking away from the camera in a shot taken at some distance and from behind. William, who looked broad and tall in his tailcoat, walked beside the svelte Kate, who suddenly seemed impossibly glamorous and possessed the silhouette of a 1940s starlet. Their heads inclined towards each other as William's hand hovered tenderly at the small of Kate's back. Not even the most hardened of cynics could deny that this was the image of a couple both intimate and in love.

CHAPTER 9

ROYAL MARRIAGE BUSINESS

'Marry Prince William? I'd love that.
Who wouldn't want to be a princess?'
BRITNEY SPEARS

By the summer of 2006, nearly four years into their relationship, any photograph of Kate that appeared in a newspaper or magazine would do so under the caption, 'princess-in-waiting'. For the media, it was only a matter of time before Kate Middleton would be William's bride.

In March 2006, the newspaper I was then working as royal correspondent for, the *Evening Standard*, ran a spread of pictures of Kate wearing a fur hat at Cheltenham races and pointing out that her fashion sense mirrored the controversial regal fondness for animal pelt. Seasoned royal watchers were less moved by her choice of hat than by the fact that she was pictured in the same exclusive members' enclosure as Prince Charles and his new wife Camilla, now Duchess of Cornwall. William was not with Kate on this occasion as he was continuing his rigorous training at Sandhurst Military Academy. Yet there was Kate, laughing and smiling and utterly at ease with the royals and their entourage. It only served to underline the extent to which the so-called Firm now embraced Kate. Later, when a reporter from the *Standard* asked a Clarence House official for an on-the-record comment about Kate's fur fashion accessory, the response was as intriguing as it was revealing. They could not comment on the issue, the representative explained, as Kate was a private individual and 'not yet' a member of the Royal Family.

Was it not for that tantalising 'yet' it would have been a predictable rebuttal. As it was, it suggested there was an inevitable outcome of William's relationship, that it would only be a matter of time before they would be commenting on her behalf as a fully signed-up princess and member of the family.

Media obsession with the marriage of an heir to the throne is nothing new, nor is the public's fascination for the partner he or she chooses. Perhaps only the modes of expression differ. Today people can make their views known through opinion polls commissioned by journalists to break down into percentages the nature and strength of the general view. When Henry VIII dumped his Spanish first wife, Katherine of Aragon, to wed and crown his ill-fated second wife Anne Boleyn, mother of Queen Elizabeth I, things were less scientific. The people gathered on the foul-smelling streets of London to witness the lavish ceremony that took place on 29 May 1533 and to register their displeasure at both Henry's decision to divorce and, worse still, at his choice of new bride.

Of course King Henry VIII could and did wed, divorce and even execute his wives pretty much at will (in fact two were executed, Anne Boleyn and her cousin Katherine Howard). Henry, an absolute monarch, was not truly concerned about any public backlash. The problems for a young prince today, placed under the scrutiny of less reticent and at times downright aggressive media and the public, are far more intense and pressing. Little wonder, then, that the modern royals have not completely abandoned the methods of their more ruthless forebear. On the day of Prince Charles's wedding to Camilla, for example, there was genuine concern that ardent supporters of the late Princess Diana might ruin the day with noisy protest – so much so that a 'friendly' crowd of charitable workers and those known to support the couple were given tickets and allowed to congregate behind barriers inside the walls of Windsor Castle. The cameras were then carefully positioned to ensure these positive pictures were the ones beamed around the world when the couple emerged after the ceremony.

Outside, uniformed police as well as undercover officers guarded the route. The only person with an anti-Camilla poster was politely asked to take it down.

For a 21st-century prince, finding a balance between public role and private life is all but impossible. In spite of what has gone before, the vast majority of the public still expect their royals to marry for love. This means that a royal's most personal choice is laden with public repercussions and judgement. Set against this is the knowledge that love can make fools of us all. William is aware of this. Whereas marrying the wrong woman can be a cause of heartache and financial strain for the average man in the street, for the future king and his family the impact of getting it wrong can be cataclysmic on the institution they represent. Finding a bride is a fraught business – it is also vital.

An heir to the throne may raise a great deal of money for needy causes and draw attention to important cause dear to his heart. Then again, he may strive to implement some level of social change through various schemes and enterprises. He may even represent his crown and country abroad with distinction, supporting his sovereign, shaking hands and giving impressive and thought-provoking speeches before graciously posing for photographs with paupers, presidents and politicians. But no matter how much heat and noise he may generate – and with his penchant for firing off letters to Members of Parliament and espousing his views on topics such as organic farming, complementary medicine, genetically modified crops and the state of modern architecture, the present incumbent, Prince Charles, certainly does a great deal of that – one simple fact remains: the heir to the throne must find a suitable partner and breed. In this respect, he is little more than a farmyard stud, albeit from a top bloodline, in a well-tailored Savile Row suit.

If anybody knows how important the heir's choice of bride has always been both constitutionally and personally, it is William's grandmother and sovereign, Queen Elizabeth II. She need only look, helplessly, to the generation that preceded her and to the one that followed to see in these bookends of her reign concrete proof that the moments in recent history that have brought the

Royal Family to the lip of destruction are those precipitated by the wrong choice of bride. Getting it wrong has brought the monarchy to its knees and laid it bare to ridicule from the people, whose support is necessary if this unelected and undemocratic institution is to survive.

Picking the right bride to become a princess and a possible future queen is not a decision to be taken lightly. A 21st-century princess is a different species from the ones of old. In the past, the system was tried and tested. A prince would marry for political and dynastic reasons, not for love. He would marry a daughter of a foreign king to forge an alliance between nations or pick from a host of suitable, not-too-distant cousins raised to know the score. In time, and in awareness of their respective jobs, they might grow to love each other. Princes found their passion in the arms of their mistresses, usually a discreet aristocrat and invariably somebody else's wife. Newspaper proprietors of old, usually barons and earls themselves, would instruct their editors and reporters to ignore any royal extramarital activity.

In this century money talks and sordid sex secrets sell newspapers. Such deals for discretion have long been torn up. Royals and their affairs, as far as the tabloids are concerned, are fair game. For a modern prince like William the past failures of his ancestors must play heavy on his mind. The consequences have, after all, been almost fatal to the institution he will one day head. The crisis that accompanied Edward VIII's abdication in 1936 and thrust William's great grandfather George VI onto the throne shook the monarchy to its very foundations.

There is no tradition of abdication in the British Royal Family – and for very good reason. In some European countries, such as Holland, an ageing monarch may routinely retire. But it has been drummed into William from an early age that in Britain the only routine separation of monarch from throne comes with death. William as a child may have fought against his birthright and even dreaded it, but his duty was fully explained and his destiny mapped out for him. The abdication of Edward VIII, less than a year after he had ascended the throne, stands alone in British royal history, a cataclysmic event, once unimaginable, now unforgettable. For the generations that have only ever lived through the reign of his niece, Elizabeth II, it is almost impossible to imagine just how devastating Edward's departure was.

Today the Duke of Windsor, as Edward became after his abdication, is eulogised rather romantically by some as the king who renounced the throne for love. Films, dramas and documentaries have been made about his and Wallis Simpson's gripping love story, which all seem conveniently to ignore her later infidelities with younger, sexually exotic men, perhaps because they do not dovetail with the love story we all in our hearts want to believe. What we do trust, however, is that Edward loved American divorcée Wallis Simpson beyond reason and because of that love he abandoned his birthright and the heavy burden of responsibility that comes with it. In his riveting memoir, *A King's Story* – the only book ever written by a king and ever likely to be – Edward reflected that, whatever one's station in life, love must conquer all.

However, there was precious little romance in his sombre 1936 speech informing the nation of his decision to abdicate – perhaps because Prime Minister Stanley Baldwin insisted on having the final say on the wording. There was no romance in his meetings with Baldwin, who relieved him of any hopes of making a queen of Simpson. He told the King, 'The British public will not have her'; and there was no romance in the transference of the burden of monarchy onto the less sturdy shoulders of his younger brother, Bertie, then Duke of York, and soon to be King George VI.

That act – that the much-maligned Wallis herself had counselled against offering to leave the country for good – tore violently across the empire and the country, striking painfully at the very core of the Royal Family. The institution did not so much wobble as threaten to keel over. It fell to the current Queen's father, the then Duke of York, to lead his small family out of the dust storm. Still mourning the death of his own father, Bertie, as he was known by his family, guided his wife – the stoic former Lady Elizabeth Bowes-Lyon, later Queen Elizabeth, the Queen Mother – along with Princesses Elizabeth and Margaret, blinking into the harsh light of a public life and office for which none had been prepared.

117

As King George VI, he was suddenly the defender of a monarchy in crisis, a monarchy that some genuinely believed to be on the cusp of destruction. With hindsight, it is easy to wonder why there was so much fuss. For the Royal Family, and for the stoic new Queen Consort and her daughters, the answer was and is extremely straightforward. The fuss was all about the wrong choice of bride.

In 1996 Elizabeth's youngest child Prince Edward produced and presented a television documentary on the life of the Duke of Windsor, called *Edward on Edward*. It charted his great-uncle's love affair with Wallis Simpson and followed him into exile in France. It was one of the best productions by his controversial company, Ardent, well researched and ably fronted by Edward. But, for all the sympathy Prince Edward personally expressed, there was notably no hint of the Duke of Windsor's behaviour being in any way forgiven or sanctioned by any member of the Royal Family. The Queen did famously visit him before his death, during an official visit to France in May 1972, and when his body was brought back to burial at Frogmore afterwards his wife was pictured walking in the grounds of Buckingham Palace. But these were acts of common Christian decency on the part of the monarch, his niece. They were not signs that all was forgiven.

Time, for the Queen at least, has done nothing to heal those wounds. Edward VIII made a bad choice, and the Queen's life and those of her children have been defined by it. To a woman as imbued with a sense of duty as the Queen, this fact is compounded by her knowledge that Edward VIII's true crime was that he failed in his duty. He failed to do the one thing that the Prince of Wales simply must do: choose the right woman to be his bride. It was a failure that would, in turn, be repeated by his great-nephew and William's father, Prince Charles. That bears down on Prince William as second in line to the throne with all the weight and inevitability of history.

In the wraithlike figure of Wallis Simpson, King Edward's error was further compounded by the empire's absolute rejection of her. With the still dazzling figure of Diana, Prince Charles's marital folly was compounded by the world's absolute acceptance of her.

The danger was not that he would renounce the throne and his people but that they would renounce him. It was a fear to which Charles reacted at times petulantly and rashly. Charles's desperate attempts to regain public favour – or rather the attempts of those working on his behalf – led him and his court into the previously uncharted territory of spin, at times running the risk of damaging not only his mother but the institution of the monarchy itself.

Pragmatists may argue that the marriage of Charles and Camilla on 9 April 2006 – a month after I exclusively broke the story of their engagement in the *Standard* – was the perfect compromise. Unlike his great-uncle, Charles played his cards with a cool head. He was able to have it both ways, the love of his life as well as the chance to reign. Camilla, the restyled, revamped and rehabilitated Duchess of Cornwall, has proved a success. The heir to the throne, so often presented as a middle-aged eccentric, now seems complete with a woman at his side that he not only loves but who believes in him and his many crusades. Charles's succession was a matter of great debate in the months following his divorce from Diana, when damaging revelations of infidelities and the casually inflicted cruelties of their marriage abounded. The debate also resurfaced after Diana's death in 1997.

These days, it may not be a notion greeted with universal joy, but few genuinely believe that Charles's crown would pass directly to William instead. After all, if Charles was so inclined it would require an Act of Parliament not only here but in the realms and dominions. It would also need the Queen to agree it. Crisis over then? No, not quite. Charles may feel entitled to his happiness (of the entire Queen's offspring he must surely empathise the most with his great-uncle's situation) and as a mother the Queen will want her children to be settled in their personal lives and happy. Unlike his great-uncle, Charles has been allowed to marry his divorcée and keep his position. But it raises the question: at what cost?

The Royal Family, and in particular the court of the Prince of Wales, has been stripped bare for public ridicule, examination and disapproval. The impact has been profound. Spending is scrutinised and tax concessions criticised. There is at times in the country a sentiment perilously close to republicanism. The previous two men to hold the title Prince of Wales have failed catastrophically in their sole duty to choose a suitable bride. Could the family withstand a third generation making the same mistake? It hardly seems a chance they are likely to take.

Queen Elizabeth has taken a conspicuous interest in her grandson's romance with Kate Middleton. The parallels between William and Kate and the generation preceding them cannot be lost on the monarch. William was 23 and Kate 24 when their love became truly apparent, the same ages as Charles and Camilla were when they first fell in love. The monarch may not be given to whimsy but it must be difficult to resist wondering, What if . . .? What if Charles had got it right first time around? Then again, there is also the nagging uncertainty: What if William does not?

Prince Charles is understandably determined to shield his elder son from the pressures of such thoughts, from the clamour of the press and the exigencies of royal duties too soon. But already, and perhaps unfairly, William has been touted as a more appealing monarch than his father when his time comes. And, although 88 years and two days separate William from his great-great-uncle Edward VIII, he can expect to receive all of the eulogies bestowed upon his notorious ancestor in his prime.

Outside the palace walls the world in which William exists has been transformed beyond recognition. Yet the imperative that underscored King Edward VIII's life, and the necessity that has governed Charles's, remains William's solemn duty. If he is to avoid the tortuous scandals of the preceding Prince of Wales he must find a girl he loves, make sure she is single, respectable and suited to a public role, and produce heirs – preferably male, though that may become less important if the oft-mooted end to male primogeniture is realised in William's lifetime. If his predecessors' failures are anything to go by it is a career path that is nowhere near as simple as it sounds.

Sticking to his narrow job description is not made easier by the fact that William, as heir to the throne, automatically becomes the country's most eligible bachelor. Eligible bachelors are catnip to a host of decidedly ineligible females. It's easy to go wrong and in these times of telephoto lenses, leaks and appalling betrayals it is easy to get caught if you do. Yet, despite their relative youth and reports of the occasional trial separation, William and Kate's relationship did survive the transition from university life into the real world and now to marriage. In the process William's 'adorable' Kate, whose role in William's life started innocently enough as just a bit of student fun, has been recast in a far more significant part – that of princess and our Queen in waiting.

CHAPTER 10

INTO THE REAL WORLD

'At the moment it's about having fun in the right places,
enjoying myself as much as I can,'
PRINCE WILLIAM, AFTER TAKING HIS FINAL UNIVERSITY EXAMS

If it had been any other couple embroiled in an intense argument, nobody would have given it much notice. Nevertheless, the two people sitting side by side in the Volkswagen Golf in the midst of a furious exchange were not just any couple, but Prince William and his girlfriend, Kate Middleton. Instead of making the most of their time together, they were locked in an animated row, their expressions strained and their body language anything but intimate. The noise may have been muffled by the closed windows of the locked car but their vocal disagreement was still audible and it was hardly surprising that it caused a stir.

It was the first time these two intensely private people had been caught in such an unrestrained and unguarded row. Their public lovers' tiff was all the more extraordinary because William and Kate had been at such pains to conduct their relationship in secrecy bordering on paranoia over the previous year. Unbeknown to the passers-by who feigned disinterest as they hovered near the couple's car, William and Kate had made a pact never to betray the slightest hint of emotion towards each other in public. Until this moment they had never come close to breaking it. But, on this soft English summer's day in 2004, at a private polo match at Coworth Park near Ascot in Berkshire, that pact was undone.

'It was clear to anyone who walked past that they were having a pretty major set-to,' said an eyewitness. 'We all wondered what it was all about.' Neither William nor Kate like scenes, and the fact that they had taken their discussion to his car showed that they needed some privacy to talk. So what could have happened to provoke such an outburst?

The speculation was predictably swift. Perhaps, like any young couple together for more than a year, they were going through a difficult patch. The relationship had bloomed in the relative seclusion of William and Kate's close clique of university friends, but the price of privacy can be claustrophobia. It was inevitable that irritations and frustrations would come to the surface at some point. Some observers went further and theorised that this tiff signalled the end of the romance only months after it had been revealed. One contemporaneous report suggested that they had agreed to a trial separation.

This was the type of speculation normally associated with a married couple of several years. Of course, such doom mongers were proved wrong. But it was true that William and Kate were feeling the strain barely a year into their affair. Some pressures were self-generated, not least William's insistence on conducting their relationship in almost paranoid secrecy. Others were circumstantial, as university course work mounted. Some were simply par for the course in a maturing relationship, as reality, for prince or pauper, often falls short of romantic expectations.

That day, as they engaged in their fraught tête-à-tête, many issues collided. It seemed that William was conscious that the end of his university life was no longer a distant possibility. Three-quarters of his course was done, the sand was rapidly running through the hourglass. William, then just 21, was said to have told Kate that he wanted them to 'cool it' for a while. He wanted to turn his attentions more seriously to his studies. Already tutors and lecturers were beginning to remind their students that finals were rapidly approaching. That in itself wasn't a problem as far as Kate was concerned.

She had the same stresses and workload ahead of her as William. If anything, she always seemed the more studious of the two. What apparently troubled her far more were William's plans to travel overseas when his studies were over. Instead of staying with her in Scotland during the month between the end of final examinations and graduation in June he wanted to head off on his own.

Worse still for Kate was William's claim that he felt claustrophobic and hemmed in by the relationship. At a time when all around him students were playing the field, swapping partners with remarkable regularity, he had fallen into a comfortable coupling in his early years of university. The house they shared on the outskirts of town was more suggestive of comfortable middle age than wild student life. It was a sprawling 18th-century pile, a four-bedroom home on the Strathtyrum estate flanked by orchards and fuchsia bushes whose inside was a blend of faded grandeur and shabby chic. When William, Kate and their friend Fergus Boyd moved in it must have seemed the ideal party house, complete with cavernous kitchen, plenty of floor space for guests to bed down and no neighbours to bother with noise. But, though they entertained occasionally, the house gradually turned into more of a retreat as the relationship slowed to a comfortable drift. William would not be the first person to wonder whether he was missing out on the rather innocent hedonism of university days by settling for somebody too soon. Might he have met the right girl at the wrong time?

A senior palace aide told me that the discussions had been very serious. 'Prince William thinks the world of Kate Middleton but he has confided to at least one of his best friends that the relationship has been getting a little stale and he thinks they may be better suited as friends. He has been unhappy in the relationship for a while, but the last thing he wants is a high-profile split in the crucial months leading to his finals. The truth is he thinks that when they graduate in the spring they'll go their own ways.'

This seemed to be the death knell for their romance. For *any* young woman who had invested so much time and emotion in a university relationship this would have been a terrible blow, but to Kate it must have been a bombshell. Hers, after all, had been a high-profile relationship with the future King played out in the newspapers. The prospect of being thrown from the regal stallion at the final furlong (in racing terms, of course) must have been simply devastating. There had been no hint of any such storm clouds looming on the horizon at the beginning of the year. After their spring holiday at Klosters, when snaps of William and Kate on the white, picture-postcard slopes had first revealed their love to the world, they could not have seemed a more united couple. I was there to observe and record and at the time there was no doubt that William had eyes only for Kate.

Over that summer they had gone on to enjoy yet another luxurious holiday together on the remote sun-kissed island of Rodrigues in the Indian Ocean and perhaps unreality had set in. They spent their days snorkelling and scuba-diving, sipping cocktails at beach cabana bars and stretching out on the sands on those long and lazy sunny days. It was by all accounts a blissfully happy time. They had been joined by six other friends and luxuriated in the chance of some downtime away from the goldfish bowl of university life.

William had been there before, in September 2000, when he had swapped the rigours of training with the Welsh Guards in Belize for the white sands of Mauritius during his gap year. The palace had dressed it up as an 'educational trip', announcing that the prince was working on an 'undisclosed project' with the Royal Geographical Society. To some of us it seemed more likely that he was simply working on his tan. It was certainly far from all work and no play, despite the predictable protestations from palace aides that this was an 'important period of personal development'. Quite!

However he spent those sun-baked days in 2000, William could not wait to return to the islands of the Indian Ocean once more. When he did, ahead of his final year at university, he chose the speck of land only a short hop from Mauritius to romance the girl from whom he seemed inseparable. He had loved the harmonious, simple way of life the last time he was there. William's trip may have had more than a dusting of luxury, but still he was struck by the diverse cultural backgrounds of the people he met. It was an environment that left an indelible mark on the barefoot and laid-back prince, and one he wanted to share with Kate. He felt sure that she would love it.

The coral reefs off Rodrigues are among the most beautiful in the world, and the island itself, just east of Mauritius, is remote and hilly and has tracts of rocky coast that give way to breathtakingly beautiful white sands. It echoes to the song of rare birds and is known as a perfect retreat for nature lovers seeking peace and tranquillity. It was the perfect venue for lovers of a different nature, too. It earned Portuguese explorer Diego Rodrigues a footnote in history when he discovered the island in 1528. Almost five centuries on, it would make its way into William and Kate's shared history, providing the backdrop for their carefree break that August. It may have been midwinter in the southern hemisphere but it was still balmy and warm.

It was a blissful time in William and Kate's relationship. William sought to impress Kate by tearing up the coast on his motorbike or diving from launches into the Indian Ocean. And there was still the spark of new passion in evidence, however carefully their group of friends sought to shield the couple from lurking paparazzi. But they were comfortable in each other's company, too. The clumsiness of early intimacy was long gone. So it seemed all the more perplexing when, after that holiday, William's ardour towards Kate began to cool. During the rest of the summer break Kate did visit William at Highgrove, but she was far from a permanent fixture at his side. Perhaps he felt the situation was getting a little predictable, a touch stale. Back on English soil, perhaps the prospect of a future with Kate seemed less golden than it had before.

They began to row. William began to strain on the leash of their relationship. A less understanding or less resilient young woman might have baulked at William's apparent need to stretch his wings. She might have issued an ultimatum, made hysterical demands or dug her claws ever deeper into her prized catch, and she might have blown it as a result. But not Kate. At this crucial moment she showed herself once again to be remarkably confident. She was naturally upset and fearful that William was trying to extricate himself from the relationship but she is said to have told him that she valued his friendship so highly that she was prepared to accept his rather unreasonable terms. She was even said to have considered quitting their shared student house in an effort to embrace William's expressed need for time and space.

It all seemed terribly grown up and reasonable. But others sensed that William's protestations of feeling trapped, of wanting to focus on exams and of increasingly regarding Kate as a friend, told only half the story. Equally, Kate's surprising tolerance went only part of the way towards explaining the real situation. According to some there was another topic up for debate: Jecca Craig.

Among William's travel plans was a trip to Kenya to visit Jecca on her parents' wildlife reserve in the foothills of Mount Kenya. The enigmatic and beautiful Miss Craig was always a bone of contention for Kate. She did not want to appear desperate but nor was she about to allow William to walk all over her – or to walk away from her. Everybody has their limit when it comes to tolerance and understanding; Kate's seemed to stretch as far as Jecca.

After that volatile debate in the car William scrapped his plans to return to Kenya. However, it's doubtful that Kate allowed herself to celebrate too much at having won the day. She must surely have known that putting her foot down was a gamble. And there would be many more anxious months ahead before she would be certain that it had paid off. As summer gave way to autumn the steady drip of disaffection between William and Kate continued. Towards the end of August William took the potentially provocative decision to travel to Texas and to the home of another intimate female friend, Anna Sloan, a stunning blonde Southern belle who had been studying at nearby Edinburgh University.

Kate had been assured that her boyfriend and Anna had never been more than friends. According to some of her circle, Kate also knew that, while she had been dating Rupert Finch, William had made his move on Anna only to be coolly and firmly rebuffed. William, more than most young men, was not used to being told no. For him it was a novel experience and perhaps all the more titillating for it.

Another significant moment in their relationship came in September, when William apparently snubbed Kate by deciding to go on a boys-only sailing holiday around the Greek islands. Adding insult to injury, he allegedly insisted on an all-female crew. His girlfriend was far from impressed. Kate was irritated and humiliated and must have been left wondering whether William was in some cowardly fashion trying to push her beyond endurance, prompting her to break off their relationship.

Many young women in love may have found it a step too far, for, while William no longer planned to travel to Kenya and spend time with Jecca, she had not disappeared from his life. Ever since she had been first romantically linked with William, Jecca had accrued the sort of social standing that Kate, even as William's steady girlfriend, was still denied. Jecca's effortless beauty was praised in glossy magazines; her bohemian sense of style, in stark contrast to Kate's safe, well-groomed Sloaney look, was lauded. She was compared rather romantically to a deer that shivered in the light of publicity, shied away from attention and craved privacy and nature. By now she was a student of anthropology at the University of London and a deer well and truly stalked by the more unruly elements of the press. The bible of British society, *Tatler* magazine, named her in its *Little Black Book* of the most eligible women in the country. Inevitably, she turned down the invitation to attend the starry party to celebrate the book's launch and her inclusion. Kate didn't even warrant a place on the list. However much Jecca may have hated the attention of the press, it must have rankled rather more with Kate.

When William and Kate got together it had simply been assumed that any romantic ties between Jecca and William had been severed. But towards the end of 2004 people began to wonder. In September, William turned up for the wedding of old friend Davina Duckworth-Chad, to whom he had also been romantically linked. According to one guest, 'I didn't see any sign of Kate. But Jecca was there.' By this time Jecca and William were in regular contact, speaking on the phone and exchanging emails. It could all have been entirely innocent, but who could have blamed Kate for feeling threatened? In November 2004, Jecca's presence at the society wedding of Edward van Cutsem and Lady Tamara Grosvenor provoked a storm of media interest. The van Cutsems are close family friends of Prince Charles, and William acted as an usher at the ceremony. Kate was there. But it was Jecca, in brown suede and turquoise-trimmed coat, boots and Jackaroo hat that drew admiring glances and knowing looks.

Later that month one newspaper went as far as to claim that William's intimate friendship with Jecca was back on and had in recent months become far more intense. One who had noticed a shift in tempo said, 'Their closeness has never been a secret. William is extremely fond of Jecca. But he does seem to be spending rather a lot of time talking to her at the moment.' Would it be surprising if these cosy chats with the honey-skinned Jecca had, over time, led to a distinct frostiness between Kate and William?

It is worth remembering that when it comes to William nothing is ever quite as it seems. He guards his private life with a jealousy that borders on paranoia. In the second half of 2004 he had gone to extraordinary lengths to keep himself and anyone close to him out of the public gaze. He sought out ever-more exclusive and excluding events to attend with Kate and ever-more secluded venues to take her to. By necessity, William can be extremely cunning and actively revels in the intrigue of creating a smokescreen of uncertainty about his private life. It is a game he continues to play to this day. And he rather enjoys the feeling that he is winning.

'Ordinarily it would be very strange to leave one's long-term girlfriend out of the wedding of a close friend like Davina,' one of their circle of friends told me at the time. 'But I would not put it past him to choose deliberately not to take Kate with him, both to protect her from attention and to add to the confusion about their relationship, which suits Wills just fine.'

But by the end of 2004 there was no avoiding the fact that reports of difficulties between William and Kate were more frequent and certainly more persistent. Irrespective of who you are, affairs of the heart are never straightforward; for William and Kate all the natural complications and doubts were multiplied by the scrutiny of others and pressures peculiar to William's position. He is a good-looking and athletic young man and could have his pick of any of the beautiful girls of his generation. At times the ever-so-dependable Kate must have seemed ever so slightly dull. This is what some people close to William began to suggest.

William may have the reputation of being the quieter of the two brothers. It is Harry, after all, who is more often pictured falling out of nightclubs or was snapped kissing his mini-skirted girlfriend Chelsy in public – but William is no prissy prude by any stretch of the imagination. He enjoys a party like any young man his age and he is not averse to the company of racy and confident girls. At times it seemed that sensible Kate may have cramped his style. He also has the perfect get-out-of-jail-free card – he could tell Kate that he was unable to invite her to certain events for her own protection. This would leave him free, like his father before him, to nurture intimacies with more than one girl at once should he choose to. Old habits, especially familial traits, die hard.

But those close to William point out that part of his anxiety during this difficult time stemmed from a more serious concern and sense of his future. William knew that, as future king, once he reached a certain stage of intimacy with a girl it would be hard to turn back. He did not want to make the 'wrong' move. Getting too close and too settled too soon might have seemed to him to be just that, even though his feelings for the girl were powerful.

If this was the case, then Kate's response to her royal boyfriend's uncertainties was a textbook example of how to keep hold of your man. She played it cool. This, remember, is the girl who, when asked if she felt lucky to be dating a prince, rightly and confidently responded, 'He's lucky to be going out with *me.*' It may have been a bit of bravado but Kate was sharp enough to know that being clingy and needy wouldn't wash when it came to holding onto a prize catch like William. She gave him the time and space he wanted, but she put her foot down just enough and no more.

Only three people will ever really know whether Jecca held William's affections for a time over the summer of 2004 and how close William and Kate came to calling it a day. But Kate can rest assured that, as autumn turned to winter and the year drew to a close, she was safe and secure in her lover's arms and affections once again. More than that, after the blip, she was woven ever tighter into the fabric of his life.

Like so many waning royal love affairs, theirs rekindled in the beautiful surroundings of the Scottish Highlands, where William had first romanced her in the early days of their relationship and where friendship had given way to passion. In February 2005 William and Kate repeatedly returned to their Balmoral hideaway to take a break from university life, travelling on at least three occasions to the cottage given to the princes as a bolthole by the Queen. And their intimacy was clear for the world to see in March 2005, when he invited Kate to join him skiing in Klosters on his father's annual family ski break with his sons, prior to his wedding to Camilla. I was on that trip as a professional observer and saw, albeit from a reporter's distance, how William was back to his old attentive ways with Kate. The chemistry that may have briefly waned was certainly back. 'Wills only has eyes for Kate,' gushed the *Daily Mail*, going on to note that Kate's presence on the ski slopes at such an important moment in the life of Charles and his sons meant that she had been given 'the royal seal of approval'. It certainly seemed significant. At one jolly lunch, William was seated next to his father but might as well have been in the room with Kate alone, as she was the centre of his attention throughout.

At last, the 22-year-old prince seemed more relaxed with Kate in public. There were still some attempts to protect her from press attention. Most mornings as the royal party walked to the cable car to the slopes, William would stroll out ahead, leaving Kate to avoid the spotlight. It might have seemed rude to the uninitiated but it was William's way of trying to keep her literally out of the picture.

While William may have seemed anxious, Kate seemed perfectly at ease. At times William managed to push aside his natural misgivings. In the midst of a large group of family and friends he openly showed affection for Kate. At one stage she happily sat on his knee as they petted each other playfully. His father was there and he too seemed utterly relaxed with Kate in his presence. On that trip more than on any previously, Kate showed just how far she had come from student love interest to established partner. She chatted animatedly to Prince Charles as they gathered to eat in a mountainside restaurant. On another occasion, she was seen deep in conversation with Charles as they rode side by side in a gondola taking them up to the slopes.

It was the first time that Prince Charles had been photographed with his elder son's girlfriend, and confirmed for the cameras and accompanying reporters what I had been told several months earlier: that Charles thoroughly approved of William's choice of partner. By now both he and Camilla had had several opportunities to get to know her. They found Kate charming company and had both grown fond of her. She was at ease in the bosom of William's family and happy in the company of Harry and his friends, too, although on this occasion Chelsy Davy had turned down an invitation in favour of staying in South Africa. The trip that March was the clearest sign yet for royal observers that William had made a conscious decision to introduce Kate to the other life that he had, the life that awaited him once he left university – and the life that could possibly be awaiting Kate as well. After those fraught six months or so the previous year it now seemed unequivocal: Kate was the real deal.

In May 2005, William was putting down his pen after his last gruelling geography exam. Kate had completed hers too, including a well-received dissertation entitled ' "Angels from Heaven": Lewis Carroll's Photographic Interpretation of Childhood' (Kate later agreed to make it available to future students on the university website). Unlike William's university contemporaries – perhaps Kate included – who all desperately needed to attain a good grade to help them with their chosen future career, there was for the prince only personal pride at stake. Whether he got first-class honours, a 2:1 or scraped through with a third was pretty irrelevant as far as his career path to kingship was concerned. Sandhurst, a commission with one of the Guards regiments and then the fast-track into royal duties would follow on from graduation regardless of whatever the University of St Andrews examinations boards thought of his final performance. But William, a proud and intelligent young man, was desperate for academic success. He was determined not to perform poorly – an eventuality that would inevitably have been met by howls of derision from certain corners of the media and public. William, probably the most academically gifted member of the Royal Family in recent times (a comment that some may think damns him with faint praise), was not about to let anybody down, least of all himself.

He had prepared himself diligently for these exams and as he finished them he let out an audible sigh of relief. Ahead of him were three weeks of festivities and fun, culminating in a lavish graduation ball at the university on 24 June. There would be a traditional ceilidh band, a pop group and disco. And his beautiful girlfriend Kate would be on his arm.

On the night itself, students who had arrived as visions of glamour afterwards stumbled out into the early morning and picked their way across the litter-strewn quadrangle. They linked arms and walked towards the stretch of beach known as Castle Sands. The more foolhardy among them took the headlong plunge into the freezing waters that glimmered as the dawn began to break. Kate, William and flatmate and confidant Fergus Boyd stayed on dry land, wandering down the sands and trying, no doubt, to ignore the fact that day was breaking and, with it, a new era in their life was beginning. In many respects Kate and William were no different now from any other young couple facing the prospect of testing their university romance in the outside world to see if it could stay the course. Neither of them knew what lay in store, only that they were prepared to give it a go. So many university relationships flounder once lectures and common rooms are swapped for working lives. Both were fully aware that their intimacy would diminish; the routine of their lives would never again be quite so in tune as it was through university days. But they agreed that whatever happened they would always be the closest of friends and have no regrets.

William knew that his time on easy street was at an end. He had relished the relative anonymity that full-time education had afforded him. For him, graduating had more resonance than for his contemporaries. Whatever he did now, the reality and expectations of impending royal duties could no longer be ignored. At the very least he would face familial pressure to step up to the mark and shoulder his duties.

A few weeks earlier he had already acknowledged this point and expressed some anxiety, candidly admitting that he was wary of taking on public duties, 'because I don't want to start too early and then be stuck doing that for the rest of my life'. His university peers might envy William's financial security, as they struggled to find jobs and started paying off loans and eating further into hefty overdrafts, but they at least had the freedom to try on for size different careers or ways of life. Not William. Once he embarked on public life he would effectively be starting on an apprenticeship that would end with his kingship. And, even though the prince had learned to combat his self-consciousness with age and experience, he was discouraged by what he had seen of his father's attempts to try to turn that apprenticeship into a meaningful role in its own right. As one of his aides told me at the time, William was put off by what he saw as the relentless belittling of his father's efforts. Would that be his lot, too? If he tried to adopt his father's combative stance when he became Prince of Wales, tried to be a figure with something to say, something to contribute, would he be faced with the same negative treatment?

According to this senior aide, 'William is very loyal to his father. He is irritated by what he sees is the unfair way the Prince of Wales is constantly held up to ridicule; he is also frustrated that admirable aspects of Charles's work, such as the Prince's Trust, do not receive the recognition they deserve.'

This is a familiar and rather boring complaint aimed at the media, and one I feel compelled to say is unfounded. The Prince's Trust has received extensive and positive coverage over many years and, thanks to the dedication of impressive figures such as the affable Sir Tom Shebbeare, who was the hands-on motivator responsible for much of its success, it has been praised, winning Charles a great deal of respect in the process. It seems a shame to me that the view of the moaning minions at Clarence House, whose constant swipes at the press are clearly a reflection of their boss's own frustrations, appear to have rubbed off on William. In truth, the merry-go-round of royal courtiers changes every two or three years before they depart, clutching a gong and an updated CV. Then a new batch of eager-to-please clerks arrive, excited by the idea of working with royalty, and then complain about the same things as if they have just invented the wheel!

As one now liberated palace official told me, 'Prince William would do well to read the papers and check these things out for himself instead of adopting the head-in-the-sand approach favoured by his father and the yes men at the palace. Some of them, senior aides too, are scared of their own shadow and would never dream of criticising the prince for fear of losing their job and considerable perks and kudos that go with their position. Frankly, some of them give the term "lackey" a bad name. The result is that all this whining has made William determined to ensure that he puts off that side of the job for as long as he possibly can instead of, as the Queen would want, embracing it.'

But, with his university days all but over, William's apparent reticence to assume the business of being a key member of the Royal Family would only ever become more exposed. William had managed to reach the end of his university days – and the grand age of 23 – without actually doing a great deal of anything in the way of public duties for the family. His father, conversely, was a far less natural student but was, by then, something of a veteran on the royal circuit. He carried out his first overseas engagement in Australia at the age of 19 and was invested as Prince of Wales at Caernarfon Castle two years later, in 1969.

One royal official at the time explained to me, 'The difficulty for Prince William is that all he wants to do is to keep his head down. He is really torn. He feels very strongly that he has enough of his adult life ahead of him to grow into the role that has been mapped out for him. And if he does not raise expectations about himself too early he might just achieve a degree of normality.'

Prince Charles and his aides have always defended William's stance. His situation is, they say, very different from that of his father, who even as a teenager was heir to the throne. It all seems so much semantics to me. William's place in the succession is writ large in his present as much as his future. On the eve of graduation, opinion polls continued to give out a message that frankly left the young prince in a state of despair. Time and again polls showed that almost half the population would rather see William succeed to the throne instead of Charles, prompting calls for the 'mollycoddled' young royal to finally step out of the shadows. Even Harry had done more photo and interview opportunities than William had at that stage. It was inevitable that, even before his degree results were though, commentators would begin to ask, 'Where does William go from here?'

On 23 June 2005 William graduated in front of his father, stepmother and royal grandparents – as well as several hundred other equally proud parents. Looking nervous and biting his bottom lip, William waited his turn along with 30 fellow geography students. They hovered by the side of the stage in Younger Hall, William dressed in white bow tie and black silk academic gown with cherry-red lining. As the dean of arts, Professor Christopher Smith, called out the name 'William Wales' from the lectern, the prince stepped forward to a prolonged burst of applause and flash photography from the audience. In the front row of the lower balcony Charles and Camilla, who had until then exchanged banter and laughter, fell silent. Sitting beside them, the Duke of Edinburgh studied his programme of events intensely. The Queen, in a brilliant lemon outfit and recently recovered from a cold, adopted that familiar stern look.

William walked to the centre-stage pulpit, grasped its brass handrail bearing the university crest and knelt before Sir Kenneth Dover, chancellor of St Andrews. The ceremony was perfunctory. As with all other graduates, Sir Kenneth tapped William lightly on the head with the ceremonial birretum, a 17th-century scarlet cap rumoured to contain a fragment of the trousers of John Knox, the great Presbyterian reformer. 'Et super te' (meaning 'And upon you'), Dover intoned as the cloth touched William's head. Then James Douglas, the university bedellus – a kind of glorified head butler – hooked the prince's red and black academic hood over the kneeling supplicant's shoulders. This act signified that, after four years' study, William was now a master of arts. Within moments the master was offstage and being handed the scroll of his degree certificate. The culmination of four years of work was over, just like that. William emerged with fellow graduates into the hazy sunshine of the town's main street. Their cosseted undergraduate life was at an end.

William was met by the noise of hundreds of people lining the streets in scenes reminiscent of those that had accompanied his arrival in St Andrews. He graciously glad-handed the crowds on his way to the town police station to thank the Fife Constabulary for looking after him. His student days had been a success, despite the rocky start, and with his upper second he had outranked his father's lower second from Cambridge. As she watched, the Queen would have been the first to point out that there are no academic courses on how to be head of state.

After the ceremony an official thank-you was issued by Clarence House on William's behalf. It said, 'I have thoroughly enjoyed my time at St Andrews and I shall be very sad to leave. I just want to say a big thank you to everyone who has made my time here so enjoyable.' He declared afterwards, 'I have been able to lead as normal a student life as I could have hoped for and I am very grateful to everyone, particularly the locals, who have helped make this happen.' More revealing was a chance remark he made to a guest following the ceremony itself. Blinking in the sun as he joined his fellow graduates meeting proud relatives on the clipped grass of St Salvador's quadrangle, he told one guest with some trepidation that it was time for him to go forth 'into the big wide world'. He would not do so alone.

Seated five rows in front of the prince and graduating 80 people ahead of him was the young woman who, more than anything or anyone, had shaped William's student life. Wearing high heels and a sexy short black skirt beneath her gown, she was called to the stage as Catherine Middleton. She smiled broadly as she returned to her seat, catching William's eye as he flashed back a proud smile.

'Today is a very special day,' William said, 'and I am delighted I can share it with my family, particularly my grandmother, who has made such an effort to come, having been under the weather.' It was a predictably stiff summation of events. Far more natural was the affection with which the Queen patted her grandson's shoulder as he kissed her on both cheeks before she departed. Revealingly, far more natural was the smile on Kate's face as, at William's urging, she introduced her parents to their monarch. It seemed the most normal thing in the world for her to do. But it marked a departure for Kate. She and William had taken a momentous step towards adulthood together that day and Kate was now well and truly part of the fold.

'You will have made lifelong friends,' Dr Brian Lang, vice-chancellor of St Andrews, told the new graduates in an address before they left Younger Hall that day. 'I say this every year to all new graduates: you may have met your husband or wife. Our title as "Top Matchmaking University in Britain" signifies so much that is good about St Andrews, so we can rely on you to go forth and multiply.'

His words were met with laughter of course. But there must have been a few couples in the auditorium that day who prickled slightly at his words and wondered if they referred to them. Were William and Kate among them?

Leaving the security of St Andrews was going to prove a challenge to them both. They had endured a rocky spell in their relationship already but more trials would lie ahead. William could not postpone for ever either duties or decisions. Kate was a bright determined young woman. She had already invested much in William, but her friends were clear that he would be wrong to assume that she would hang around indefinitely in the absence of any commitment. As for William, he was a young man still struggling to carve out his role in life and horribly conscious that the constitutional clock was ticking. 'I have so many things I want to do,' he said. 'I'm scared, really scared, that I won't have time.'

CHAPTER 11

PRIVACY OF A NUN

*'The thing is with me, I look on the brighter side of everything.
There's no point being pessimistic or being worried about too
many things because, frankly, life's too short'*
Prince William, interviewed in 2004

As the sun went down over the plains on a beautiful Sunday evening in July, the trio sat on the veranda of their Masai lodge sipping sundowners and admiring the breathtaking views of the Kenyan wilderness. When he had bid farewell to university life William may have worried that he would not have time to do the things that he really wanted to before royal duties took over his life. For now, and for Kate, there was still time to hold back the flood of reality just a little while longer.

And this was about as far removed from the reality that awaited both William and Kate as one could possibly get. The air vibrated with the sounds of Africa. In the mid-distance zebras drank from a watering hole and giraffes tugged leaves from the high branches of the trees that grew in lush abandon. Elephants called and rhinos and lions prowled, hidden, in the bush. It was a scene awesome enough to make even a prince feel a certain insignificance about his place in the world.

As the sun disappeared below the horizon the party tucked into a lavish barbecue served on a wooden platform that jutted out into the air. It was easy to see why William might choose this isolated hideaway thousands of miles from home for a romantic interlude with Kate after the pressure of university exams was over. Perhaps it was a little more surprising that the love-struck couple were joined in this blissful moment by Jecca Craig, the enigmatic beauty to whom – it had been widely speculated – Kate had nearly lost her prince barely a year earlier. The reality was that, however romantic the setting, this was more of a group affair than a holiday *à deux* for William and Kate. It was perfectly natural that Jecca should have been there as a guide for the pair and the friends who joined them. Their destination, after all, was her parents' ranch of Lewa Downs, where some five years earlier William had spent an enjoyable month working on the estate as part of his gap year. His late mother had once observed that William was like a 'caged lion' in the confines of London, in the stiff collars and buttoned-up life of the city. And still, so many years on, William found something irresistible and liberating in wide-open landscapes – whether those of Gloucestershire close to his father's Highgrove home, the bleak moorland of the Balmoral estate or the heat-soaked African wilderness.

Earlier in the day Jecca had driven William and Kate around some of the estate. Her family had settled in Kenya in 1924, it was her home and something of a second home to William who had travelled there almost every year since his first trip to the region. A dozen or so friends tucked into the barbecue that evening. It was the sort of elegantly decadent scene reminiscent of days of empire and the so-called Happy Valley set. The whole thing was a treat from the prince to his closest companions – including his best friend Thomas van Straubenzee, himself then romantically linked to Jecca. Prince William had splashed out £1,500 to hire Il Ngwesi for the night. Most of the party had arrived there on foot shortly after lunch following a six-hour trek through the bush with armed guards. Situated on a hill next to the Ngare Ndare river, Il Ngwesi's six 'bandas' – thatched open-plan cottages – are designed to allow the occupants to make the most of the scenery, a breathtaking sweep from the snowy caps of Mount Kenya and down across the plain. It was simply blissful. But it was an escape that inevitably had to come to an end.

Back in Britain, as late summer gave way to autumn 2005, the uncomfortable process of trying to assimilate real life with royal life was, for Kate, about to begin in earnest. Neither she nor William could have reckoned on it as they luxuriated in their last Kenyan sunsets, but in just a matter of weeks back home the strain would begin to tell as Kate's 'double' life would put pressure on her personally, cause tensions between palace and press and take its toll on her and William's relationship. How could it not? After all, one day Kate would be taking tea with the Queen at Windsor Castle, the next she was catching a ride on a bus, seated next to a complete stranger who was oblivious of the esteemed company she was getting used to keeping. When she was by William's side she was treated accordingly, afforded every courtesy and even the security of a member of the Royal Family itself. She was taken to the best restaurants and the most fashionable clubs and through it all she was embraced by the phalanx of armed Scotland Yard security men. The privilege, and the glamour, would be enough to turn many a young girl's head. But not Kate. She had been raised wisely and brought up to keep her feet firmly on the ground. But, while her sensible nature may have helped steady her, the turbulence of this strangely conflicting life was still difficult to deal with – especially since her relationship with William was now considered to be moving to a new stage.

In September 2005 I received a tantalising telephone call from a senior Buckingham Palace insider. The source seemed quite upbeat. The news was happy. The informant said that I should be 'on my toes' when it came to Kate. 'The relationship,' the source said, 'had gone to a new level.' When I pressed the informant further a story unfolded that made me begin to appreciate just how important Kate was and went a long way towards hinting at just how important she may yet become. I was told that Kate had had a 'series of private meetings with the Queen'. The two – joined by William – had had at least two intimate dinners in recent months and the Queen had developed a 'warm and relaxed relationship' with her grandson's girlfriend. One of the dinners was said to have taken place at Windsor Castle. This is the Queen's favourite royal residence and the one that she truly regards as home. This was significant in itself.

'Keep a close eye on the situation,' I was told. 'The fact that Kate has met with Her Majesty several times and has dined with her privately should not be underestimated. Her Majesty takes a loving interest in her grandson and heir and she is delighted he is so happy with Kate. Kate has a wonderfully relaxed manner and to be so relaxed in the company of the Queen is a good thing. It speaks volumes about how the Queen feels about her.'

It was a very important steer and proof, as if proof were needed, that in the world of royal reporting the story does not stand still for long. Outside castle walls Kate continued to act like an ordinary girl: independent, intelligent, possessing a certain degree of class perhaps, but not so very different from swathes of London-smart young women. She was often spotted browsing in shops on the fashionable King's Road, sometimes alone, sometimes with her mother or friends, before heading back to the Chelsea flat where she was now living. There was no armed guard by her side. She was equipped with only her wits and growing savvy. This, by the autumn of 2005, was the dichotomy of Kate Middleton's new life. There is no more vulnerable or conflicting position than this, to be hovering, half in, half out of the Royal Family. But, for the most part, Kate coped remarkably well with her newfound and always shifting state.

Kate and William tried to develop their own routine. After all, whatever William's status, they were like any couple trying to figure out what their relationship meant in the real world beyond the university gates. At its core was a need for secrecy and a continued game of cat-and-mouse with the pursuing paparazzi. William began to stay overnight with Kate at her white stucco-fronted apartment opposite a bus stop in Chelsea. They would do what any young couple might. Sometimes they would head out to nearby clubs, such as Boujis or Purple, drink vodka and cranberry and enjoy the release of a throbbing dance floor and a mindless night of fun with friends. At other times they would relax at a local restaurant. The gastro pub the Pig's Ear, discreet, classy, and known for its good food and Chelsea-bohemian clientele, was one of Kate's favourites, and William's too. He was often seen there supping his Breton cider. On other occasions they would stay in;

William would cook as he often had at their St Andrew's house, or they would order in pizza, watch a film and try to emulate the simplicity of their university 'marriage'.

It was all a far cry from the privilege and attention that the prince would receive when staying at the home of his father or grandmother; but after four years of freedom this was how he liked it. His 'double life' was one of choice; Kate's was imposed upon her. For there was one significant difference from their carefree university days: the press, or rather the press's attitude to the couple. As far as freelance photographers were concerned the gloves were off. William – and by extension Kate – was no longer shielded by agreements fixed by courtiers. Editors were now ready to test the water and see just how far they could go and just how much money they could make in the process.

At university the press had fulfilled their gentlemen's agreement and kept their distance. They had allowed William to go about his daily business free in the knowledge that he and his companions were not being followed. Now the paparazzi were out in force and Kate, for the first time, would learn just what it really entailed to be the beautiful girlfriend of a future king. Her Chelsea flat and its environs may have been vetted by William's Scotland Yard security officers but nothing stops a paparazzo with the scent of his prey – and his pay – in his nostrils.

Up to five such astute photographers had tracked Kate down to her home, having trailed doggedly after her through town. They sometimes worked as a team, thus reducing the risk of missing a picture – but it meant having to share the spoils if successful. They would pitch up outside in the early hours of the morning, sitting quietly in their cars, sometimes with blacked-out windows, engines off, patiently waiting and watching. As soon as Kate or William emerged they would act – firing off a few frames from the distance. If Kate was on her own they would invariably follow. Her photograph had now earned something of a premium – not as much as the Royal Family and their advisers might estimate, but enough to make securing and selling it a worthwhile venture. Glossy magazines and newspapers had woken up to the fact that Kate was now newsworthy. Their readers wanted to know more about her: what she was wearing, where she shopped for her clothes, where she had her hair and makeup done. It all became part of an almost daily news diet.

Kate's arguably stunning image began to appear alongside snaps of footballers' wives and girlfriends or the latest girl band member or pop sensation. At first the pair let it ride. To some extent William was of the opinion that the media attention went with the territory – for him, after all, it always had and it was the brief respite during student days, rather than this renewed onslaught, that marked a break from the norm. Besides, when they were together it was easier to handle. There was always a waiting car and a royal bodyguard on hand to deal with any eventuality. Pictures of William and Kate climbing into a car after a night out together had rapidly become a staple of the picture editors' morning schedules. It was more difficult for Kate, though, when her protective boyfriend and his security entourage were not there to assist her. She had become unnerved as some of the photographers began to follow her more openly. It was as though she were being stalked – not aggressively but a tricky situation nevertheless. The photographers were professionals and knew the rules. To some extent Kate had to work them out as she went along.

As early as August 2005 she seemed to be making some headway as far as learning the ropes was concerned. At horse trials at Princess Anne's estate of Gatcombe Park, Kate revealed a flicker of an incipient confidence when it came to dealing with the press. She and her mother Carole were enjoying a wonderful day. The green-Wellington-boot brigade was out in force and she and Carole mingled with spectators among the stalls between watching the competitors.

It was the sort of event that might make a few society snaps for a high-end glossy, or perhaps the sporting pages of a newspaper. The Princess Royal's daughter, Zara, an accomplished equestrian competitor, was competing that day. A handful of experienced photographers had turned up on a hunch that there might be richer pickings in the form of Kate. Their instincts were proved right. The photographers included Mark Stewart, an affable and experienced royal photographer and veteran of many official tours. He spotted Kate in the crowd. She and Carole had made their way to the hospitality tent, an area where free drinks and food and a degree of comfort were guaranteed.

The two women spent a few minutes flicking through celebrity magazines and, by the time they were ready to leave, Mark Stewart and a fellow freelance photographer, the equally experienced David Hartley, were poised and waiting. At first Kate went to walk the cross-country course. She was wearing tight-fitting designer jeans, a stone heart pendant and a suede jacket. She looked fabulous but she was always on the move and surrounded by hundreds of fellow spectators. The photographers were following but never quite getting the clear shot they needed. By now several other snappers had cottoned on to the women's presence and one of them decided to intervene. Walking towards Kate and her mother, he asked the two women to pose. Kate remained cool. Mark tried to reason with her: 'Could we have a picture, Kate? This is getting silly.' But she point-blank refused to pose. The royals hate staged photographs. 'We are not performing monkeys,' Prince Charles once proclaimed, and here was Kate following a similar routine. She now knew what was expected of her by her boyfriend's family and she was not about to let him, or them, down.

She stepped forward a couple of paces, smiled disarmingly and responded politely but with defiance: 'If I do it now I'll have to keep doing it at skiing or every time.' One of the photographers among the group tried a different tack and tried to flatter her into submission. 'You're so beautiful Kate; you'll look great in the pictures,' he told her. She fluttered her lashes, flushed slightly pink, but said nothing. The photographers got the pictures of Kate at Gatcombe but they were candid shots, not posed. Kate had quietly and charmingly had her way. And she had surprised and impressed the experienced snappers in the process.

But, however apparently confident Kate seemed that August afternoon, it was a brittle display. As she and her mother retreated into the crowds her heart must have pounded, her palms felt clammy and her cheeks remained just a little flushed. She had seemed far more assured than she really was. For the rest of the day she would be looking over her shoulder, ill at ease with the awareness that she was in the spotlight. It was inevitably a topic of conversation between William and Kate. It cannot have helped ease any niggling worries that, as a backdrop to Kate's burgeoning celebrity, Lord Stevens's Scotland Yard inquiry into the death of Princess Diana was rumbling on through the newspapers.

At William's behest, Clarence House officials tried to form a strategy to cover Kate. They wanted to prove harassment, so privacy specialists from royal lawyers Harbottle and Lewis were called in to advise. Everyone at the palace, including Prince Charles, knew how fraught any sort of legal recourse could be. In October Harbottle and Lewis sent newspaper editors a pre-publication warning, suggesting in the strongest possible terms that Kate should be left alone and that some of the photographers who persistently pursued her had breached guidelines from the Press Complaints Commission. William was determined to push things further. He was being briefed on privacy issues by Paddy Harverson, his father's communications secretary, and was interested in finding out how a landmark ruling won by Princess Caroline of Monaco in a Strasbourg court the previous year might impact upon him and his girlfriend. The ruling, after years of alleged harassment by the paparazzi, effectively banned the German press from publishing photographs of Princess Caroline and her children. Might William be able to argue the same for his girlfriend? He discussed the problem with Kate and her family and within weeks had instructed royal lawyers to examine the possibility of taking some form of legal action through the courts to place Kate firmly off limits. In December 2005 the broadsheet *Sunday Telegraph* was tipped off about the move, and its chief reporter, Andrew Alderson, penned a report that Clarence House would be proud of.

'William may turn to the human rights court to protect Kate,' it read. The information could only have come from William's own officials, and the *Sunday Telegraph* is a favoured publication for official leaks. The article continued, 'Prince William is personally masterminding attempts to ensure that his girlfriend, Kate

Middleton, can pursue a "normal" life and career away from the prying lenses of the paparazzi. The *Sunday Telegraph* has learned that the prince has mastered complex privacy laws and may ask lawyers to go to the European Court of Human Rights if the situation worsens. According to his friends, Prince William feels that Miss Middleton's future happiness and the survival of the relationship depend on protecting her from overly intrusive photographers.'

It read as a barely concealed threat to Fleet Street's tabloid editors to consider themselves put on notice – if they continued to publish images of Kate the palace would use the courts to act. When I checked this story out at the time one courtier told me, 'Actually, the level of intrusion has calmed down quite a bit but it's something William is very concerned about. He can cope with it but he's always been anxious about the impact on others who have suffered intrusion simply because of being linked to him.'

William's concerns may have been understandable but they also proved a source of slight tension between him and his father. Prince Charles sympathised with Kate's lot but he felt recourse to the European Court of Human Rights was ill-advised and could open a whole new can of worms for the Royal Family, who, after all, depend on positive publicity for their very existence as a privileged, expensive and unelected institution. Besides, Prince Charles has never been a great fan of laws that he views as all too often abused by the undeserving at the cost to the greater good and to the detriment of his country's sovereign laws.

Much to the relief of all, it seemed that, as Christmas approached, the problem was abating. Reporters and their editors did seem suitably chastened. But just before Christmas, as the palace began to relax, I revealed a story that put privacy issues back in the spotlight and sent alarm bells ringing all the way to SO14, Scotland Yard's elite Royalty and Diplomatic Protection Department. I revealed that William had demanded to know how photographs pinpointing the location of his girlfriend's London home had come to be printed in a downmarket German magazine. The pictures showed William leaving the apartment following a night spent there with Kate and crudely indicated the exact location of the flat with a big red arrow and the caption, 'Das liebesnest' – the love nest. Senior protection sources condemned the story, printed in the Hamburg-based *Das Neue*, as 'grossly irresponsible' and the episode prompted an immediate review of the prince's security. William was furious at the magazine's 'stupidity' in publishing such personal information at a time when security fears in the capital were at their peak in the aftermath of the city's 2005 bloody 7/7 bombings by terrorists.

Kate and William had been back in the real world barely five months and already it seemed to be closing in on them and threatening their relationship. William knew that his father was uncomfortable with his proactive approach to the press and it was a source of some friction between them. But it was not the only element of William's life that seemed out of kilter. This period of adjustment was proving tense and uncertain as far as his continued relationship with Kate was concerned. In September I had been told to keep an eye on the situation and had been informed that the relationship was moving rapidly on.

But by the following month nothing seemed so certain. The affair had been careering along at such a clip it now seemed perilously close to coming off the rails. William and Kate had had a rocky patch while they were still at university. Now, it seemed, they were due another period of uncertainty. Since they were no longer restricted by cohabiting full time, it was always bound to be a testing period for the young lovers. It may not have been his intention, but William was seeing less of Kate. She, not wishing to appear needy, again drew on past experience and did her best to let it pass. But it was not easy. However much they tried to keep their relationship to themselves, it was out in the open and subject to scrutiny. Seasoned observers, well acquainted with the rhythm of the relationship, were not slow in picking up when something was going awry. My long-term friend and colleague, the royal writer Richard Kay, was one of the first to draw attention to it. 'Even now, when miles from a permanent union,' he wrote, 'Kate Middleton is finding that being a woman in the life of a prince can be a lonely business.'

Kay, whose sources are impeccable, noted that two separate

Above: Kate at a concert but apart from Prince William.   © *PA Photos*

Below: Working at her parents' firm Party Pieces in the summer of 2008.

Above: William and Kate together in 2009.

Above right: At the wedding of friend Chiara Hunt in Salzburg, where the guests included James Blunt and Ben Fogle.

Below: Prince William mid-match at Tidworth Polo Club.

bove: At a spring wedding in Scotland in 2010.

elow: Kate and friends waiting for a glimpse of William.

Kate caught in 2008.

ate with (right) Isabella Calthorpe. © *Rex Features*

William and Kate in August 2009.

Above: Harry and William on a Royal visit together.

Below: Kate going out in 2006.

© *Rex Features*

Kate in a pensive moment in 2008.

episodes gave a 'startling insight' into how William may have wanted the relationship to work if it were to fit into his image of a serviceable royal union. The setting for the first episode was a rowdy pub in Cornwall, the Chain Locker in Falmouth. It was a drizzly lunchtime and the wood-panelled bar was heaving. Pints of beer were being downed by the dozen and glasses smashed on the cobbles outside. There, in the midst of the hurrah, was William, casually dressed, his dark baseball cap pulled low over his eyes, red faced and slightly the worse for wear, though the landlord would later comment that the prince remained 'very polite'. William was celebrating the return to shore of his friend Oliver Hicks – a grizzled-looking young man, complete with sandy beard – who had just returned from four months at sea undertaking the Herculean task of rowing solo from North America to the Isles of Scilly. In the process he rowed into the record books for the dubious honour of completing the journey more slowly than anyone before him. Hicks is a good friend of William's, and of Kate's. But Kate was nowhere to be seen as William knocked back pints and roared manfully at his friend's achievement. Afterwards, 30 or so of the revellers went back to Hicks's parents' house for bangers and mash and champagne, and still there was no sign of Kate.

Twenty-four hours later, Kay pointed out, Kate was present but relegated to a walk-on role when William and she were guests at an £80-a-head charity ball in aid of the Institute for Cancer Research. William was not even on the same table as his date. 'So what might be going on?' Kay asked in his column in the *Daily Mail*. 'Only the most starry-eyed romantic would say that the couple's relationship is permanent. William is only 23 and he has made it clear he has no wish to marry for some years.'

It was a fair observation, but one that I felt had taken a logical point and stretched it to a conclusion too far. I believed it underestimated Kate's resilience and William's dependency and, at the risk of sounding like a starry-eyed romantic, I felt it underestimated the power and passion of young love. Nevertheless, it must have made uncomfortable reading for Kate, who was described in Richard's missive as 'a wallflower' – hardly the sort of summing-up that will sit well with any girl, let alone a sexy, confident creature like Kate. It is bad enough for a man quietly to sideline his partner, but when he leaves her exposed to public humiliation the sparks are likely to fly. And there was no doubt that at this juncture the friction between Kate and William was visible. Worse still, it was drawing comment.

Loyal friends naturally toed the party line. 'They are together,' Oliver Hicks insisted when asked about Kate's absence from his post-Atlantic celebrations. 'I spent the weekend with them,' he continued. 'The reason they never confirm their relationship is because they don't want to make it open season for people to ask questions.' It was the stock response by most of their friends and a reasonable enough point. Everybody acknowledged that William is by nature a cautious young man. I witnessed time and time again that his modus operandi was always to try to shield Kate from too much attention by keeping apart from her. But it didn't quite wash this time. After all, on the night of the Institute for Cancer Research ball in the Banqueting House, Whitehall, William and Kate were surrounded by many of those friends. There, of all places, was their chance to be open and expressive of their feelings for each other.

Instead, if anything, William's behaviour in front of Kate that evening seemed designed to do everything possible to unsettle and even upset. He found time to chat to various attractive young women, including a striking young blonde with whom he joked and flirted for a good 25 minutes. He felt relaxed enough to perform an impromptu *Zorba the Greek* routine, dancing with his arms around the shoulders of a group of young men. But he did not find time to dance with Kate more than once, and when he did it was a brief and half-hearted affair. On a table for ten that included the Duke of Westminster's daughter, Lady Tamara van Cutsem, the Earl of Home's daughter, Mary Douglas-Home, Lord Beaverbrook's daughter, Charlotte Aitken, and television presenter Ben Fogle's girlfriend, Marina Hunt, William seemed happy to whoop it up with 'his sort' and leave Kate to find her own way through the evening. For once, Kate let her disappointment glimmer through. One onlooker commented, 'I saw William with Kate in the hall just as the disco ended and she didn't look at all happy. I would say she was miffed that he'd spent the evening enjoying himself with everyone except her.'

But, however much may have been read into this collision of events, the reality was, it seemed to me, that the relationship was still very much on. Yes, William and Kate were going through a rough patch, but it was a blip that bore all the trademarks not of a move to split but of a move to commit more deeply. William's relative waywardness and Kate's uncharacteristic petulance in public seemed to me the classic unease of a couple aware that the stakes were getting higher as their commitment to each other became more profound. This, for both of them, was uncharted territory, and with the circus that accompanies William's status it was never going to be plain sailing. For Kate in particular this was a time of negotiation, of working out just what space in William's life she could expect to occupy and just how much she would have to grin and bear. William's duties, his demanding family and the looming prospect of training at Sandhurst all conspired to squeeze her out in so many ways. Kate would have to be strong enough, and wise enough, to recognise how much of her boyfriend she could claw back for herself and how much she would simply have to make do with what was left.

By November 2005 it seems she and William were back on an even keel. For the first time William acknowledged that he and Kate were 'going steady'. His admission came as the New Zealand All Blacks rugby team visited Buckingham Palace. All Blacks forward Ali Williams, whom the prince had met during his visit to New Zealand to watch the British Lions play, asked William about Kate. 'He said it was going well, going steady,' the rugby giant told reporters.

Meanwhile, in a concerted effort to prove that she was anything but a pushover, Kate set about establishing herself professionally. She abandoned plans to work at a London art gallery and decided instead to look at setting up a company to design and sell clothes for children. Her own parents' business experience and the extent to which she had helped them herself were elements on which she could draw. Kate was showing herself to be a free and independent woman with a determined streak. She was neither the sort of girl to let her relationship slip away nor the sort to allow William to take it, and her, for granted. Once again her strategy worked. Just as slackening her grip on William had brought him back to her side in university days, turning her attentions to her own life away from William seemed to reinvigorate and strengthen the couple's bond. William's articulation of their relationship was a massive step forward and it led some to speculate that more was to come. There was a real sense that, wobble over, the relationship was picking up speed once more – and with such momentum it had to be going somewhere.

It was only a matter of time, it seemed, before the 'M' word was mentioned. When it was, it came in the form of a snippet in the *Mail on Sunday*'s feisty gossip columnist Katie Nicholls's page. 'Prince William's turbulent relationship with Kate Middleton is more gripping than any soap opera,' she wrote. 'Whether they will stay together is the question on everyone's lips,' she continued before taking the giant leap and claiming that senior courtiers at Buckingham Palace had started discussing the prospect of a marriage and that 'contingency plans' for a wedding had been put in place. She allowed herself the safety net of pointing out that the palace plans for all eventualities (preparations for the Queen Mother's funeral began in 1969), before going on to suggest that an announcement was being readied for spring 2006, with a wedding in the autumn. Of course it was wildly speculative, but it was not entirely without foundation. And it showed just how far Kate Middleton had come in the few short months since graduating from university.

However keen she and William may have been to maintain her privacy, by the end of the year even the broadsheet newspapers – known for their restraint in comparison with their more energetic cousins the tabloids – were publishing profile articles about Kate. The *Independent on Sunday* referred to her as 'Her Royal Shyness'. William, they claimed, frequently conveyed the impression that, if the monarchy could be persuaded to call it a day before it was his turn to lift the crown, he would happily step out of the aristocratic limelight. He was, they said, a commoner by instinct if not by birth. This seemed to me a theory too far. However much William was a product of both his mother's and father's opposing influences, he was a royal through and through. His desire for privacy and for his version of normality was, if anything, akin to wanting to have his cake and eat it too. His attraction to Kate and his continued relationship with her was, perhaps, evidence of a certain fascination with 'normality' but he could hardly be the sort of 'republican prince' envisaged in the article. Still, it was clear that William felt irresistibly drawn to the daughter of decidedly middle-class, self-made entrepreneurs in a way that he was not when in the company of, say, some obscure Ruritanian princess with a triple-barrelled name and several shaky connections to the extended family tree.

Under King William, commentators mused, and possibly Queen Catherine, we might yet see a move away from the present, expensive, fake-ancient patronage and pageantry (much of which dates back no further than the 19th century and Queen Victoria's adoration of pomp and history, however faux). In its place we could expect a move towards a more modern Scandinavian-type monarch, but perhaps at the cost of being far less secure.

Undeterred, the *Independent on Sunday*'s article ran, 'The People's Princess may be replaced, in Kate, by a real princess of the people: a non-blue-blood. For republicans who prefer to be citizens rather than subjects and who hoped, after Diana's death, that the demise of the monarchy was imminent it's not the happy-ever-after they envisaged. But it might yet be for William.'

But even as the newspapers got ready to crown Kate and lauded her for her normality it was this, not her proximity to royalty, on which she seemed determined to focus. Speaking of her plans to design her own range of children's wear with her parents, one friend revealed, 'She had this fashion idea and she's decided to see it through. She's always loved clothes and has a good eye for design. Working with her parents means she won't be spied on if she and William do stay together. Kate believes she can make good money as well.'

She had William's backing, it seemed. 'He's determined she should be able to lead a "normal" life,' another source told me. Yet this harping on about normality was beginning to irk some sectors of the press. Kate's normality might appeal for now, but it would begin to pall pretty quickly if she, or her boyfriend's emissaries, turned it into a weapon with which to jab back even the best-intentioned of press enquiries. In a matter of months the palace had fired a variety of warning shots across the bows of Fleet Street's finest and it seemed that they were playing a dangerous game in the process. In his desire to protect Kate and to indulge her fantasy that it was possible to date the future King and still lead a life unaltered by that reality, was William really doing Kate any favours? The sheltered university days were over. Their relationship was moving on to another level. Kate might still cling to her identity as a private individual but her relationship, their relationship, was not a matter for them and them alone.

There was a genuine argument that some coverage was in the public interest. As 2005 drew to a close William and Kate were running a real risk of making enemies of a press that was very favourably disposed to them both. If William did not help Kate acknowledge the press and deal with it, he risked alienating the media. However much he may have felt that the press intruded upon his mother's life, the advisers who counselled William so assiduously on matters of privacy might have served him just as well with a gentle reminder that Diana, more than any royal in recent history, recognised the press as a force not only to be reckoned with but to be courted, wooed and won over. The young royal's truculence had begun to irritate senior Fleet Street executives. For the first time Kate came under fire – and from a dangerous sniper, too: Fergus Shanahan, deputy editor of the *Sun*. His words were eloquent and blunt, his readers many. Under the headline Kate Middleton wants the privacy of a nun, he launched the first overt criticism of a young woman who had until then been something of an enigma. He wrote, 'Kate Middleton wants the privacy of a nun. Yet she chooses to go out with Prince William, the world's most eligible young man. She can't have it both ways. She complains about photographers, but what does she expect if she dates a future king? The Royal Family is the circus that no longer puts on any performances for the paying public, and the punters are rapidly losing interest. If we go on like this, nobody will care enough to resist scheming antimonarchists who want to scrap the Queen and install a Labour puppet as president. Kate wouldn't like it, but headlines are what the monarchy needs if it is to survive.'

It could not have been put more succinctly, and senior figures close to the Queen sat up and took note.

CHAPTER 12

IN THE ARMY NOW

'The last thing I want to do is be mollycoddled or be wrapped up in cotton wool, because, if I was to join the army, I would want to go where my men went, and I'd want to do what they did. I would not want to be kept back for being precious, or whatever – that's the last thing I would want.'

PRINCE WILLIAM TALKING ABOUT HIS MILITARY CAREER

Prince William put his arm around Kate, pulled her towards him and kissed her full on the lips, apparently oblivious of anything or anyone around him. Perhaps it was the mountain air or his determination to enjoy his last moments of real freedom before starting his military training; or perhaps he was simply too exuberant and too in love to let this impulse pass without action. Unbeknown to them, his touching moment of romance was captured on film and was destined to be recorded as their first public kiss – the first time that the young lovers had let their guard down and shown their intimacy.

After four years together, their commitment to keeping their distance from each other in public was such that at times they ran the risk of seeming rather staid and middle-aged, a couple so comfortable with each other that one might be forgiven for thinking that all passion was a thing of the past. But this moment in January 2006 put paid to that notion. If they were worried about privacy, for once it took a back seat to the overriding mood of the moment.

Separation was looming, with William only days away from starting his military training at Sandhurst Military Academy. His brother Prince Harry was already a cadet there and well into the year-long course on which William would soon embark. No doubt Harry had filled William in on some of the rigours that awaited him. But in the meantime William could turn his attentions to Kate and to a carefree skiing holiday together in a modest chalet in Klosters. The location may have been a familiar enough choice but William and Kate's pre-Sandhurst break was actually a far cry from his family holidays there with his father, who, over the past 17 years, had always telegraphed his arrival by pitching up at the five-star Walserhof Hotel with a sizeable entourage in tow. This time the tone was low key, simple and normal.

Much to the young couple's amused delight, they had initially given the media the slip as scores of photographers and reporters had made the expensive trek from Britain to the Swiss ski resort of Verbier. They had followed a hunch that the young lovers might return to one of their favourite haunts over the New Year. But William and Kate had shunned the resort's bars and restaurants, intent on spending as much time together in cosy intimacy as possible. For the press it was a costly error and no doubt William and Kate rather enjoyed the thought of the assembled media all those miles across the Alps, replete with skis and salopettes, wanting for nothing but the all-important story.

When the press pack finally did track them down they got the perfect story in the form of that first kiss. William's romantic gesture had come on the penultimate day of their holiday. After an invigorating morning spent tackling some of the resort's most challenging black runs, they had decided to go off-piste on Casanna Alp to enjoy the powder before stopping for a bite of lunch. And then came that kiss. One onlooker said, 'As Kate caught her breath, William placed an arm around her shoulders and pulled her close for a long, slow kiss on the lips. It was very romantic and lasted several moments.' They had come a long way together: from the heights of young passion to the lows of trial separations, uncertainties and wobbles. Now, as this open, confident kiss signified, William knew he had found a girl he could love and who loved him in return, not for his status, wealth or title, but just for himself. William knew that he would soon begin the toughest physical test of his life at Sandhurst and that he would effectively be banned from seeing Kate for five weeks. (Cadets are not allowed any leave until the first five weeks of their training is completed.)

With their thoughts turning towards the immediate future, William and Kate allowed themselves to consider more distant possibilities. 'Although their lives are about to change, they are determined not to let that spoil what they have got. They know they have got something really special and nobody and nothing will come between them as long as they are honest with one another,' a close source told me at the time.

Amid the 'Kiss me Kate' headlines that accompanied the pictures of that kiss among the snowy peaks came more and more speculation that maybe, just maybe, the romance was about to move up another notch. The idea of William and Kate formalising their relationship was not just the subject of idle gossip or tabloid tittle-tattle. It had been discussed by William's wider family, too. One former lady-in-waiting to the Queen let it be known that the young couple had support from the very top of the Royal Family. A confidante of the Queen, she revealed that now Charles and Camilla were happily installed as a married couple and the shadow of Charles's first disastrous marriage was shortening. The Queen's view was that everything could go well for her grandson. William's relative youth was, to her, a boon not a drawback.

According to this source, 'The Queen thinks that one of the reasons Charles's marriage to Diana didn't last was because he waited too long and, at 32, was too set in his ways.' Remember, this is the young man who at 19 turned up at university dressed like a city gent and with all the stiffness and formality of a middle-aged stock broker. Thirty-two may not sound terribly old to most sensibilities, but by then Charles had acquired a certain form and shape to his life that he was unwilling, or unable, to change. He had also acquired Mrs Parker Bowles. But those days were long gone. In January 2006, as William anticipated the beginning of his military training, he had, perhaps for the first time, a father who was in a position to press upon him the merits of a happy marriage; a father who was to some extent already doting on Kate with the benevolence of a fond, even rather relieved, father-in-law.

On 8 January 2006, the day before Kate's 24th birthday, William arrived with his father at Sandhurst Military Academy for the start of his 44-week officer training course. He was the most senior member of the Royal Family to train at the academy and he was taking his first step towards accepting the future inheritance that would make him head of the armed forces. But in the first instance the 23-year-old prince, one of 269 other officer cadets to enrol at the famous Surrey institution that day, was faced with the less than grand ordeal of having his head shorn of hair: exposing, in the process, that other Windsor crown to be handed down by his father – his bald patch.

William was assigned to a company and platoon and banned from leaving the camp for the next five weeks. He underwent a gruelling schedule, which saw him living in the field, improving his fitness and polishing his boots until they gleamed. By the end of his first term the second in line to the throne would be proficient in using a hand grenade, an SA80 5.56mm rifle and a Browning 9mm pistol. He would have absorbed lectures on first aid, tactics and war studies given by some of the country's most knowledgeable officers and more fearless taskmasters. Lieutenant Colonel Roy Parkinson, an instructor at Sandhurst, laid it on the line. He told the media who had gathered at the academy to witness the prince's arrival that Prince William would get 'very little sleep' in the first few weeks of training. Officer Cadet Wales, as he would be known, would receive no special treatment and his drill sergeants would not go easy on him. 'We receive people from all backgrounds,' Parkinson explained, 'but background goes right out the window once training begins. It's a team effort here. If someone steps out of line they're stamped on, whether they're a prince or not.' In the next day's papers one wag predictably joked that the prince's time at Sandhurst was going to be a 'battle of Wills'. Ahead of him lay one of the toughest experiences of his young life, physically at least.

Just six weeks into training he faced one of the most grim and notorious exercises, the 'Long Reach' – a 24-hour march in sleet and snow on the Welsh hills. Carrying a pack as heavy as himself, deprived of sleep and on minimal rations William was testing to the limit his resolve and physical and mental reserves. Pictures appeared of him, his body bowed against the icy wind as he and his platoon struggled through awful conditions. However, there was never any question of his following his Uncle Edward's lacklustre performance while training and failing to be a Royal Marine. The army's motto is 'Be the Best', and William had to prove himself equal to that challenge. He had once flirted with quitting university but he knew now that, however tough the task, quitting was not an option. After almost a day and night slogging through the bitterly cold Black Mountains of Wales, pale and exhausted and surviving on bites of chocolate and precious little else, there was a real determination about the young prince. He had inner strength and he wanted to prove to himself and to his fellow cadets that he had what it takes. At one point, close to collapse during one steep climb, he sank to his haunches to gather his breath. Typically, he urged on his fellow cadets before gathering himself up and getting back on track. This was, after all, a team-building pursuit during which the young cadets marched more than 65km (40 miles), navigating between nine checkpoints and sleeping, when they could, under the stars. Such are the demands of the exercise that up to a third of the 269 cadets who started failed. William was not among them.

While William threw himself into military training, Kate had her own battle on her hands. In some respects hers was the more perilous of the two. For, while William's life was mapped out and rigid in its military discipline, Kate faced the rather daunting prospect of working out just what to do with herself while he was at Sandhurst. Her position in his life was still, officially, rather up in the air. She still had to contend with the life of contradictions presented by her strange, uncomfortable status of middle-class-royal-in-waiting. 'She is not and never has been somebody who would rest on her laurels,' one source close to the couple admitted at the time. 'But it's fair to say that this was a difficult period for both of them. William had his route pretty much mapped out.' Kate did not. She loved him of course, of that she was certain. But she could not sit around waiting for her prince to come home and sweep her off her feet. She had already toyed with and rejected the idea of working in an art gallery; this after all was a girl with a degree in art history from one of the most respected universities in the country. She was no fool, happy to while away her hours dreaming about her prince. She resurrected her idea of setting up a business venture of her own, working in the meantime with her parents at Party Pieces. But, more than ever, she found that her movements were scrutinised, however robust previous attempts to deter paparazzi and reporters may have been.

As she was by now well aware, the smallest detail could be spun into a story, however throwaway it might seem. The salon where she had her hair and nails done was now news. It provided a light-hearted moment when Kate, out with her mother in London's Sloane Square, found herself accidentally and somewhat prematurely ascending a throne of sorts. At Richard Ward's upmarket hair-and-beauty emporium, a favourite salon of Prince Edward's wife, Sophie, Countess of Wessex, and Prince Marie Chantal of Greece, the spa treatments involve sitting on a raised 'throne' while having a manicure. The gossip columnists thought it hilarious when this detail emerged about the young woman who, as far as they were concerned, was destined to be the future queen. Even Kate must have seen the humour in the moment. 'Kate drops in with her mother Carole,' said an inside source at the salon. 'She's very down-to-earth. You wouldn't say she was a preener by any means, but she always looks great.' It was true. Kate always seemed to hit the mark. She was just glamorous enough. Her association with royalty lent her a certain sparkle, but in her own right she possessed that tantalising blend of understated style and a glint of self-confidence that turns a pretty girl into a sexy young woman. She never looked as if she was trying too hard. But she was never caught on camera looking anything other than great.

Now that William was away from her side for prolonged periods, the issue of Kate's security became more pressing. Privacy had always been a much-used word by William when it came to his girlfriend, and he understandably wanted to shield her from unwarranted or overly aggressive press attention. But in the post-7/7 era there are darker forces to be reckoned with and more serious threats from which to protect a girl whose significance to the second in line to the throne had, after all, been so publicly and openly sealed with a kiss. With each day that Kate's relationship with William continued and deepened there was a growing concern that she could be a terrorist target.

The concern was not just the subject of conversation around the breakfast table at Highgrove or at Clarence House, but at Scotland Yard, too. How could they justify spending millions investigating the death of the Princess of Wales in a car crash (especially when most right-minded people believed it was the result of chauffeur Henri Paul driving drunkenly and recklessly) while not addressing the very real possibility that the girlfriend of the future king could be in danger? Scotland Yard acted and set contingency security plans in motion after consulting William's own personal protection officers. The hierarchy of the Royalty and Diplomatic Protection Department wanted to know just what the problems facing Kate were when she was not with her royal boyfriend.

The very fact that Kate's security became a matter of private discussion and strategy at a time when there had been a directive from the government to try to reduce the royal security bill, not increase it, was intriguing. I learned that even the level of protection of the Queen's granddaughters, Princesses Beatrice and Eugenie, had been notably reduced. They no longer automatically qualify for royal bodyguards when they travel abroad. Each case is assessed on its merit and necessity. One senior Scotland Yard source told me, 'It is my understanding that the princesses do not get protection from SO14 while they are abroad. In fact they only get minimal protection while in the UK. It is the same for the Princess Royal's children, too, but given their closeness to the throne Beatrice and Eugenie in the past warranted personal protection from Scotland Yard.'

Sure enough, during a holiday in Zermatt in the New Year of 2006, the princesses enjoyed evenings out in bars, returning home without a bodyguard. It struck me as an extraordinary state of affairs in the wake of the London bombings when royal security has been described as being at its tightest since the height of the mainland IRA attacks. Set against this backdrop, the fact that Kate's security was being discussed with a view to action was more significant than ever. It may not have been a hearts-and-flowers demonstration of love but royal romance is about nuts-and-bolts logistics, too. As a rule, officers from SO14 are assigned only to senior members of the Royal Family; traditionally, Kate would be considered for such status only if she and William were to become engaged. One security source told me at the time, 'The decision to hold the security review demonstrates that officials believe the couple is in a genuine, lasting relationship.' As we would see in November 2010, this belief was well founded.

In February 2006 I broke the exclusive story that Charles was considering providing Kate with a personal bodyguard. I had been told that former Superintendent Colin Hayward Trimming, the man honoured for his role in the Tumberlong Park attack on Charles in Sydney, Australia, in January 1994, when an intruder ran towards the prince firing a starting pistol, was called in to review the security situation. Hayward, one of the smoothest bodyguards to ever grace the elite Scotland Yard unit, known as 'Haircut 100' by his colleagues due to his close attention to his appearance, had advised in the selection of officers to oversee security for Camilla Parker Bowles before she and Charles wed. Informed security sources had told me that what was being considered was an 'interim measure' opening the way for full Scotland Yard protection at a later date should it be needed. Though it may have been outside their remit, Scotland Yard had, even before the announcement of the 2011 wedding, been carrying out a feasibility study on keeping Kate secure in the event of a 'credible threat' to her safety. This and the news that Charles was considering paying for Kate's protection was explosive stuff: after all, it was impossible not to draw a parallel between it and the fact that, before his engagement, he had paid for former SO14 protection officers to protect Camilla. I knew my source was rock solid.

All the national daily newspapers followed the *Standard*'s lead the following morning. My claim that the move would increase speculation that the couple were set to formalise their relationship could not have been more accurate. More and more, in spite of their relative youth, media commentators felt that it was a case of when, not if, William and Kate would announce their engagement. This renewed talk of marriage, coupled with issues of security that raised the spectre of the taxpayers footing the bill for another member of the Firm, was met with predictable churlishness by republicans. Even those close to government seemed keen to stick their oar in. Gordon Brown, then Chancellor, was unwittingly plunged into a row when one of his most senior advisers went on record to say that Prince William's children should attend state schools. As he was not yet even married it seemed the socialist thinker was getting ahead of himself. When former Labour minister Michael Wills, Gordon Brown's chief speechwriter, launched an astonishing attack on the institution of monarchy, his focus fell on William himself for the first time.

With the future of the monarchy firmly in his sights, Wills demanded a massive shake-up in the powers and privileged lifestyle of the Royal Family. It must have been particularly odd for William and Kate to hear Wills effectively lay out his plans for 'their' children. Among the most controversial of his notions was that future heirs to the throne should send their offspring to state primary schools rather than elite establishments such as the £16,000-a-year Ludgrove Prep School in Berkshire attended by both Harry and William until they reached 13 and transferred to Eton College. Wills was adamant that it was wrong that the next heir to the throne should enjoy an education denied to all but a tiny proportion of the population. He also launched an extraordinary attack on Prince Charles himself, accusing him of failing in his constitutional duty to maintain political neutrality. With his opposition to Labour's hunting ban, Charles had overstepped the mark, according to Wills, who was speaking at the left-wing Institute for Public Policy Research in London, and claimed to be voicing the views of many traditional Labour voters. He went on to demand that the ancient Coronation Oath should no longer force the monarch to uphold the Protestant faith or bar Catholics from becoming kings or queens, and he claimed that primogeniture, which states that male heirs take precedence over their sisters, ought also to be scrapped. It was an embarrassing outburst as far as Gordon Brown was concerned, placing one of his key advisers so firmly in the republican, or at least antimonarchist, camp. He issued a statement insisting that he had never discussed such matters with Wills, but the tirade marked a watershed as far as William and Kate were concerned.

Their relationship had become caught up in a political debate. Their romance was exposed as a union with political as well as personal ramifications. The longer they existed in the real world, the less they could run away from that reality. If Kate were to be protected properly, in all senses of the word, she and William would have to face up to it or call it a day – and they showed no signs of doing the latter.

Wills had gone on to outline a series of gimmicky ideas that he felt would improve the image of the royals and bring them firmly into line. He said that all new citizens from foreign countries should be invited to a Buckingham Palace garden party to meet the Queen and her immediate family, and he suggested that the ceremonial post of lord lieutenant held by the Queen's official representative in each county should be changed to something more reflective of society as a whole.

However off message Michael Wills's words may have been, they came at an interesting point in William's life and, in the year of the Queen's 80th birthday, they served as a reminder that, however popular the younger royals might appear, they – especially William – could take nothing for granted. Being Princess Diana's boy was not enough to guarantee him limitless public indulgence. He would have to prove himself. There may have been a flood of affection and respect for the Queen during her 80th-birthday celebrations, but the ripples of public goodwill did not always extend to the far reaches of her family. Truth be told, they still lapped uncertainly at Charles's and Camilla's feet.

William's decision to join the army had marked a compromise on his part and an acknowledgement of his royal duty. He had resisted pressure to join the Royal Navy, a move that would require months at sea, away from his 'adorable Kate'. Joining the army had been a victory of sorts for William. But he still had many personal bridges to cross as he faced gruelling training, miles away from Kate. Each mud-soaked step, each teeth-chattering night in the wilds, each barked order obeyed, served to remind him that this was not the life he would have chosen but one forced upon him by birth. William let it be known from a very early stage that if he were to enter the army his ultimate aim was to join the Army Air Corps as a helicopter pilot. He was not interested in taking the more traditional route of serving in a Guards regiment, as his younger brother Harry had done when he joined the Blues and Royals.

In fact it was Harry, rather than William, who proved himself a natural soldier and leader of men. This came as a surprise to critics who always considered Harry something of a joke. He had long since been regarded as the feckless younger brother, with no real job, no real responsibility and absolutely no qualms about capitalising on the fact. But at Sandhurst Harry knuckled down and bloomed. He impressed his superiors and proved popular with his peers, though he was far from a saint. 'He can be a lazy little shit,' one senior officer admitted. Yet, for all that, Harry's time at Sandhurst passed in the sort of uneventful fashion that must have had Clarence House aides offering prayers of thanks on a nightly basis.

As the brothers endured their personal trials at Sandhurst, Kate's profile was about to rocket with one picture that underlined just how much she was a part of the royal firmament, with or without the presence of her royal boyfriend. The moment came on 17 March 2006 at the Cheltenham Gold Cup races. Camilla was due to present the winner's trophy and so the engagement was down in her and Charles's diaries as an official event. Kate had arrived for the famous Friday race day with a girlfriend and her girlfriend's parents, entering through the punters' entrance and mingling with the rest of the day's spectators. She was particularly smartly dressed and looked stunning. Veteran royal photographer Mark Stewart spotted her in the crowds and mentioned her presence to Amanda Neville (now Amanda Foster), a friendly long-serving member of Prince Charles's press team. According to Stewart, Amanda looked a little surprised by the news that Kate was at the races as well as her royal boss.

By the second race Kate, much to the photographers' surprise, had appeared on the balcony of the royal box, where Lord Vestey, a friend of the prince, was hosting a lunch for Charles and Camilla. Camilla's daughter Laura and Laura's then fiancé Harry Lopes were there, as were Tom Parker Bowles and his wife Sara, Zac Goldsmith, Ben Elliot and Thomas van Straubenzee, one of William's best friends, who was locked in conversation with Kate. It was the first time that Kate had been invited to adopt such an elevated position on her own. She had arrived. It was Camilla's most high-profile social engagement yet, but she did not seem bothered by the presence of the younger woman who threatened to steal her limelight. Quite the opposite: she appeared warm and welcoming. If anybody could understand the nerves that Kate might have been experiencing it was Camilla. She was a past master – or rather mistress – when it came to hovering publicly on the edges of royalty.

The pictures from that day, with Kate in full view, seemed to present a 'new' Royal Family of sorts. It was fresh and surprisingly attractive, more representative in its blended nature of the social realities of its subjects. Here was a ragtag group, each member with a tale to tell: some of marital strife and infidelity, some of young love, some of privilege squandered but recovered. Here was a new cast, or at least assorted members of the old cast, playing new roles: the mistress as wife, the petulant prince as doting stepfather, husband and, perhaps, father-in-law-to-be.

'It was astonishing to see how relaxed and comfortable Kate was around the heir to the throne,' said Mark Stewart. 'It just goes to prove how serious her relationship with William is. It also shows how fond Camilla is of her, too. After all, it was Camilla's first year of presenting the Gold Cup but she didn't appear to be remotely put out at being overshadowed by Kate's presence.'

Unsurprisingly, Kate's impromptu appearance in the royal box sparked a betting frenzy, with at least one bookmaker forced to slash the odds on Kate and William getting engaged before the following year's festival from 40–1 to 25–1.

A few days later she was back in the spotlight. After years of determinedly keeping a distance while out together in public, the couple again threw caution to the wind, no longer caring who knew they were an item. Kate, casually dressed in jeans, sweater and a quilted waistcoat and boots, turned up with a girlfriend to watch William when he returned to Eton College from Sandhurst to turn out for an old boys' team in the Field Game – a cross between rugby and soccer using smaller, hockey-sized goals. However, it was not the fact that she was there that surprised onlookers, but her carefree open show of affection. She strolled over to the prince, dressed in his blue sports kit, gave him a loving kiss and playfully ruffled the thinning hair that had been cropped by the army barber.

'They looked really comfortable together,' said one onlooker, 'and when the match was finished he gave her a hug and she immediately placed her hand on the small of his back. They looked perfect for each other and appeared totally at ease and in love.'

Shortly after this it transpired that Charles had given William and Kate permission to share a room when she stayed over at Highgrove, where she had become a regular visitor. Admittedly, the 'not under my roof' rule might have been a bit rich coming from a man so notoriously caught out committing adultery. Still, it was a telling detail and was read as a step towards Charles's acknowledgement of both his sons' increasing maturity and the seriousness of William's relationship with Kate. William's grandmother also showed her conviction in the significance of Kate to her grandson when she ensured that the young couple would have a secure and romantic bolthole on the Balmoral estate in the Scottish Highlands. Work began on an £80,000 facelift for a beautiful, if faded, 120-year-old cottage hidden away on a secluded corner of the Queen's estate and just a short stroll from Charles's own Aberdeenshire retreat of Birkhall – a place much loved by both him and Camilla and where they intended to spend each New Year together following their marriage. For Charles the Balmoral estate had for a long time been somehow symbolic of much that was wrong between him and Diana. He loved the wilderness and could spend hours up to his waist in the waters of the River Dee, casting his rod and waiting patiently for the fish to bite. Diana simply did not get it. She, by contrast, loathed the long country miles, the long country hours and what she regarded as the achingly stuffy remoteness of the place. But Birkhall and Camilla was a very different prospect. To Charles it is a place that has always represented the freedom to be truly himself. There, he and Camilla are simply Mr and Mrs Wales, happy to spend hours walking across the moors. Perhaps part of Charles's affection for Kate stemmed from his recognition that in her William had found somebody who could happily share the remote Aberdeenshire landscapes that he loved, somebody who would walk by his side as far as he wanted and curl up in front of a roaring fire at the end of the day. The fact that, along with the Queen, he gifted the couple a Highland 'home' was massively significant. The Queen picked up the bill but it is fair to say that she would not have dreamed of offering the place without the blessing of William's father.

The cottage, set on a part of the estate known as Brochdhu, had lain uninhabited for many years. It had been used as a game store for years but now the royal residence was to be refurbished with all modern conveniences, including a large round bath big enough for two. A second-storey extension provided two large, airy bedrooms, with stunning views across the pine trees and over the Highland estate. Triple-glazed windows would keep out the bitter chill of Scottish nights and a luxury kitchen and wood-burning stove were installed. In a nod to logistics, not comfort, a wooden security fence had to be installed.

But for all this apparent finessing into stable coupledom – the domestic bliss of a Highland getaway, the shared bed at Highgrove, the embracing of Kate by the extended Royal Family, the logistics of protection and William's apparent shouldering of some of his royal burden through officer training at Sandhurst – there is still a wild streak that runs through the second in line to the throne. It is often overshadowed by his more exuberantly headline-grabbing younger brother, but it is one that, according to some well-placed observers, could become troublesome if not curbed. It is the streak of rebellion that has led some royal insiders to express a degree of concern over what would happen if William were not to marry Kate. It is not that marriage to Kate would be seen to clip his wings, but her influence on William is a positive one. She knows how to have fun, she loves to dance and flirt and drink into the night, but she has a limited tolerance for that side of life. William's capacity for high living and rebellion is more ample. The older he gets the more senior courtiers start to worry that this throwback to the sometimes wayward Diana, combined with a hint of petulance inherited from his tantrum-throwing father, could turn their great hope for the monarchy into another liability. Prince Charles has always wanted his son to enjoy as much of his time as he can before the duties of royal life bear down on him. But there comes a point when the reality must be faced.

When a child's desire conflicts with their safety it is a matter of understandable and profound anxiety for any parent. When the child in question is the future king, that anxiety takes on a whole new significance, as William was to demonstrate in the early months of 2006 with his growing passion for motorbikes. Years earlier, in her authorised biography *Diana: Her True Story*, William's mother had intimated that she longed for the day when she could walk along a beach without her policeman following on behind. Her comment, a rather dramatic cry for freedom, may have been a little disingenuous, as her long-serving senior Scotland Yard bodyguard, Inspector Ken Wharfe, would often allow her to do just that, on condition that she keep in touch by radio and ensure she was disguised with a headscarf. She once wandered onto a nudist beach on Studland Bay and roared with laughter down the radio as she told Wharfe where she was. Perhaps the desire is genetic; perhaps it is simply symptomatic of anyone whose life is led in a goldfish bowl. Whatever the reason, according to those close to him, William has expressed a very similar longing for anonymity and freedom. But, whereas his mother hankered after a quiet stroll, William's expression of this need comes in a far higher-octane guise. Whenever he can he dons his leathers and helmet and roars off on the open road on his Honda CBR 1100XX Blackbird. It is one of the fastest super-bikes on the road, capable of speeds of more than 260km/h (160mph). It is little wonder that William's obsession became a source of anxiety for both Charles and the Queen, who at first viewed William's new hobby as a bit of fun not dissimilar to Prince Philip's penchant for getting behind the wheel of his green Hackney taxi cab and driving through London. But, given what happened to his mother and given the far higher risk of his own flirtation with 'normality', William's need for speed has potentially far more serious consequences for the future of the monarchy.

Prince Charles was torn between mollycoddling his son and opening him up to such danger by giving him his head. He believes that there is no point in wrapping a young man in cotton wool, but William is no ordinary young man. His determination to shrug off danger, almost to kick out at those who are inclined to restrict him, is both a flaw and an attribute. His approach to motorbikes was a case in point. 'Riding a motorbike,' according to William, 'can be dangerous, but so can a lot of things, really. Admittedly, there are more risks involved in riding a motorbike than there are in a lot of things. It is a risk, but as long as you've had sufficient and thorough training you should be OK. You've just got to be aware of what you're doing.' But William's rapid acceleration from smaller bikes to a more powerful Triumph, then to the Honda Blackbird, was, by the spring of 2006, proving a headache for the family and his police minders alike. Just as protection for Kate covered many aspects of life – from privacy to basic, physical safety – so, too, did the danger that William appeared to be inviting into his life with his insistent pursuit of speed. On one level he was risking death and injury to himself or others; on another he was risking giving his guards the slip, unwittingly or otherwise, leaving him exposed to other threats. Truthfully, it was the simple anxiety over his ability to control such a ferocious vehicle that caused his protection officers most concern. Officers from SO14 did not feel that William had the training needed to manoeuvre such a bike safely. They felt that he was an accident waiting to happen. In May 2006 high-level sources made it clear to me that something needed to be done. They felt that the prince was underqualified and needed to be sent on a specialist course at the police training college at Hendon, north London, to ensure he could cope with his powerful new machine. Precautions were taken and one of Charles's guards – Inspector Ian McRae, an expertly trained motorbike cop as well as a member of the elite SO14 – was assigned to head up a team of four to accompany William when he hit the road on his bike. Any warnings his father or security personnel may have offered fell on deaf ears, and his determination to ride his super-bike anyway – with the throwaway remark, 'My father doesn't want to keep me wrapped in cotton wool' – showed a side to William rarely seen in the controlled environment of organised interviews.

'William knows his mind,' one former courtier told me. 'He will not be deterred by anyone, maybe with the exception of the Queen. He has the utmost respect for her, and, if she insisted that he did something, I am sure that he would comply.' Nobody, except those who have lived with the responsibility, could ever really know what it is like to be born a future king or queen. There are times when you must ask, 'Why me?' and reject it outright. All you can do is turn to those who, like you, have had to deal with it. In William's case this is his father and grandmother, and that is what he has always done. But, however much he may seek their guidance and respect their words of advice, there is a rebel that lurks in William. It was one that came to the fore like never before that spring. In April he was busy getting himself into another sort of trouble – far less threatening perhaps, far more normal for a young man of his age, certainly, but surprising nonetheless as far as the vast majority of the public were concerned. On the 14th and 15th of that month it was William and not, for once, his younger brother whose partying thrust him into the front pages of the morning tabloids.

It should have been all about Harry. Friday, 14 April was, after all, the day that he passed out at Sandhurst, the day that Officer Cadet Wales became Second Lieutenant Wales of the Blues and Royals and paraded in front of the sovereign – or 'Granny', as Harry called her. There had been the predictable, good-natured jokes at the young royal's expense: 'A red-faced Harry passes out; no, it's not what you think' – that sort of thing. In fact, after completing his 44-week training, Harry deserved his moment of self-pride and recognition and he deserved it to be unsullied by bad behaviour or scandal. It was a shame he did not receive it. The Queen gave a speech to the cadets where she described the parade as a 'great occasion'. 'This day marks the beginning of what I hope will be highly successful careers,' she said. 'My prayers and my trust go with you all.' She then presented the prestigious Sword of Honour to the best cadet and also handed out the Overseas Medal and the Queen's Medal, before addressing the newly commissioned officers. It was the first time in 15 years that she had attended a parade, and there were no prizes for guessing why she had chosen to present at this one.

The passing-out parade was Harry's graduation moment, the revelry that followed his graduation ball. It is, of course, a well-rehearsed tradition at Sandhurst and the day began well enough with the ceremonial Sovereign's Parade. Harry had, in accordance with custom, invited a party of ten family and friends to join him. His girlfriend Chelsy Davy was not among the elite group who watched Harry march, as she was spending the afternoon at the hairdresser in anticipation of the lavish black-tie event that evening. But Prince Charles was there along with Camilla, Harry's former nanny Tiggy Pettifer (née Legge-Bourke), family friends Hugh and Emilie van Cutsem and Prince Philip. William was there of course, along with the rest of the officer cadets, standing to attention and beaming with pride as his brother passed out. Kate had been invited to the afternoon's events but, much to the surprise of many there, she did not turn up.

According to one person who was there, 'Everybody was expecting her but she did not show. In fact she was still expected at about five p.m. that evening but, to be honest, I think there was a little bit of relief among the top brass that she did not come because the thinking was that, if Kate did not go, William would not and it would be less of a nightmare in terms of security later on. It made sense that William and Kate would not want to upstage Harry and Chelsy either, as it was Harry's day.' If the desire not to overshadow her royal boyfriend's younger sibling had been behind Kate's decision not to go to the ball that evening, then her sacrifice was in vain.

Once the passing out ceremony was over Harry and his fellow new officers changed into the mess suits that, until then, they had not been entitled to wear. Dressed in the tight-fitting trousers, stiff waistcoat and bright-red dress jacket, Harry looked every inch the officer as he chatted happily with the men of his platoon at the drinks that preceded the evening's party. His grandparents had expressed their pride and left early, as did the rest of his personal party of guests, except Chelsy, who had passed on the day's events in favour of the evening's festivities.

After drinks in their individual platoon houses the cadets and their guests headed across to the college's gymnasium where the real party was waiting to happen. It may sound rather low-rent, the equivalent of a school disco held in a gym, but the building had been transformed into a breathtakingly lavish venue. A series of covered walkways connected the network of themed rooms that had been plotted throughout the vast space to cater for every taste and mood. In one area a live band played in front of a chequered dance floor, surrounded by high tables, uplit in red. In another there was jazz. Elsewhere the partygoers could play roulette or blackjack in the casino, drink vodka from an ice bar or eat chocolate from a chocolate fountain. Outside, the discipline of military life had been turned over in favour of an amusement park, complete with roller-coaster thrill rides and a hamburger van. It was an extravagant setting, but Harry had eyes only for Chelsy. She was dressed in a sheath of turquoise satin that clung to her curves, scooped low at the back to show off her flawless tanned skin, and flowed, mermaid-like, out and down to the floor. Her makeup was minimal and her earrings simple. She had flown into the country the previous afternoon, landing at Heathrow, and was met by the sort of security usually reserved for members of royalty, heads of state or – for that matter – wanted criminals. It had been weeks since she and Harry had been in each other's company, so there was little wonder that they seemed reluctant to take their eyes, or hands, off each other.

'Harry's bodyguards stood around him as he and Chelsy danced and kissed. They were snogging, hugging and holding hands, massively and openly affectionate,' one partygoer recalled. 'I suppose he's used to that by now but it did seem odd. He was joking with other cadets and is obviously very popular. He was happy to talk to anybody who approached him, although he did seem keener to talk to the girls.' He posed happily for pictures when asked by pretty guests and laughed good-naturedly when one girl, the worse for wear for drink and urged on by her friends, cheekily took a pinch at his bum. 'Instead of being annoyed,' one girl said, 'Harry just pinched her bum back and she ran off giggling.' At midnight the party moved outside, where a vast display of fireworks lit up the night sky and the new officers ripped the velvet strips that had been covering the officers' pips on their suits. It was a traditional rite of passage and a moment of whooping celebration amid an increasingly chaotic party as some cadets and their guests were by now showing signs of flagging.

Among the strugglers, to the dismay of his senior officers, was Prince William. Harry was drinking and smoking and partying with the best of them. But he was, those who witnessed the brothers maintained, a perfect gentleman throughout. He was not brash, or loud, or inappropriate. He was focused on Chelsy. He was proud of his achievement and that of his brothers-in-arms. The same could not be said of William and some of his civilian friends who had pitched up to join the fun. One college source recalled, 'One of William's civvy pals impersonated a brigadier all evening and tried ordering people about. He and the royal gang thought it very funny. Another found it highly hilarious to brag about a stag-night encounter with a prostitute and losing his wallet. Nobody else found them funny.'

Their behaviour was found so distinctly unfunny that, as 2 a.m. approached, William was advised by a senior officer that it would be best for him to call it a night. It was a humiliating rap on the knuckles for William and worse was to come. Hours later, Sandhurst's commandant, General Andrew Ritchie, rang Clarence House and apparently demanded an explanation for the raucous behaviour of the previous night. Pictures appeared in a morning tabloid of William, apparently the worse for drink, having a go on one of the thrill rides. Reports about 'upper-class twits' and the older prince's behaviour soon began seeping out. Harry had by all accounts been 'as good as gold' and had played by the rules. William had not.

Twenty-four hours later William and Harry, joined by Kate and

Chelsy, were continuing the party back in London and were pictured having a boozy night out at their favoured club, Boujis, in South Kensington. William was seen leaving with Chelsy, not Kate. Harry, it seemed, had sneaked out of a back door. It was the princes' way of playing with the waiting paparazzi, throwing them off their guard. Harry had something to celebrate: Sandhurst was over and he and Chelsy would soon head off on holiday together. But for William things were different. For once, he was the brother who seemed selfish, thoughtless and downright badly behaved. He had gone too far the night before and here he was carrying on as if he could do whatever he pleased without fear of criticism. It may sound harsh and some would argue that William was still just a high-spirited young man approaching his 24th birthday having fun with his brother and their girlfriends. Possibly, but he was not beyond reproach, either. With his lack of self-control and his inability to rein in his friends, William had spoiled Harry's moment of glory. He had turned the story away from his brother in the most negative fashion. Significantly, Kate had not been by his side when it had happened. Would William have been in the same position had she gone to the ball? It seemed unlikely.

Suddenly and subtly it became clear that the balance of their relationship had changed. Once, Kate's glamour and image was dependent on William's presence. But the night of Harry's passing-out suggested that this had begun to work both ways. The public liked Kate and they had a limited tolerance for playboy princes, whatever their parentage. Kate was now irrevocably linked with William as far as press and public were concerned. Could it be that we all liked William a little bit more with her by his side?

William was always very keen to stress his youth when it came to talk of marriage and his royal duties. He may cite the fact that the average age for marriage in Britain is 32 and claim that, at 24, he had many years of bachelorhood to look forward to. But there was nothing average about William or his position. This is something that William – like his late mother – does not want to hear. Diana famously parted company with William's first nanny, Barbara Barnes, when she pointed out that in trying to raise William as a 'normal' little boy Diana was fighting the forces of nature. Diana had a clear idea of how she wanted her sons to be raised. Barnes, a traditionalist, protested, 'The princes need to be treated differently because they *are* different.' She may have been speaking out of turn but she was speaking the truth: William was not and never would be 'normal'.

CHAPTER 13

THE WAY AHEAD

'She's been brilliant, she's a real role model.'
PRINCE WILLIAM COMMENTING ON THE QUEEN

They arrived at Kew Palace to the strains of Bach, Wagner and Donizetti played by harpist and flautist. The music played as the light began to fade in the exquisite Royal Botanic Gardens that surround the palace, and the family progressed through the Queen's Boudoir, known as the Sulking Room, and on into the King's Drawing Room. The table was set to perfection – bathed in the soft light of a myriad candles. Spring blooms brought fragrance and colour to the room; silverware placed with military precision shone and glassware gleamed. This was the scene of a very special dinner, in honour of a truly remarkably woman, and everything had to be perfect. It was the evening of 21 April 2006 and the guest of honour was Queen Elizabeth II, there to celebrate her landmark 80th birthday in the bosom of her close family.

Appropriately for a woman proud of her Scottish ancestry, the menu included a starter of timbale of organic Hebridean smoked salmon. There was juniper roast loin of venison from the Sandringham estates served with a port-wine sauce, steamed young cabbage and spring vegetables, and fruits from Prince Charles's Highgrove estates were used in the dessert. William sat next to his grandmother. His father sat on the other side of the woman who had reigned supreme as monarch and matriarch for

53 years. She must have surveyed the family gathered around that burnished table with real delight and not a little relief that, after a bumpy start to the year, here at last was an occasion that had drawn together her family in undiluted joy, pride and celebration.

The event's co-hosts, Charles and Camilla, had been first to arrive, swiftly followed by William and Harry, the Duke of York and his daughters, Beatrice and Eugenie, looking elegant and more grown-up than ever. After them came the Earl and Countess of Wessex and then the Princess Royal with her husband, Rear-Admiral Tim Laurence, and her children, Peter and Zara Phillips. The children of the late Princess Margaret, Viscount Linley and Lady Sarah Chatto, the Queen's nephew and niece, were also among the guests.

Throughout the dinner a selection of Handel's *Water Music* was played by 12 musicians from the London Chamber Orchestra, conducted by a thrilled Christopher Warren Green. As the meal drew to a close those present raised their glasses in a toast to a 'wonderful' monarch and a 'darling mama and grandmother'. The day had been one of great pageantry and joy. Earlier, the focus of world media attention had fallen on Windsor. Again, I was commentating on a historic royal event, standing on a box, perched high on the roof of the Best of Britain shop opposite the castle and a temporary set for CNN. As the Queen emerged, the band of the Irish Guards, resplendent in scarlet tunics and bearskins, oompahed out 'Happy Birthday' on the stroke of noon before the Queen began a walkabout through the town centre.

Around 20,000 people had congregated behind police barriers. Some were so eager to catch a glimpse of the Queen on her birthday that they had pitched up six hours earlier and patiently waited as the crowds grew and the hour drew near. From my vantage point I could see how the street before the castle teemed with red, white and blue patriots. Some gripped the steel barriers in excitement; others waved miniature flags or held banners aloft. Flowers were thrown and gifts proffered as the Queen, dressed in cerise and with a sprightliness that belied her years, walked past. She walked by the bronze statue of Queen Victoria outside the King Henry VIII gate dominating the front of the castle – set high above the tarmac road and walkways and the High Street and seeming to survey the scene with imperious approval. It was hard to believe that our own smiling monarch was now just one year shy of the age reached by her iconic great-great grandmother.

As I described the events, I recalled for my global audience the Queen's own words, spoken on another momentous birthday, her 21st, 59 years earlier. Then, where other young women entering adult life might have looked forward to all the freedoms that brings, Elizabeth had earnestly acknowledged that hers would be a sort of living sacrifice to the state. 'My whole life,' she selflessly vowed, 'whether it be long or short, shall be devoted to your service and the service of our great imperial family to which we all belong.' We may not use words like 'imperial' these days, but the notions of 'devotion' and 'service' have also been cheapened by a culture where fans pledge devotion to the latest pop idol on a weekly basis and where service is something consumers demand in a fast-food joint. But the passing of time has done nothing to diminish that heartfelt promise made by a young woman who, despite her tender years, had unswervingly accepted her destiny to serve her country for the rest of her days. It was an awesome undertaking and a solemn vow that, all these years later, as she met her subjects in Windsor, she was continuing to fulfil.

Her father had once reminded her that, while she may meet thousands of people in her life and not recall their faces, the moment when somebody meets her would be one they would remember for ever. He told her she must never be unkind and always be giving of herself and her time. She was just that on that overcast Windsor day, extending her walkabout, which, given her age, was no mean feat.

The next day the newspapers couldn't get enough of it. The People's Queen, declared the *Times*; the *Daily Telegraph* continued the theme saying, 'Prince Charles led the nation in paying tribute to his "darling mama".' In typically over-the-top fashion the *Sun*, screamed, 'The ecstatic cheers were heard from here to New

Zealand.' It concluded that doubts raised not so long ago about the future of the monarchy were now history.

The palace could not have had better headlines had they written them themselves. There was a real sense of the historic nature of the day. Even before the celebrations were coming to an end, as the fireworks exploded in the skies over Kew Palace ahead of the family dinner and the band of the Royal Marines played a medley of everything from Elvis to the Beatles, I was personally overwhelmed by the feeling that this spectacle marked the beginning of the end of Elizabeth's great reign. To me this landmark birthday was about more than the moment of celebration and more than an expression of relief at another milestone reached. It was a transition, a passing from one royal order to the next.

Those closest to the Queen, such as her cousin Margaret Rhodes, loyally declared that Elizabeth would never quit her post. 'I'm perfectly certain the Queen will never retire as such,' she said. 'Because it's not like a normal job and to the Queen the vows that she made on Coronation Day are something so deep and so special that she wouldn't consider not continuing to fulfil those vows until she dies. I am sure she will never abdicate.'

I am quite certain she is right. The spectre of the abdication of her uncle and her determination that it must never happen again has defined Elizabeth II's long and eventful reign. 'She is completely haunted by it,' the late political historian Professor Ben Pimlott claimed. But it wasn't the well-rehearsed claim that the Queen would never give up her crown that resonated for me, but the words 'as such'. The Queen 'will never retire as such'. Those two little words conveyed so much and suggested to me that the Queen's role was in a state of flux. 'I sometimes wish,' her second son Prince Andrew said in a television interview marking the birthday, 'that the people round about my mother would remember her age.' The Queen may be remarkably fit and industrious but the time has come to acknowledge her advancing years and make some concession to her age. Yes, she will remain Queen until death, but more and more responsibilities will pass to her son and heir Prince Charles – and, in due course, to Prince

William. The long-haul foreign tours for one will become the domain of Charles and Camilla, then William and his princess bride and eventual Queen Consort, Kate Middleton.

Some senior palace courtiers and political figures still fear that Prince Charles's years may spell trouble for the institution of the monarchy. Most rather blindly just hope and pray that the Queen's remarkable good health continues. Many who have watched the royal players at close quarters fear for the future. Dickie Arbiter, a former assistant private secretary to the Queen, who worked closely with Prince Charles for many years, told me, 'There are those inside the palace and out, myself among them, who say, "God Save the Queen" and really mean it. Perhaps because they're worried about what comes next.'

Poll after poll has shown that the people love the Queen and are tantalised by the thought of Prince William succeeding his grandmother. The reaction to Prince Charles is more complex, veering between animosity and tolerance. He is still not a figure who inspires real public affection. As for Camilla, her presence on Charles's arm is no longer met with hostility, and there is an increasing acceptance of her as Charles's wife, even a creeping warmth, but the public do not want her anywhere near the throne or crowned as Queen Consort, which is her entitlement. Nearly a decade and a half after her death, Diana continues to haunt Charles and, no matter how hard Camilla tries, or how fervently the Clarence House PR machine pushes, Camilla can no more shake her predecessor's ghost than right the wrongs of the past.

Marriage to Camilla has not killed Charles's hopes of being king one day and it has not destroyed the monarchy, as scaremongers and traditionalists once asserted. But nor has it been the absolute salvation for which Charles might have hoped.

On Charles and Camilla's second foreign tour of Egypt and India in March 2006 there was a real sense that the royal roadshow had come off the rails. After 16 years of following members of the Royal Family on official tours abroad I saw this one for what it really was: tired, badly organised and giving out very mixed messages. One minute Charles and Camilla appeared like a couple of ageing tourists, dubbed 'Fred and Gladys', their pet names for themselves, by the press back home. The next they were staying in the splendour of the maharaja's palaces in Jodhpur and Jaipur.

The trip to India hardly spawned thrilling copy but was generally well received and written up positively for the newspapers in Britain and India. Extended picture captions and fluffy broadsheet stories praising Charles and Camilla accounted for the majority of coverage. But unlike state visits abroad with the Queen, which are as a rule sedate and structured, this one was a shambles, not just for the press but for the royal couple, too. In one village, in the Rajasthan desert, Camilla looked on the point of collapse as she struggled to cope with a hectic schedule in soaring temperatures. She was a trouper, really trying to make it work for everyone and not let down her husband, who, after all his years of experience, took it in his stride. But they both looked worn out – likeable and friendly but somehow outdated. As I watched them tramp around dusty desert forts I recalled a conversation I'd had with a fellow Air India passenger on the flight to the pink city, as Jaipur is known.

'Why does he always stay with princes that lost their titles years ago and don't exist any more?' my fellow traveller asked. It was a fair point, and, as I arrived at the Maharaja of Jaipur's residence, I was struck by how stuck in a different era it all seemed. The black-and-white pictures on the walls framed the scene and set the tone perfectly: there was Earl Mountbatten and his wife Edwina, Prince Philip in another, elsewhere a young Charles and Diana. The photographs were fuzzy, slightly out of focus, almost dirty. I was on the official joint visit when Charles took his then wife, Diana, to India in 1992 and now the pictures looked as out of date as the snaps of the last days of the British Raj. Was it possible that the same thing could happen to the British monarchy if, like the old Raj in India, it was no longer representative or relevant?

If Prince Charles and his new wife should prove a tainted, outmoded vehicle to transport the monarchy into a new era, is William really the modernisers' dream ticket? When the Queen inherited the crown it was handed down to her from a thoroughly respected King. When William receives the crown what condition will Charles and Camilla have left it in? Charles has made some headway in terms of public popularity, but he still has a long way to go if he is ever to convince the majority of his subjects that he is not simply a pampered, self-indulgent man. It is all too easy to fondly imagine that the Queen will simply carry on, ruling victorious *ad infinitum*. There are certainly courtiers who wish that this were possible.

The very nature of palace life conspires to give a sense of permanence, filled as it is with pomp and the ceremony handed down through the ages, unchanged and unchanging. The minutiae of the Queen and her court's daily routines are so predictable that they convince the observer it is unthinkable that things had ever been any different – or will ever be. At home in Buckingham Palace the Queen's day begins in the same way as it has for the past five decades of her reign. A police sergeant sits at the door of her first-floor suite; he carries a gun, is in uniform – and wears slippers. The footwear is his one concession to the hours of his nocturnal watch and his highly polished shoes are tucked neatly beneath his chair. Further along the hallway sleeps Philip in his own private suite.

Occasionally, the solitary officer rises to patrol the corridor as he waits for the guard who will relieve him of his watch. He is just one of scores of security men in the grounds and around the perimeters of the palace. The life of a monarch is one of great privilege and awesome limitations: both protected and confined.

There is rarely a truly private moment in the palace. By 5 a.m. the first shift of domestic staff are making their way to their posts along the network of passageways and tunnels below the Royal Family's rooms. There they will embark on preparations for the separate beginnings of the sovereign's and Prince Philip's day.

At 7.30 a.m. precisely, a maid bearing a tea tray walks briskly along the first-floor hallway. She is known to the watchful officer, who stands by as she taps lightly on the Queen's door before entering. Her every move is part of a rigid morning ritual. Nothing is unrehearsed. From the maid's steps as she pulls back the curtains to reveal views across Constitution Hill, to the temperature of the bath she draws in silence, to the tea that she pours – made by R Twining & Company of the Strand, London, and blended exclusively for the Queen. The palace steward, the most senior domestic servant in the palace, has drilled everything sergeant-major-like into this loyal servant. She serves the Queen's tea – milk, no sugar – and offers a courteous 'Good morning, Your Majesty'. Prince Philip's day begins in a similarly measured fashion with the first of many cups of coffee, a blend specially made for the Royal Family by the Savoy Hotel Coffee Department.

Everything is just so, planned and executed with rigid precision. This carefully choreographed morning routine, the pomp and the ceremony and the strict codes that govern each and every member of the royal household, all conspire to create an illusion of permanence where, truth be told, none exists. As she entered her 81st year, the Queen did so in the knowledge that decisions had already been taken that would change the face of the monarchy. The key players had already been put in place – perhaps even down to William's future consort, who, as we now know, will be his beloved Kate. After all, William is a man who, unlike his grandmother, was born to rule. Like his father, he has been primed for the main job all his life. While the prospect of William's future reign must stretch out before him, with each passing day Charles must watch his own future tenure dwindle and shrink. For the Queen, as far as her role in royal history is concerned, the end game has already begun.

I felt it as I watched her celebrate her momentous birthday on that overcast April morning and I have watched the cogs turn quietly as the royal machine prepares to change gear. One well-placed source told me, 'The decisions have already been made and the process in which the Queen will step back and out of public life has already been set in motion. The Queen is 80 and Philip, while he's remarkably fit for his age, is an old man. The key to the monarchy as the Queen sees it is making changes without anybody seeing the joins.'

That's exactly what's been happening and she is effectively moving into semi-retirement. The Queen realises her place in history and knows that the time has come to adapt or risk the monarchy falling into disrepair. A handover of power is happening right in front of us and only the very few within the Royal Family and their closest confidants and advisers are even aware it is happening. The changes are subtle but seismic.

It's powerful stuff and nothing has been left to chance. It never is. After more than a decade reporting on some of the family's most torrid and turbulent times it has become abundantly clear to me that, while the Queen is keen to set herself at the head of the archetypal nuclear family, hers is anything but, and conducts and governs itself unlike any other family. The future of the Royal Family is governed and set by senior family members along with the aid of a clique of key confidants and advisers. They meet twice a year and form the powerful group in the monarchy's inner sanctum known simply as the Way Ahead Group. In a family where information is exchanged in letters more often than in conversations, where phone calls are placed via siblings' private secretaries rather than made direct, and where diaries have to be cross-referenced and memos checked, the Way Ahead Group is their version of sitting around the kitchen table and thrashing out differences of opinions and plans for the future. Lord Airlie, one of the Queen's favourite peers and then Lord Chamberlain, set up the group in the early 1990s. Not even the prime minister knows the details of this elite group's discussions. MPs may debate the merits of the monarchy and social commentators such as Michael Wills may pontificate, but it's the Way Ahead Group that meets behind closed doors at the heart of the royal establishment and makes the decisions that have shaped the Royal Family – with varying degrees of success. Politicians have raised what they regard as the controversial issue of bringing an end to male primogeniture, blissfully unaware, it seems, that the topic has long since been dispatched by the Way Ahead Group.

Both the Queen and Prince William are in favour of doing away with the outmoded concept, hinting at a shared vision of a modern monarchy that must warm the Queen's heart. Clarence House as done its best to scotch the notion that in Christmas 2005 William sat in on his first Way Ahead Group meeting, but I have always been less than convinced by Clarence House's take on the goings-on of the palace. One well-placed source has insisted to me that he did. If it is true then, in this seemingly arbitrary detail, lies the most significant evidence yet of what those close to the monarch already know: that the Queen has begun her retreat from public life. A new order is about to be ushered in. Charles and Camilla may be next in line but it is William and his bride who will be seen as the real future of the monarchy. Buckingham Palace, now the symbolic and practical heart of the British monarchy, will cease to be the sovereign's primary residence. Sections of it will be turned over to royal offices and much will be open to the public. It will be a sort of living museum and gallery. The Queen, meanwhile, will spend the majority of her time at her beloved Windsor Castle – riding as long as her health permits in Windsor's Great Park and enjoying the dwindling of her reign in the place that she has always regarded as home.

At its winter meeting in 2005 the Way Ahead Group agreed that Royal Family Christmases would in future be held at Windsor, rather than at Sandringham. A well-placed source told me, 'The Queen will continue to do tours of the Commonwealth as a debt of duty to her late father, but she's prepared to hand over many more onerous duties to Charles and William.'

It is no coincidence that the Queen has been spending more and more time with her grandson, of whom she is very fond. The Queen recognises a simple, for Charles painful, fact that the role for which her eldest son was born has all but passed him by, however much public opinion may have softened. History, fate and his own spoilt nature have conspired to place Charles in an unenviable position. For years his own parents seriously doubted his suitability for the throne. He was, according to one royal insider, regarded as something of a loose cannon: too quick to anger, given to tantrums and driven by an almost revolutionary zeal to 'make his mark' on the country with his various initiatives, causes and beliefs that many believed teetered dangerously on the brink of quackery.

Charles's apparent need to be viewed as a shaper of ideas and political influence was a serious source of concern to his advisers, too. Former deputy private secretary Mark Bolland has admitted that during his time in the prince's service he 'tried to dampen down the prince's behaviour in making public his thoughts and views on a whole range of issues'.

He wrote, 'The prince's expressions of his views have often been regarded with concern by politicians because we would be contacted by them – and on their behalf. Private Secretaries to government ministers would often let us know their views and, typically, how concerned they were.'

Charles may have done some good. Certainly, he has raised the debate on important issues such as genetically modified crops, religious tolerance and saving the environment, but he will have to keep all his undoubted passion to himself when he ascends the throne. He is well aware of this fact. Yet, despite the partially successful efforts to rehabilitate Charles and Camilla, the fact remains that the spotlight is now turning increasingly towards William and the court that he will establish. Whatever happens, the focus seems destined to fall only briefly on Charles and Camilla. No doubt it won't be easy for a man as opinionated as Charles to bite back his views, but he must if he is to keep the institution of the monarchy safe for the next generation – safe for William and Kate.

According to one former courtier, 'There was a time after Diana's death, and even more recently than that, when many staff at Buckingham Palace were quite convinced that they were serving the penultimate monarch, that Charles wouldn't have a crown left to hand down to William.' I do not think this doomsday scenario is given any serious credence now. However, mindful of her lengthening reign, the Queen was prompted to urge a resolution to the 'Camilla problem' through marriage. Mindful of his duty, Charles complied. This was a smoothing of the way forward to the next generation, not simply the glorious resolution of Charles and Camilla's enduring grand romance. It was made clear to Charles that he had to fit in with the bigger picture and accept the shifting shape of the monarchy as envisaged by the Queen. It was a calculated risk and it appears to have paid off. The reception to Charles and Camilla on their Indian tour was warm, if not excited; the press coverage of Camilla is increasingly gentle but never effusive. There is no escaping the lingering feeling that, while

Charles may have many supporters, his greatest asset is also his greatest weakness. Camilla as consort and Duchess of Cornwall is a constant reminder of the failings of the past. She undoubtedly gives strength to Charles but, no matter how optimistic palace spokespersons try to be, Charles and Camilla have both brought far too much baggage to the relationship for it to be presented as anything approaching love's young dream.

Still, the general feeling is that with Camilla at his side Charles is a less abrasive, spoilt figure and behind the scenes the groundwork has been laid for the shift in power from queen to Charles and so to William. Key members of staff from Buckingham Palace have been moved to Clarence House. It seems to me that Charles's court is being bolstered and strengthened as the Queen prepares to hand over much of her power.

The movements may seem mundane to the casual observer but they're worth noting because it is in these changes that the key to the bigger picture lies. Most significant in these appointments are Sir Malcolm Ross, who in 2005 was appointed master of the household of the Prince of Wales, and his dapper deputy, Andrew Farquharson. Ross, a man in his 60s was, until he switched palaces, the linchpin of the Queen's organisation, having served in her household for 18 years. It was he who organised the Queen Mother's and Diana's funerals, and who organised Edward and Sophie's wedding. His office at Buckingham Palace contained filing cabinets filled with blueprints for every conceivable royal hatch, match or dispatch. He replaced Kevin Knott, the ill-fated accountant who was tasked with overseeing Charles and Camilla's much-mocked wedding arrangements. Ross was just three years short of retirement when he made his move, an odd time, one might think, to quit the sovereign's court and take on a new and weighty role at Clarence House. His remit involves overseeing Charles and Camilla's public and private diaries as well as running their three main residences: Birkhall in Scotland, Clarence House, and Highgrove in Gloucestershire.

Meanwhile, Farquharson has ditched a powerful position as head of F Branch at Buckingham Palace, a job that meant he was responsible for the monarch's food and drink at everything from state banquets to summer picnics, for a seemingly lower-profile role in Charles's court. Both were likely to receive far higher salaries from Charles than they ever did from Buckingham Palace and some at the time suggested that they had deserted the Queen out of the disloyal urge to make a quick buck. I don't think so. These are honourable men who were always far more likely to accommodate themselves to the Queen's grand plan than feather their own nests. It is a plan that seems to involve peopling Clarence House with mature and qualified men, establishing a court fit for a king. The moves were arguably overdue. The prince's household and offices had, according to Mark Bolland, 'A longstanding reputation for being chaotic, with phone calls unanswered, correspondence remaining unanswered for great lengths of time, people being late for meetings, things going missing.' It seemed likely that the arrival of Ross and Farquharson would go a long way to clamping down on such chaos. The position of Michael Fawcett, Charles's former valet, is the subject of some controversy. Fawcett continues to work for Charles on a freelance basis, much to the consternation of the household staff, organising much of his entertainment and earning substantial amounts of money a year in the process. He even had the honour of 'overseeing' the birthday dinner at Kew palace, although Clarence House staff cooked and served the food. It seems anyone sounding the death knell on Fawcett's power may have spoken too soon. While to some the new appointments signal 'the end of the old order', according to one royal insider this statement may be a little premature. Save for the perceived weakening of Charles's favourite, Michael Fawcett, these new appointments and the increased palace confidence they signal are a triumph of sorts for Charles – a man who bemoaned the fact that he would truly be appreciated only once he was dead and gone. 'Right now a complete transformation is taking place at the heart of the monarchy,' explained one royal observer at the time. The Queen is about to step back, Charles is considered a safe pair of hands but the real focus, the real hopes for the future of the monarchy, are on William – and Kate.

The Queen has been spending more and more time with her grandson and he has increasingly started to undertake the duties of his public life that, for a while, he seemed to be avoiding. He was deemed to have conducted himself brilliantly on his first official tour in New Zealand in 2005. He has been to Sandhurst, which showed that he finally accepted the fact that as future head of the armed forces he must have a uniform himself. Significantly, he also took on the presidency of the Football Association. That has always been a position relegated to a more minor royal in recent years. William took over from his uncle, Prince Andrew, but just look at the timing: his incumbency came in the year of the World Cup and it is a role that both George V and George VI took. The role is very much part of William's presentation as a modern monarch in the making. The message his presidency gave was clear: he doesn't just play polo, like his father, but he's into football as well (although Kate's not so keen and, when asked why she did not play polo, she told writer Kathy Lette, 'I'm allergic to horses'). William, for all his privilege, is a man for – if not entirely of – the people. He has trained with Premiership team Charlton and has revealed he is an Aston Villa supporter. It gives him and the Firm an edge and a contemporary feel. 'He's not outmoded, like his father may appear,' one commentator put it. 'He's very much in touch – just look at his girlfriend.'

Kate could hardly be a more middle-class consort if she tried. Her family is neither landed nor aristocratic. And she is from the sort of 'stock' that a previous generation of royal heir would have been allowed to consider only as mistress material. That is not to say that she lacks the qualities laid down for a royal bride. In some respects she ticks the boxes: she has no lurid past and has conducted herself with poise and discretion through a relationship that, in all likelihood, was passionate and romantic long before their secret leaked into the public domain. Charles has pressed upon his son the notion that duty must be paramount when choosing a bride, but the rebel in William – the product of his two frankly wayward parents – makes him question whether a truly modern monarchy should endure the sort of self-sacrifice made by previous generations. He argues that he should be allowed to make his own choice in his own time and that his family, and his country, should have confidence in his ability to do so. William's stubborn determination not to be pushed around seems fair enough to contemporary sensibilities. But so too is his father's gentle reminder of the responsibility that comes with his title.

We are not prepared to tolerate indefinitely the playboy prince rolling out of nightclubs at 3 a.m. or, like his brother, thrusting his head between strippers' breasts. Bar bills of £2,500 at exclusive members-only clubs like Boujis in west London will begin to lose their novelty value. As for the Queen, too much high living is all too reminiscent of her dashing, playboy uncle and his desertion of duty all those years ago. No one has ever read a story about the Queen collapsing outside a bar. Her conduct past and present has always been befitting of a monarch. William has to look out for the pitfalls that come with confusing royalty with vacuous celebrity. If he treats his situation like the latter, the public might begin to question what they are paying for in maintaining the young royals.

The Royal Family needs a dose of youthful romance, not relentless debauchery. In the clear-skinned Kate and the strapping figure of William they may just have found it. Kate, the Home Counties girl, is, as one insider told me, 'very much part of the system now'. She has met and dined with the Queen on several occasions and has introduced the monarch to her parents. She has demonstrated an unprecedented level of self-possession for a non-royal in the company of the sovereign and she has received training from media adviser Paddy Harverson's press team at Clarence House on how to cope with the inevitable press interest that she now attracts – and will attract more of since the couple announced their engagement in November 2010.

'There is a real sense,' one aide told me before that announcement, 'that there's no reason why Kate shouldn't have the sort of impact on the monarchy and its popularity that Diana had. Only she is older, more self-assured and, let's face it, far more intelligent, at least academically, than Diana ever was.'

In William, she would have a husband quite clearly concerned with protecting her in a way that perhaps Charles just was not equipped to do with Diana. Charles will be King and Camilla will be his Queen Consort alongside him, make no mistake. William believes very strongly that his father will be a good King while he himself remains rather reluctant about rushing into an official role.

William has admitted, 'I'm very much the person who doesn't want to rush into anything without really thinking it through. I don't shy away from doing particular events but I do like to go to the ones that I really feel passionately about.'

Without doubt, William's contribution to royal life is much smaller than either his father's or his grandmother's was at the equivalent age. At some point during the day he attends to his correspondence. He does respond promptly to personal letters from family and friends, and if he has spent a weekend as a guest at someone's house he will always write a thank-you note with a fountain pen. He will also spend an hour or two studying papers that the Queen and Charles have sent him. These are not state papers but documents and articles that they have carefully selected to help him prepare for his eventual role as King. It is not a chore he enjoys, but one that he simply has to knuckle down to, one of the less glamorous trappings of royalty.

In his 2003 book *God Save the Queen: The Truth about the Windsors*, the writer and journalist Johann Hari made an astonishing claim. He said that Prince William, his father, brother and 20 per cent of the British people were all supporters of republicanism. He wrote, 'One man has the power to destroy the British monarchy – and he's not a politician. The man who will finally herald the Republic of Britain is a soon-to-be 21-year-old named William Windsor [it should be William Wales of course] – or, as the history books might record him, William the Last. It is time we all admitted three basic facts: William does not want to be king; he hates the idea of being king; he will not be king – ever.'

He went on, 'So what happens to the monarchy if William quits? Constitutionally, the throne could easily pass to William's younger brother Harry. But all the evidence suggests Harry is even more wilful, individualistic and ill-inclined to sublimate his energies into a pleasureless life of "duty". The crown could pass to Andrew

Windsor. But, really, won't most people conclude that it's time to call it a day?'

It is hard to discern the factual basis for these claims. He wanted the Royal Family out and he came up with the premise that William agreed with him in order to argue that the monarchy was doomed. Unsurprisingly, given such contentious views, the book was well publicised, however ill-founded it was. It also rattled a few cages at the palace, including William's. His response spoke volumes about his comprehension of the role that was unalterably his.

William used an interview set up to mark his 21st birthday to assert his desire to serve his country in a deliberate rebuttal of Hari's remarks. He cut to the chase: 'All these questions about "Do you want to be king?" It's not a question of wanting to be, it's something I was born into and it's my duty. Wanting is not the right word. But those stories about me not wanting to be king are all wrong. It's a very important role and it's one that I don't take lightly. It's all about helping people and dedication and loyalty which I hope I have – I know I have.

'Sometimes I do get anxious about it but I don't really worry a lot. I want to get through university and then maybe start thinking seriously about that in the future. I don't really ever talk about it publicly. It's not something you talk about with whoever. I think about it a lot but they are my own personal thoughts. I'll take each step as it comes and deal with it as best I can. The monarchy is something that needs to be there. I just feel it's very, very important. It's a form of stability and I hope to be able to continue that.'

He is seen, probably because of his youth, to be a moderniser. But, however 'radical' his choice of partner, William is far from the revolutionary that Hari has envisaged. William has said, 'Modernisation is quite a strong word to use with the monarchy because it's something that's been around for many hundreds of years. But I think it's important that people feel the monarchy can keep up with them and is relevant to their lives. We are all human and inevitably mistakes are made.

'But in the end there is a great sense of loyalty and dedication among the family and it rubs off on me. Ever since I was very small, it's something that's been very much impressed on me, in a good way. People say it's not ambitious, but it is actually quite ambitious wanting to help people. Trying to keep that going is quite tricky and it's something that, without the whole family, is harder for just one person to do. It would be dangerous to look a long way ahead and predict changes in the monarchy.'

William may be relatively inexperienced but he is young enough to recognise that the monarchy has to be seen as relevant to its people. In my view he was right to be reticent about looking ahead too far. Perhaps the death of his mother will always make it difficult for him to look to the future with any real faith and conviction. But, if he is to be a successful monarch, there are certain things to which he will have to face up – sooner rather than later. The succession is one of them.

William has grown from being his late mother's loyal little consort, to awkward teenager idolised by screaming young girls, to assured young prince. He has joked around with his father, doing more for Charles's popularity in those happy, natural family moments than a lifetime of PR campaigns ever could. He has been the naughty schoolboy, the model pupil and the student struggling for normality. Eventually, though, he will be King. 'I am worried about it,' he has said, 'but I don't really think about it too much because there's no point in worrying about things which are not really present yet. It's not that I never want to do it, it's just that I'm reluctant at such a young age, I think anyway, to throw myself in the deep end.'

The crown is an ever-present reality in William's life, however much he may try to convince himself and others of the contrary. William's place in the succession defines him and the responsibility that he faces is awesome. More and more he frets about the steady slipping away of normality that must come with the preordained path set out for him. He worries that he will be unable to remain grounded and hopes to emulate his grandmother in her strength, his father in his passion and his late mother in her empathy and warmth. He holds back and he holds his breath and hopes that he will know when, as he puts it, the moment has

Above: Princes William and Edward with the Queen at Trooping the Colour in June 2010.

© *Rex Features*

Below: William and Kate watching rugby at Twickenham.

© *PA Photos*

Kate and William at the October 2010 wedding of Rosie Bradford and Harry Mead when the Royal couple were already secretly engaged. Guests included (*opposite, above left*) Jecca Craig and Guy Pelly (*opposite, above right*). Harry and Rosie Mea (*opposite, below*).

Prince Harry, Kate and Camilla watch as William is made a knight of the garter by his grandmother.

© PA Photo

Kate in the summer of 2010
at the Beaufort Polo Club.
© *Rex Features*

Above: Kate and William at the Cheltenham Festival.

Below: The author, centre left, with William, David Beckham and Harry in South Africa in June 2010.

Carole and Michael Middleton announce the engagement of their daughter to Prince William outside their Berkshire home.   © *PA Photos and Rex Features*

Kate and William formally announce their
engagement in November 2010. © *PA Photos*

arrived to throw himself in at the deep end, not realising that he is already there. In reality, Prince William has no choice; he cannot be allowed to sink, so he must swim. The only decision still left for the young prince until not long ago was whom he would choose to swim alongside him. That decision has now been made.

CHAPTER 14
PRINCESS-IN-WAITING

'He's *lucky to be going out with* me.'
KATE MIDDLETON ON DATING PRINCE WILLIAM

It would be difficult to imagine a more idyllic setting. Before them, the turquoise waters of the Caribbean glimmered and gave way to emeralds, pinks and reds as the sun dipped towards the sea on the horizon. The sky glowed golden and above them a fan cut rhythmically through the still evening air. As they sat in the cocktail bar of the Firefly guesthouse, sipping their exotic drinks and absorbed in each other's company, the casually dressed young couple could easily have passed for newlyweds.

They would not have been the first couple caught up in the romance of the villa's hilltop location. In the background, the sound of the grand piano blended with the chatter and laughter of fellow guests and the reedy chirp of cicadas mingled with the sound of the surf as it rolled onto the white sand below. Once a private villa, the Firefly is now a hideaway for wealthy travellers and proudly boasts to be the exclusive island of Mustique's best-kept secret.

Its seclusion was one of the reasons that William and Kate chose to spend an evening there together. For close to an hour on 2 May 2006 they sat in the hilltop bar. Earlier that day their bodyguard had made a detailed reconnaissance of the location and had chosen the spot where William sipped his 'poison', a vodka and cranberry, and Kate enjoyed a piña colada flavoured with St Vincent's own special blend of rum. But what their evening lacked in spontaneity it made up for in romance. Their Scotland Yard personal protection officer kept a professional eye on them from a discreet distance so they were effectively alone, enjoying the same cherished privacy as any other young couple in love in one of the most romantic settings in the world.

Twenty or so well-heeled holidaymakers were enjoying the ambience on that same Tuesday evening. A ripple of recognition spread through the bar as the prince and his girlfriend were shown to their seats, but their fellow guests were simply too well bred to spoil their moment together.

One who was there commented, 'They were very nice and ordinary. They watched the sunset and had two drinks each.' They were anything but an ordinary couple of course, and however low-key their dress and their demeanour that evening, back home William and Kate's holiday plans were front-page news.

I broke the story of their 'secret love holiday' in the *Standard* on 28 April. William was due to fly to Mustique that morning – Kate was already there, waiting. Some days earlier, other newspapers had wrongly reported that they had planned to stay in Barbados at Sandy Lane, one of the Caribbean's most famous five-star hotels and a favourite among many A-list celebrities. The hotel has private villas where the couple, and the friends who joined them, could have enjoyed a degree of seclusion. But the speculation was wrong and Mustique, an island steeped in a history of royal romance and dipped in scandal, turned out to be a far more appealing prospect for the young pair.

Kate had travelled there two days ahead of her royal boyfriend. When boarding the flight to Barbados for the first stage of her journey she was, significantly, afforded the sort of VIP treatment at Heathrow usually reserved for royalty. She was, to all intents and purposes, a private individual boarding a commercial flight yet she was taken airside and ushered on with the sort of reverence usually bestowed upon members of the House of Windsor. From Barbados she made the short hop to Mustique by private jet.

Perhaps it was inevitable that with such a romantic destination, and such convoluted travel plans, gossip columnists speculated that this holiday was to be more than a chance for William and Kate to kick back in the sun. Some argued that this was where William would propose to Kate. It may have been wishful thinking, but on their evening at the Firefly nobody could have denied that the setting and the mood all conspired to create the perfect circumstances for William to drop to one knee and pop the question. The Firefly even advertises that it can arrange weddings for anyone who has been on the island for more than 24 hours. Perhaps William and Kate laughed as they imagined the reaction of their loved ones were they to send a 'Just Married' postcard back home. If the thought did cross their minds, or their lips, they shared it only with each other.

With the sun all but gone, William signed the bill and the suntanned lovers left their romantic moment behind and headed back to their residence, the Villa Hibiscus, and the rest of their party of friends. Set in the hillside, 80m (250ft) above sea level and overlooking the breathtaking white sands of Macaroni beach, the villa, like the Firefly, offers unspoilt views of the sea. It is owned by business tycoon John Robertson, founder of the Jigsaw fashion chain, who usually charges guests £8,000 a week to rent his holiday home. William had been given it for free, thanks to the intervention of Lotty 'B' Bunbury, one of the jet set's favourite designers, and her sister Lucy. Apparently, William had met the girls at a wedding and confessed to them how dearly he would love to holiday on the island with Kate but felt, despite his huge trust-fund wealth, that it was beyond his reach financially. He had not exactly gone cap in hand but the message permeated through. Villa Hibiscus was placed at the prince and his party's disposal and in return William offered to make a donation to a hospital on St Vincent.

It turned out to be an ideal holiday choice for William and Kate. Each day they made the short drive to the shoreline and idyllic beaches for games of volleyball on the sands. On one occasion, they took on a group of local islanders in a frisbee match. They visited Basil's Bar, the waterfront bistro on stilts that claims to be the world's best bar, and William joined two of his friends in a sterling performance of Elvis's 'Suspicious Minds'. It was an appropriate enough choice, given the colourful and scandalous family connections that the place holds for William. It was once a hangout of his exotic great-aunt, Princess Margaret, whose ties with the island stretched back to her marriage to Lord Snowdon in 1960. Her long-term friend Colin Tennant, the Scottish peer Lord Glenconner, gave the princess a wedding gift of a large plot of land on which was built her holiday villa, Les Jolie Eaux.

But it was Margaret's extramarital activities that really put the island on the gossip columnists' map. Early in 1976 her affair with baronet's son Roddy Llewellyn, when he was 28 and she 45, was exposed on a beach not far from the bar where William and Kate relaxed with their friends. Margaret and her younger lover were captured on film by New Zealand-born photographer Ross Waby, who worked for the New York bureau of News International, whose stable included the *News of the World*. Waby had cannily evaded the press ban imposed by Lord Glenconner, who then owned the island, by posing as a package tourist. He staked out the Beach Bar and managed to snatch a blurred picture of the princess sitting at a wooden table beside her long-haired bronzed lover, both wearing just swimming costumes. They were with two other friends, who were conveniently cropped out of the picture when it was published. It caused a sensation and a scandal that effectively ended the Queen's sister's stormy marriage to Lord Snowdon. On 19 March 1976, just a few weeks later, Margaret's separation from Snowdon was announced in a statement issued by Kensington Palace. Mustique was, therefore, the setting for the biggest royal scandal of the 1970s. There would, of course, be many more – but this incident provided the benchmark for the relationship between press and the royals from then on.

Three decades later there was no such scandal in the offing, but the prospect of a possible marriage proposal was enough to mobilise the paparazzi into action. The island teemed with snappers and, led by master paparazzo Jason Fraser, they soon tracked down the royal party to their villa. It was great news for the photographers, but not for William and Kate, who had settled on Mustique only after intense consultation over the best place to protect their privacy. William had apparently even taken legal advice from solicitor Gerrard Tyrrell, a leading specialist in media law and a partner in London law firm Harbottle and Lewis. He had acted for the couple before.

But no amount of Clarence House threats or legal posturing was going to deter the army of paparazzi when big money was at stake. In reality, the royal party emerged relatively unscathed. They were photographed, however, and the images of the royal lovers taken aboard a yacht were marketed by Jason Fraser for a reported £80,000. All the major titles coughed up, leaving Charles's media team powerless.

The pictures were an editor's dream. They showed the young prince and his beautiful, bikini-clad girlfriend tanned and relaxed on the deck of a sun-drenched yacht loaned to them by a billionaire. And they got even better. Not content simply to idle away the hours in the searing heat, William, wearing sky-blue swimming shorts, showed off his considerable physical prowess by literally going overboard as his lady looked on admiringly. Used to the physical challenges of military training, the prince swung on a pulley rope before plunging into the warm blue waters below. It was all so blissful and natural.

Less than a week later both bore the glow of their break in the sun when they arrived in the tiny Wiltshire village of Lacock for the wedding of William's stepsister, Laura Parker Bowles, to her boyfriend of eight years, Harry Lopes, grandson of the late Lord Astor of Hever. As the bells rang out over the village's church of St Cyriac, William and Kate seemed to have swapped one idyllic setting for another. On that sunny spring day all the disparate elements of their lives and families collided in the happiest of ways. Charles beamed with pride, the doting stepfather; Camilla looked radiant; her daughter was a vision of loveliness. Camilla's ex-husband, Andrew Parker Bowles, displayed nothing but joy and pride. The past may have held misery and betrayal but there was no rancour on the day. Here was a hotchpotch version of the Royal Family that seemed, at last, to have stumbled into some sort of happy equilibrium. And there at the heart of it was Kate.

Tanned and toned, she cut a chic and confident figure. She

appeared refined and elegant in a buttermilk knee-length dress coat, nipped in to the waist and flaring open to reveal a daring see-through lace dress beneath. On her head she wore a spray of ostrich feathers. Her earrings were simple pearls and she wore a ring on her right-hand middle finger. It was Laura Parker Bowles's day, of course, but the following morning's papers inevitably carried pictures of Kate. Even the most restrained of social commentators now seemed happy to assume that it was only a matter of time before petals of confetti rained down over William and Kate on their own wedding day. The *Sunday Telegraph*, a newspaper favoured by Clarence House officials and often used to convey their spin on royal stories, ran a front-page article under the headline: OUT OF THE SHADOWS: IT'S A CHURCH WEDDING AT LAST FOR KATE AND WILLIAM. It noted that Kate's appearance at William's side at a family wedding meant that she had taken a 'significant step forward' in her relationship with him. It was true. Without doubt, her presence on his arm at such a family event attended by the Prince of Wales, the Duchess of Cornwall and Harry showed that she was now completely accepted in royal circles. William could not expect his girlfriend to live her life in the shadows.

Later, the guests returned to Camilla's former country home of Raymill House. For many years William's father shuttled between here and nearby Highgrove, in the time when Charles's relationship with Camilla was treated as a shameful, albeit open, secret. Now their affair had been sanctioned by marriage and, on the day of Laura's wedding reception, Raymill's part in their tawdry history was forgotten. It provided instead the backdrop for a delightful afternoon of fine dining, toasts, dancing and laughter. The day was all about unions, and who would have been surprised if, as he watched Kate laugh and mingle and relax into the wedding reception, William's thoughts had turned to a wedding day of his own? But Kate and William would not be together that night. Duty called for William, and he broke away from the party, mounting his motorbike and speeding back along the country lanes to Sandhurst and to the rigours of officer training.

For the time being such enforced separations are an inevitable part of their lives but for how much longer will that be the case?

Bit by bit Kate has been elevated from friend, to girlfriend, to fiancée. Even then, there were many, including senior palace officials, who were convinced that it was only a matter of time before Kate's role in the life of the future King would be assured. Her days as William's 'princess-in-waiting' seemed to be drawing to a close and her time as his bride, future princess and, one day, queen surely about to begin. How right they were!

CHAPTER 15

MAKING THE GRADE

'A throne is only a bench covered in velvet.'
NAPOLEON BONAPARTE

I t was perhaps the most important date so far in the life of the
girl now very publicly acknowledged as William's princess-in-
waiting, a fact that Kate Middleton must surely have recognised.
The official business of the crisp clear day – 15 December 2005 –
dictated that it was William's proud hour, as he passed out at the
Royal Military Academy, Sandhurst. However, the future King
was not the only one seen to make the grade, for this was the first
time that Kate, then almost 25, would attend a public
engagement alongside the Queen and the rest of the senior
royals. The apparent significance of this 'joining the Firm' did not
pass unnoticed, and even the most hard-nosed of hacks allowed
themselves a moment of romantic indulgence: the *Daily Mail*, for
instance, in a rare moment of whimsy, observed that Kate's
scarlet coat echoed the sash worn by William that day. The
synchronicity of her wardrobe and the simple fact that she was
there on such a significant day in her royal lover's life was, it
asserted, 'the strongest sign yet that she and Prince William
could marry'.

Until that day, William's hugely protective attitude towards his
girlfriend had ensured that, given the intensity of the relationship,
they were seen out in public together comparatively rarely – save

for the occasional night out or trip to the polo. But that December day William extended his most public invitation to Kate; little wonder, then, that many people read so much into the move. She arrived with her parents, Michael and Carole, and the prince's private secretary, Jamie Lowther-Pinkerton, moments before the Windsor party. Although the Middletons did not sit next to the royal party – including the Duke of Edinburgh, Charles and Camilla – there was certain pomp to her arrival. All the other guests were already seated as Kate was ushered into her place in the front row accompanied by William's best friend, Thomas van Straubenzee, and two of his godfathers, King Constantine of Greece and Lord Romsey. Kate and, tellingly, her family were in lofty company indeed. In truth, the arrival of the glamorous, assured young woman dressed in vibrant red completely overshadowed the royals, even the Queen.

So too did her assessment of her boyfriend's appearance in his smart passing-out uniform, when she chatted with a friend after the ceremony. It seemed there was no limit to what the media – and not just the press – would do to get a story. Britain's ITV network hired lip-reading experts who discerned that Kate had apparently declared, 'I love the uniform, it's so sexy.' Whether this is what she really said, it showed that, like Diana before her, Kate was more than capable of stealing the show – even when all the Royal Family's star performers were out in force. It was something that not only members of the family but the palace courtiers noted with some trepidation.

That day, the 24-year-old William was among 233 cadets commissioned at the Royal Military Academy marked by the Sovereign's Parade. Like his younger brother, Harry, he was destined for a commission in the Household Cavalry's Blues and Royals regiment, where he would train to become a troop leader in charge of armoured reconnaissance vehicles. Unlike Harry, who was due to deploy to Iraq in 2007, William, as second in line to the throne, is barred from going to any front-line war zones. However sincere William's devotion to his military training, it is always destined to amount to a flirtation never consummated in warfare. Instead, he was expected to serve little more than a year in the army before moving on to the Royal Air Force and Royal Navy as part of his wider training as future head of the armed forces.

For all that, as he stood in the shrill winter sun that day, William looked every inch the soldier prince. Standing 6ft 3in tall, he was placed at the end of his platoon as an 'escort' to the banner, as well as acting as marker to ensure his colleagues marched in a straight line. Like his fellow cadets, he wore a smart blue uniform, cap and white gloves, but carried a rifle instead of a sword and wore a scarlet sash. He also wore the blue-and-white Jubilee medal given to him by his grandmother to mark her 50th anniversary on the throne. Reviewing the young soldiers lined up before her, the Queen paused briefly as she walked past her grandson and whispered a 'Hello' that left William beaming.

Significantly, Clarence House sources indicated that, after the parade ended, Kate and her parents joined the royal party for a family lunch for the first time. It was something Buckingham Palace later strenuously denied. Amid a row over snobbery by the royals towards the Middletons the Palace would seek to claim that the Queen had never actually met Kate's mother – a claim that dumbfounded many royal reporters, including this one. After all, at the time the Royal Family's spin machine was happy for the story of that convivial lunch to be written.

To mark his passing-out, Clarence House released photographs and footage of the prince taken on his last major exercise at Sandhurst. They also arranged for interviews with fellow cadets to be released to the press in which he was described as a 'normal guy'. Junior Under Officer Angela Laycock, 24, who was in William's Blenheim platoon, told how he fitted in with other cadets. She said, 'I've not really noticed anything different to be honest. The first loaded march, we had a bit of a detour to avoid some photographers. He's just a normal guy and gets stuck in like everybody else.' Describing how William joined in training with the other cadets, she added, 'On a riot-training exercise he was grabbing potatoes and lobbing them at the force protection people just like the rest of us.'

Of course, he is not a 'normal' guy at all, and at that moment his girlfriend was far from just a 'normal' girl. For the focus of the national newspapers was not on the royals, but on Kate. It seemed they had found their new princess. That night she and William partied at the traditional passing-out ball as Harry and Chelsy had done in such style earlier in the year at his own graduation from Sandhurst. As they sipped champagne and celebrated, there was nothing to suggest that this romance was any less perfect than it appeared. The *Daily Mail* best summed up the mood of the moment with its headline, ON WILLIAM'S BIG DAY KATE MAKES THE GRADE, TOO. The *Sunday Times* went further and a few weeks later published a piece on Kate entitled THE GIRL WHO WOULD BE QUEEN.

Perhaps it was inevitable, but as the outcome of the affair between William and Kate seemed such a certainty, his passing-out parade was also the day that focus began to shift from Kate and the Royal Family she seemed about to join to Kate and the family she was bringing with her. However uneasily the notion of class and breeding sits with modern sensibilities, it is fated never to pass without comment, especially where issues of Crown and State are concerned. And so the backlash of soft, deft blows began.

Carole Middleton, it was observed, was chewing gum as she watched her possible future son-in-law passing out. The veteran royal commentator James Whitaker, for one, suggested it was 'common'. Others pointed to the fact that Carole was trying not to smoke and therefore, as she was probably chewing nicotine gum, she should be praised rather than criticised for the lapse in social niceties. Others still viewed the whole discussion as ludicrous and peripheral. William and Kate were, after all, very much in love – weren't they?

Shortly before Christmas 2006, reports began to emerge that Kate had been invited to join William and his family at Sandringham, the Queen's Norfolk estate. It was claimed that she had refused on the grounds that she wanted to spend the festive season with her family and that she had no intention of spending it with the Royal Family until she was part of it. The story had always seemed unlikely. But it is true that the Middleton family did rent Jordanstone House, near Blairgowrie in Scotland, for the holiday. The cost was almost £5,000, but Carole Middleton believed it was worth every penny. Jordanstone House, a late-18th-century country residence with oak-panelled rooms, flagged floors and valuable antiques, puts many visitors in mind of a stately home. Perfect for a family Christmas to which Prince William had been invited. Kate was there, with her sister Pippa and brother James. It was hoped that William would join them for the New Year. And so they waited. And waited. William, it seemed, had no intention of spending Christmas or New Year with the family half the nation believed would soon become his in-laws.

It would be close to a month before Kate and William were reunited to wish each other 'Happy Christmas' in person. Behind the scenes, William was showing worrying signs of having inherited his father's penchant for prevarication. Around this time it transpired that the young prince was under pressure from his commanding officers to clarify the position with his live-in girlfriend. The *Mail on Sunday* trumpeted the story with GET ENGAGED OR COOL IT WITH KATE, AIDES TELL WILLIAM, ahead of the start of his military service proper, claiming that the prince had been counselled that it would be almost 'impossible for him to continue his relationship with Kate as it now stands'. Advisers raised the issue with William in the hope of gauging his intentions; perplexingly, they came away none the wiser.

Just a few weeks after her starring role at Sandhurst, the newspaper quoted senior sources as saying William felt he had to make a decision one way or the other. 'In frank discussions between the prince, his private secretary Jamie Lowther-Pinkerton and other key aides,' a source said, 'William has been presented with two "ideal" scenarios: he could announce an engagement in the New Year or cool his romance with Kate during his military service with the Household Cavalry at Bovington Camp, Dorset.' It was to prove prophetic and alarming stuff for Kate and apparently prompted a heart-to-heart between her and her mother. When William failed to show at the Middletons' family gathering in December, the chill thought must surely have seeped into Kate's heart that perhaps he was not as serious about her as she had once thought, or indeed as he had once so genuinely appeared. Perhaps he was having cold feet. Perhaps Kate's heart was about to be broken.

Carole Middleton is an astute, down-to-earth woman who realised she would have to have a long, hard talk with her beloved eldest daughter. Carole has the reputation of being nobody's fool. She is worldly-wise, having travelled widely during her career as a flight attendant. Therefore, when she saw what was unfolding, she made it clear to Kate that, if William did not want to commit, it was not wise for her to drift along in the relationship indefinitely. Carole has always had a special relationship with her daughter. Later, much would be made of Carole's 'social ambitions', with the suggestion that it was her fierce desire to climb the social ladder that guided her actions when it came to Kate. This is unfair. No mother likes to see her daughter taken for granted and not receiving the respect and consideration she deserves. Kate, after all, is an intelligent girl who had put her life on hold for the sake of William and her willingness to make their relationship work.

Kate's Monday-to-Thursday job as an accessories buyer for Jigsaw, the Kew-based high street store run by family friends John and Belle Robinson, was hardly a challenging role, and one that Kate had taken primarily for the freedom it afforded her to visit her boyfriend near his Dorset barracks. As 2006 turned to 2007, it must have been a difficult period of renegotiation between Kate and William as both nursed their own trepidations over just how significant their romance was and exactly where it was going. However, they had been down this rocky road before and always pulled back from the brink of actually breaking up. They still loved each other and, despite his reservations concerning commitment, William did not want to lose Kate. She was simply too precious to him. They had a shared history. They understood each other. He needed her.

At the beginning of the year, at least, these private reservations did not deter the media and everybody hoped for a successful conclusion. The speculation intensified and rumours of a possible imminent engagement led to increased paparazzi attention outside Kate's apartment. It reached fever pitch on the day of her 25th birthday on 9 January 2007, with more than 50 paparazzi and TV cameramen positioned at the door of her Chelsea flat as she walked to her car to leave for work that morning. It was a birthday surprise that alarmed Kate. She tried hard to accept with her trademark smile. The 'cult of Kate' had never been so visible or so palpable and for the first time she was elevated from 'girl next door' to commercial trendsetter. The £40 Topshop dress she wore that morning sold out within days, proving she had a following all her own. The scenes outside her flat prompted William, fearful that his girlfriend was being forced to endure the same media pressure experienced by his late mother, to express his concern at the 'harassment' of his girlfriend. He issued a statement saying he wanted 'more than anything' for her to be left alone. Her family had already employed law firm Harbottle and Lewis to urge the media, both in Britain and abroad, to use restraint. This time, however, there were not just a few freelancers on Kate's doorstep, but representatives of newspapers and those from respected agencies such as Associated Press and the Press Association. There were also at least five TV crews, including a team from ITN, which produces news bulletins for ITV and Channel 4. The BBC did not send a camera crew but used footage supplied by the agency APTN. Sky News also used footage in its bulletins. The palace sat up and took notice. Her lawyers were in close contact with the Press Complaints Commission and stopped short of making an official representation on her behalf. Sources said they hoped to use 'persuasion' rather than legal action to protect her. The similarities with the problems faced by William's mother were clear.

The ugly scenes on Kate's birthday prompted the late princess's aides to speak out in a chorus of disapproval and a call for action. My good friend, Inspector Ken Wharfe, the retired former bodyguard to Princess Diana, was in no doubt that the number of photographers pursuing Kate, coupled with the lack of any control, put her in danger of becoming the victim of a Diana-style tragedy. He said at the time, 'History appears to be repeating itself despite claims that lessons have been learned after the loss of Diana. As far as I can see, the warnings have not been heeded.' He said it was imperative for Prince Charles to employ former royal protection officers to guard Kate until she became engaged to

William and full-time official Scotland Yard security became available. After the split, he wrote to Carole offering to protect Kate until the furore died down. Patrick Jephson, Diana's former private secretary, echoed Wharfe's views: 'I think that any reasonable person would be horrified about the situation and what Miss Middleton has to endure. I think the attempts to use legal, regulatory, and informal methods to deal with the situation will help. Nothing is more effective than proper control on the ground. That is the lesson of the Diana experience, including her death. That level of control on the ground is the only method which will work effectively for Kate.'

Perhaps fearing a backlash, News International immediately announced that all its publications, including the *Sun*, *The Times* and the *News of the World*, would not use any paparazzi photographs of Kate in future. Executives at the corporation hoped this move would curry favour with senior Clarence House aides, too, and perhaps lead to their getting the tip-off about a future royal engagement. Unusually, Charles's office at Clarence House took the decision to comment on the move to back off Kate. An official spokesperson said, 'We are pleased that News International has agreed to stop using the paparazzi pictures. What Prince William wants more than anything is for the paparazzi to stop harassing her.' There was even speculation that Kate's situation was being manipulated in a test case involving harassment laws, in an attempt to protect her privacy and curtail the activities of photographers.

In the inevitable dissection of these events, many royal commentators rallied protectively round Kate. The issue of privacy and press intrusion became the focus of the House of Commons Culture, Media and Sport Select Committee for its investigation of media invasion of privacy on 6 March 2007, during which leading media figures were called to give evidence. One of those was veteran royal photographer Arthur Edwards, recently honoured with a lifetime achievement award by his peers. During the proceedings Edwards, whose astute reading of the nuances of the royal story in the previous 30 years is second to none, was met by somewhat condescending titters by committee members when he said William had told him he intended to marry Kate. As ever, he was right.

'She is a private citizen and she is in love with Prince William and I am sure that one day they will get married. I have talked to him about this. He has made it clear that he wants to get married and I believe what he says, and they should be left alone,' he said. He added that he had heard from Kate's friends about her distress at media intrusion and said photographers had followed her shopping and even climbed onto buses to photograph her. But by this time there was pandemonium. Moreover, as he tried to clarify his comments – saying the prince had said it would not happen until he was at least 28 years old – the political reporters had already left the room to file his comments to the news wires.

There was something missing in all this well-meaning attention and earnest endeavour to get it right, this time, in terms of coverage and acceptable levels of interest. I was not alone in thinking that, as she left her flat that morning, Kate seemed curiously isolated, miles from her barracks-bound boyfriend. Yes, William had swept in to make his statement and attempt to redress the balance, pull the press up short, and remind them that this girl was very special to him. But there were some who felt this 'chivalrous' gesture was rather too little too late. Might Kate have felt so too?

There are also those who believe Middleton is enigmatic at best, boring at worst. 'What are her interests?' asks a newspaper editor. 'All she seems to do is go to the gym and go to either Boujis or Mahiki [the current favourite nightclubs for wealthy twentysomethings in London]. She does not have a job. She does not go to the theatre. We don't really have any idea of who she really is, and what we do see is rather shallow.'

Then came another signal that perhaps Kate was positioning herself for a change in status. In May, it emerged that Kate had asked people to call her 'Catherine'. The press were quick to point out the obvious: 'Catherine' is a far more regal name than 'Kate'. A defensive Paddy Harverson, Prince Charles's communications secretary, strenuously denied all these reports. Nonetheless, *Sunday Express* columnist Adam Helliker, who wrote the

'Catherine' story, insisted he had heard about – but had not seen – a 'gentle' email sent by Kate to her friends, saying she was reverting to the name she had had until she was in her mid-teens. Helliker said, 'It was just a very jokey thing.' He defiantly stood by his story. Another, potentially more damaging, report emerged soon afterwards and claimed that Kate's lack of industry was causing the Queen some irritation. The report stated that the Queen wanted Kate to get a full-time job. In fact, she was quietly working, as her lawyer Gerrard Tyrrell confirmed, already: getting up each morning in Bucklebury, driving to the Party Pieces office in Reading and putting together the catalogues for her parents' company. She also took a technology course to learn how to make digital catalogues. Under the circumstances, it was probably about the only job Kate, as a princess-in-waiting, felt safe doing.

'She's been offered every job under the sun,' I was told. Everyone from Russian oligarchs to top fashion designers wanted her. But Kate was well aware that taking such positions could open her up to accusations of using her association with William for financial gain, an accusation that could come back to haunt her. Until William formalised their relationship, she was left in an awkward spot. She was not officially entitled to any royal benefits paid for by the taxpayers, such as security, yet she perhaps more than some of the minor royals was more exposed. She had no spokesperson and or official guidance on what to wear or how to conduct herself in royal circles. Yet, because of her boyfriend, she was already a celebrity, having to cope with the difficulties that fame brings. Her main lifeline was the media lawyer Gerrard Tyrrell, whose clients included British model Kate Moss and Roman Abramovich, owner of the Chelsea Football Club. Any time Kate felt harassed, as she claims she did on her 25th birthday, it was to Tyrrell that she turned. His response was often swift, sending letters to newspaper editors warning them that Kate was a 'private' citizen and as such had a right to privacy. One of Prince Charles's former aides said he was a very *laissez-faire* father' to his two sons. 'He likes Kate a lot, but she won't be getting any "training" or guidance as to how to behave.'

In March, around the time William started army training in

Dorset, the couple attended the Cheltenham Gold Cup races in traditional tweed suits. The press covered their attendance ironically, noting how much like Charles and Camilla – nicknamed 'Fred and Gladys' – the pair looked in their old-fashioned clothes. William was said not to be amused. A few days later Kate, looking far more youthful and modern in a warm coat and Russian-style fur hat, went to the races on her own. Lord Vestey, a friend of Prince Charles, was hosting a lunch for Charles, Camilla, Camilla's children, Tom and Laura, as well as Zac Goldsmith and Camilla's nephew Ben Elliot, among others. When the royal party heard Kate was there, she was invited to join them in the royal box. There was speculation, however, that William did not like just how comfortable Kate had become in the royal-family fold. It did not bode well.

He knew there was no chance, as future King, that he would get to see actual combat, unlike his younger Harry, who would serve in secret in Afghanistan in 2008. Nevertheless, William had to go through the motions. After all, he would be head of the armed services and he needed first-hand experience of the military. And so it was that, in January 2006, William followed his younger brother to Sandhurst for a year of army training, to be followed by five months' training at Bovington in Dorset, and then he would join the Household Cavalry regiment in Windsor.

During his time there, he undertook attachments for four months with the Royal Air Force and then two in the Royal Navy during 2008, though inevitably his training in each branch would be far less arduous than that required of ordinary soldiers, aviators, and sailors. It was announced in September that William would be postponing a life full of charity work to begin an 18-month training course in January with the RAF's Search and Rescue Force.

He was following a clear career path, but Kate was less sure of what the future held. She was interested in fashion and photography, but, as the prince's girlfriend, she needed to accommodate his schedule. Once he started at Sandhurst, the couple would meet either at Highgrove or at the Middletons' house in Bucklebury. Kate's parents also bought an apartment in Chelsea. Whenever the prince was in London, this became the place where he could completely chill with the woman who had been his stalwart and lover. They could pop to the local restaurant, put his head on her lap, and just relax. However, while her prince was away, life in London during the week was lonely and stressful for Kate, who began to be followed by paparazzi on shopping excursions and photographed on nights out. Again, she went to lawyer Gerrard Tyrrell. She had a hotline to him, should she need it.

Unlike Diana, Kate has almost never seemed to be rattled by the cameras. Photographer Niraj Tanna revealed, 'Even in the early hours of the morning, when William and her pals look a little worse for wear through drink or just tiredness as they leave their favourite nightclubs, Kate always looked immaculate.' She would never let herself go. She would drink cautiously and carefully touch up in the women's toilet before facing the cameras that would inevitably be waiting for her.

In July, her boss at Jigsaw, Belle Robinson, gave an interview about Kate, portraying her as down-to-earth, even though Kate had asked for a job with 'an element of flexibility to continue the relationship with a very high-profile man and a life she can't dictate', according to Robinson. Yet the older woman liked her part-time employee. 'She sat in the kitchen at lunchtime and chatted with everyone from the van drivers to the accounts girls,' Robinson told the London *Evening Standard*. 'She wasn't precious. Many people have distorted it to say we're friends with her parents, but I've only met them four times. I have to say I was so impressed by her. There were days when there were TV crews at the end of the drive. We would say, "Listen, do you want to go out the back way?" And she'd say, "To be honest, they're going to hound us until they've got the picture. So why don't I just go, get the picture done, and then they'll leave us alone." '

Throughout 2006, Kate and William tried to keep their heads down with regard the media. They were tracked down and photographed mostly on holiday, leaving nightclubs or on the polo field. Harry, too, was caught, having been out partying perhaps a little too often. These images increasingly began to leave a somewhat negative impression – the British media referred to the young princes as 'boys' or, even worse, as 'playboys'. It did not sit well. The future hopes of the British Royal Family were being openly mocked in lots of circles as just a pair of silly Sloane Rangers spending oodles of cash celebrating on chav cocktails. For young men purporting to be serious soldiers they appeared to spend an awful lot of time in nightclubs. Interestingly, of the tight-knit royal clique who hit the clubs with increasing frequency, perhaps the most aware of the bad impression they were creating was the media-astute Kate. On holiday in 2006, Prince William and Guy Pelly, an old friend in the group, often simplistically referred to as the 'court jester', were racing around on mopeds at the villa of Kate's uncle, Gary Goldsmith, on Ibiza. Kate came out of the house and, matron-like, told them to stop. Anyone, after all, could be watching. Like chided schoolchildren, they did what they were told. William may not have liked it, but he could not fault her judgement.

Kate's confidence in her role as the royal girlfriend steadily grew. She was more self-assured – buoyed by the confidence her mother instilled in her. She met the Queen, who liked her, as did Charles and Camilla. Harry, according to one friend, took longer to warm to her. Kate, with her demure outfits, fitted jackets over a dress, drop pearl earrings and self-control, was the complete opposite of Harry's blonde Zimbabwean girlfriend, the wealthy Chelsy Davy, who dresses in a far more provocative style. Chelsy never shied from photographers with a glass in one hand, a cigarette in the other. At times, she may have looked like an unmade bed, but she has raw, earthy sex appeal – something Kate lacks. The passionate attraction between Harry and Chelsy fizzled, but in public, at least the same could not be said of William and Kate.

CHAPTER 16

END OF THE AFFAIR

'Now it has been announced, they should be allowed to get on with their lives.'
PRIME MINISTER TONY BLAIR'S COMMENT AFTER
WILLIAM AND KATE'S SEPARATION

When he entered the Kensington nightclub Boujis without Kate on his arm, William was a beacon for the attentions of young women. He was used to being 'ambushed' by well-heeled socialites keen to rub shoulders, and anything else. In the past, the dashing prince had come to accept the flirtatious attentions of pretty teenagers as an occupational hazard. Urged by their pals to dress up and party in the prince's favourite nightclubs and, more to the point, in the prince's eye line, they fluttered around him on a regular basis. He, in turn, would brush them off with aplomb, without hurting their feelings but, crucially, at the same time not upsetting Kate. However, on this particular February evening William's demeanour was rather different. He was happy to play and his interest in one particular girl caused quite a stir and led to wild and inaccurate rumours that he had been seen passionately kissing a blonde.

The girl in question was pretty PR girl Tess Shepherd. When a newspaper reporter approached her at her flat in Fulham, west London, just a few days after the alleged incident, Shepherd proved understandably reticent. 'It was very flattering,' she reportedly said, 'but we were all dancing with him, there were three of us. He was twirling me around. It's not true that I kissed

223

him.' Shepherd, who was dating another man at the time, was embarrassed by the entire episode, which appeared to have been blown out of all proportion.

The claims may well have been exaggerated. By now Kate was accustomed to her boyfriend being a target of, often ruthless, female attention. She was not used to its being paraded in such a public and therefore, for her, humiliating fashion. It would require a steely self-confidence on Kate's part not to feel, at the very least, put out by William's apparent willingness to whoop it up like a single guy while still, to all intents and purpose, she was supposedly the love of his life. Those who know Kate best claim that she tends not to believe stories generated by the rumour mill, and it would seem a sensible strategy. On the surface at least Shepherd's so-called 'encounter' with the prince appeared to be one that Kate regarded with a pinch of salt as, a few days later, she headed off with William to the slopes of the exclusive ski resort of Zermatt for what was billed a romantic break. Would it be the place where William finally popped the question? Certainly, by February Kate had been half expecting a proposal. In public, at least, it appeared William only had eyes for Kate as he romanced her on the slopes.

They were photographed in a loving embrace, and openly hugged each other in public for more than a minute. The tender moment came as they left a mountain restaurant to ski back to the village of Zermatt. It was the fourth day of the couple's week-long holiday with pals on the slopes of the Matterhorn. A fellow diner at the Blatten café said, 'They were so happy together. It's obvious they have that special chemistry. There were at least 70 other people having lunch but William was happy to show her affection in public. Throughout lunch Kate gazed at William and had a permanent smile fixed across her face.' While members of their party such as Thomas van Straubenzee and Guy Pelly were out enjoying the nightlife, William appeared happy to stay in with Kate at their £5,000-a-week chalet. Perhaps it is no wonder that British bookmakers William Hill stopped taking bets on whether the couple would get engaged – saying it was a certainty – and predicted they would wed the next year.

All seemed well, but in private there were reports of heated rows, strained conversations and, perhaps less dramatic but infinitely more significant, a lengthy 'state of the union' heart-to-heart. Apparently, William's decision to bring his friends on the trip disappointed Kate, who felt she had seen very little of her boyfriend in recent weeks. What many saw as an idyllic romantic break was, instead, according to one of the couple's friends, the holiday that proved to be the straw that broke the camel's back. Frustrations and irritations came blisteringly to the surface: 'Things were not right in Zermatt. Kate had hardly seen William and really wanted to talk things through. The fact they were in a big group was a source of friction between them.' The source added, 'Kate is a very motherly person. She's caring and, while William was at Sandhurst, this side of her shone through. When she did see William, he was sometimes so exhausted he would fall asleep on her lap. He would drive to her house straight from exercises – often when he had been sleeping in ditches for days. He would turn up in full combats and often stinking from the training. Kate would have a mug of tea waiting for him and then he'd climb into a steaming hot bath.'

Nevertheless, what had once brought them together was now pulling them in different directions and they seemed to hunger for different things. At 25, half a year older than her boyfriend, Kate suddenly seemed startlingly more mature than William, who felt 'mothered' by her. As a result, all the fun had gone out of their relationship. Eventually the pair sat down to talk about their future. One friend said, 'No one knows exactly what was said between them, but William and Kate talked for hours about their future. It's fair to say each of them wanted different things. They're a lovely couple but they simply met five years too soon. William feels too young and doesn't want to give up the freedom that life in the army allows. Kate, meanwhile, is ready to take the next step. They were a normal couple who wanted different things. It's sad for them, but then it's sad for any young couple who break up after a number of years.'

The relationship limped on for several weeks afterwards, but the painful split had begun on that holiday. Deep down, whether they acknowledged or accepted it at the time, something between William and Kate closed. The week after they returned from Switzerland, they spent the day together at the Cheltenham racing festival. In addition, it was clear from their body language that not all was well. What had once been so easy and natural now appeared stilted. It was the last time the couple were pictured together in public. It was also to prove a source of irritation between the prince and Kate. When they arrived at the race meeting that day, William was dismayed to find a battery of media photographers and TV crews there because he had been assured he and Kate would be in a secure corporate area of the racecourse. 'It put him in a real huff,' said one of his circle of friends, 'and he told her that he didn't think she should go again.' On Gold Cup day, when he was back in Bovington Barracks, Dorset, on a tank commanders' course, she did go again, joining the royal box for lunch. Apparently, Princess Anne was not best pleased. William was also apparently both unsettled and irritated at Kate's decision to go alone and go against his specific advice. Then, it seems that he knew what she did not, that their relationship had all but run its course.

Ten days later, shortly after William joined an army training course at Camp Bovington, Dorset, the death knell was finally sounded on their relationship. On 25 March he went out on what would prove a fateful night out with fellow officers from the Household Cavalry. They went drinking in the Walkabout bar in the centre of Bournemouth, Dorset. His behaviour that night was not that of a man involved in a serious relationship destined to end in marriage. He looked to everyone who saw him like a single man on the prowl. An attractive student told a reporter, and therefore the world, how William took her back to his barracks after they had danced in a nightclub in front of astonished revellers. She told how William had betrayed Kate's trust. The prince, who was drinking pints of Stella Artois and shots of sambuca, apparently spotted blonde 19-year-old Lisa Agar in the Elements nightclub in Bournemouth on the Friday night. They gyrated hip to hip on the nightclub's podium, 'bumping and grinding', before the prince invited Agar to return to his barracks 20 miles away.

Agar, who sported a pierced lip, spoke later about William's drunken antics and her intimate evening with him in graphic detail – too graphic even for a prince to deny, and too detailed for a girlfriend not to believe, even if she wanted to. Lisa explained, 'He was very affectionate and touchy-feely. Moreover, he definitely was not a shy boy. Not once did he talk about Kate. It was as though she didn't exist. I spent almost the whole time at the club with him – we drank, we danced, we went back to his place.'

The sexy six-foot student Lisa was wearing black leggings and a pink figure-hugging top in the club. 'We stood next to each other at the bar and he was having shots of sambuca. His friend, who I was dancing with earlier, introduced us and he said, "Nice to meet you." He was warm and friendly. Not shy as I thought he would be. After he finished his drinks, Will walked on to the podium with four other blokes and started dancing there. Will downed four shots of sambuca and drank at least six pints of Stella. He was laughing the whole time – as drunken people do. I could see Will was watching me,' she said.

It was then that William apparently looked down and yelled out, 'Lisa, come up here and let's show them how it's done!' Agar said he then strolled over to her and pulled her onto the stage. 'It was a very small podium, only big enough for four people at a push, so we were very close,' she said. 'We were dancing directly opposite each other. I kept nearly falling off the podium, so he would gently hold my arm and steady me. It was sweet. We had enough of dancing on the podium, so jumped off, went to the bar for a few more drinks, and just danced on the floor. He was a really good dancer.' She claimed the normally egalitarian prince then looked at her and told her, 'You're too good to be in here.'

'I was very flattered,' she said. 'I thought he was joking, but maybe he wasn't.'

At the end of the night, when the club was closing at around 3 a.m., they all left together. 'Everyone was getting a bit tired and drunk,' Agar said. She walked with William and his party to the waiting royal protection cars, an Audi and a Land Rover. 'Will jumped into the front of the Audi and asked, "Lisa, what are you going to do? You must come back to the officers' mess with us!"

'We went back to the officers' mess at Bovington Camp and it was all very fancy and William had arranged for one of his friends to wait at the entrance and swipe us in from inside.'

After that night of heavy drinking, the stories of the partying prince began to emerge in the press. Worse was to follow. A compromising photograph was published showing William with his hand on the breast of another student, Ana Ferreira – but we should note it could just have been the angle that the picture was taken. Kate was understandably humiliated by the stories and in an emotional telephone conversation the two agreed to meet privately to thrash out their problems. On 31 March, they joined their friends Hugh and Rose van Cutsem for dinner in the Cotswolds. It was clear to both of them that their love affair was going nowhere.

On 3 April, Kate and her mother Carole flew to Dublin to see an art exhibition while again William had another boozy night out with his army friends. It was now only a matter of time before the truth was out. Within days the story was breaking and William and Kate would have the most difficult conversation of their young lives – one during which, one close to both claimed, a decisive William made no attempt to 'gild the lily'.

On 12 April, Kate attended a dinner party with her pals in London. One of her friends asked her outright how things were going with William. To their surprise, she responded coolly and unemotionally: 'It's finally over between us.' There was no remorse, no tears, just a matter-of-fact response. A well-placed source told me afterwards, 'She was cool and quite relaxed when she told everybody. They were all a little surprised by how unemotional she was. She almost seemed relieved it was over and it was out. Everyone is focusing on how William dumped her. The truth is it was not like that all. It was by mutual consent.'

Who could blame Kate if her sadness was mixed with a little relief? She, after all, had behaved with utter decorum and dignity throughout their relationship. Perhaps she relished the prospect of being able to let her hair down. That night, after the dinner party was over, the girls headed for Kitts nightclub on Sloane Square, a place that promised the hedonistic party spirit of the Caribbean with polished British service. Named after the island of St Kitts, it boasts an eclectic list of cocktails such as the Hans Sloane, mixing Caribbean rum and chocolate, and is exotically decorated with Poinciana flowers around the curved bar. Perhaps it reminded Kate of her Caribbean sojourns with her prince. If that was the case, she did not show it. While the country laboured under the illusion that William and Kate were still very much together, Kate enjoyed a lock-in with her pals until the early hours.

The *News of the World* was the first to wake up to the story of the split. As it was Wednesday the editor, Colin Myler, a Fleet Street veteran who had previously edited the *Daily Mirror* and *Sunday Mirror*, was in the unenviable position of not being able to publish until Sunday. All he could do was wait and hope no one else got to the story before he could publish. By the Friday, however, after Kate's confession to her friends, the rumour mill was working overtime. It was only a matter of time before the story broke.

William felt emotionally claustrophobic. Kate felt lonely and isolated in London. Something had to give. Within days, it did. On 14 April 2007, the story of the break-up was leaked to the *Sun*. Even before it was published there had been rumours that William had been enjoying nights on the dance floor in both London and Bournemouth, near his army barracks, with pretty blondes.

Kate's patience was at breaking point. Her friends rallied to her side, pointing the finger firmly at William, saying his immaturity was to blame. One confided, 'When they went on a skiing holiday in February, William insisted on taking the gang along. You had people like Thomas van Straubenzee and Guy Pelly there, all keen to do some hard partying. Kate could hardly get a word in. She had been hoping for a romantic break . . .'

The friend said there were blazing rows and William responded by asserting what he believed was his right to go on benders with his friends.

The story reached the newspapers and, within days, the love affair that had so enchanted the nation was at an end. On the other hand, was it? The parting prompted speculation that, in the final analysis, the Royal Family had decided Kate was too much of a commoner for their taste. William's friends reportedly made dreadful remarks about Kate's mother, Carole. The truth was simple. William felt the 'fun' had disappeared from their relationship. At 24, he felt pinned down, as if his future were being mapped out. He sat her down and told her it was over. 'He didn't gild the lily,' a close source said. It was, as far as he was concerned, all happening too fast.

William felt he was just too young to contemplate settling down to marriage. He was just doing what normal 24-year-old blokes do, and being 'nailed down' did not feature in his plans. It was characteristic of William, a man who may listen to advice but always did what *he* wanted in the end. Kate was 'devastated', as she had always believed they would marry. William's rash decision had come completely unexpectedly for her.

There was speculation that William himself felt that their different backgrounds could not be ultimately reconciled. There were cruel jokes about Kate's breeding. However, after further investigation, I am satisfied that this is false. It emerged that a showdown forced by Kate three weeks earlier triggered the decision to end it. After William's public partying with the blonde student at his barracks, Kate flipped. It was understandable. After all, despite the young woman in question describing him as the 'perfect gentleman', there was that photo of him with his arm around another young woman, an 18-year-old Brazilian student, amid the claims he had apparently cupped her breast in the photo. Kate had sought 'assurances' from her boyfriend personally. They were not, however, forthcoming. Was it a mistake to press him? Kate did not think so. However, it was certainly not an ultimatum, more a test, to see where she stood in the relationship. William responded saying he was not ready for marriage. It had clearly spiralled out of control.

William let his father know what was happening – and, as a matter of courtesy, the Queen and Prince Philip, too. Their advice was sensible and compassionate. All three made it clear that he should not feel pressured into getting married. Underpinning their wise counsel was the view that William should be straight with his girlfriend of four years, a young woman who was held in affection by his family. Their advice, echoed by that of his closest friends, prompted William to take decisive action.

His decision was set against a background of constant pressures, those caused by the long periods of separation related to his army career, those caused by living in the spotlight, having every move scrutinised, and, perhaps more pertinently, those caused by William's insistence on behaving, at times, as if he were a single man. Indeed, the catalyst for Kate's commitment showdown was William's boozy nightclub outing in Bournemouth with his army friends. Harmless enough in itself, in Kate's eyes it somehow typified his cavalier attitude to their relationship. She had long learned to ignore the prince's wandering eye and the attention he received from adoring females. Nevertheless, cumulatively, it was beginning to take its toll.

News of the separation appeared to take the nation by surprise, although, as friends of the pair observed, there had been a number of clues. In particular, they pointed to the decision to spend Christmas apart and William's failure to turn up at a Middleton family house party over New Year. It left those in the couple's circle of friends, and indeed many beyond it, pondering one question: would William come to regret his decision? William had a reputation for stubbornness.

It was at around the same age that his father let a young Camilla Shand slip through his fingers because he was equally indecisive and perhaps enjoying bachelorhood too much. The comparisons that followed were inevitable. In the immediate aftermath of the split, Kate sought refuge at the place that had always been her sanctuary: her family home in Berkshire. She emerged only once, disappearing in a Land Rover Discovery with her parents. Wearing dark jeans and check shirt, she hid her eyes with dark glasses. She had obviously been crying and did not want to show it. William stayed away from the media spotlight with his regiment in Dorset.

Officially, Clarence House said nothing. They would not comment on William's private life. The media guidance offered from senior aides was that the decision to split was mutual and amicable. Within hours, the story changed. Suddenly, there were reports that courtiers and other unnamed friends of William's had swayed him with snobbish views about Middleton's background, in particular her mother's early career as a flight attendant. The Queen reportedly frowned on Carole Middleton's middle-class manner of speaking. For example, she reportedly says 'pardon' instead of 'what' and 'toilet' instead of 'loo'. No sooner had the media reported the story than the inevitable backlash started, fuelled when official spokesperson Paddy Harverson told those who bothered to ask that the reports about snobbery were not true.

It was very hard not to sympathise with Kate and her family as the weeks of commentary about their role in a possible class war escalated – until, that is, Kate seemed to take matters into her own hands and turned all the press attention to her advantage. Quite suddenly in May, looking thinner and dressing younger, she was photographed frequently going out, mostly with her sister, Pippa, a dark-haired beauty who had just split up with banking heir J. J. Jardine Paterson. As they entered the Mayfair jewellers Asprey one evening to celebrate the launch of *Young Stalin*, a book by brilliant historian Simon Sebag Montefiore, the atmosphere turned electric. Photographers went berserk, clicking madly. Both young women looked stunning, but Kate particularly so in an ivory sheath that set off her tanned, glowing skin and streamlined figure.

Suddenly it seemed the so-called 'scissor sisters' were everywhere, turning up a host of society gatherings and very much in the public spotlight. William, back in his army barracks in Bovington, alone and no doubt teased about the headlines by fellow officers. Unsurprisingly, he began to realise his mistake. She was a beautiful eligible, single woman who would not be short of offers to escort her to the various hotspots of London. He wanted her back. After all, whom else did he know as well? Whom else could he trust? Who else wanted to take on the role of royal consort? Who else loved him for himself, not for who he was?

Kate's decision to go partying a couple of days earlier had gone unnoticed in the press. However, William's behaviour would not. The Prince headed for the Polynesian-themed London club, Mahiki, owned by Piers Adam and Nick House, at 11.30 p.m. on Friday, the eve of the story's breaking in the press. He went to a private table, where he met up with an eight-strong group including his friend Guy Pelly. As Fleet Street's night news desks became aware of the story, William was drinking heavily and dancing through the night. Apparently oblivious or just careless of any adverse publicity he might receive, at one point William reportedly shouted out, 'Let's drink the menu!' and proceeded to do just that. Going through the cocktail menu is known as doing the Mahiki Trail and is based on a map. If guests finish 18 of the powerful concoctions, costing from £9 to £50, they get the club's infamous Treasure Chest – a £100 cocktail free.

On top of this heady mix, Wills and his friends also managed to drink six magnums of 1998 Dom Perignon champagne at £450 per bottle. It was his first night out since splitting from Kate and he apparently told one friend, 'I'm really happy. Everything is fine. I am going to enjoy myself.' In case there was any doubt about his feelings, it was reported that he went on to yell, 'I'm free!' before performing his version of the unusually tall Liverpool and England footballer Peter Crouch's famous robotic-dance goal celebration. It was an over-the-top display that made the prince seem in danger of being judged harshly as crass and unfeeling. If, after all, it were really so easy for him to be without Kate, why on earth had he continued the relationship for so long, encouraging thoughts of engagement, marriage and family? In the cold light of morning, the once seemingly modern prince seemed a very old-fashioned cad.

Certainly, it left an unfortunate impression of a feckless prince, quite different from the reality of the young man who had had sober conversations with his grandmother and father only days earlier. For, shortly before the Queen left Windsor Castle to stay with the Earl of Carnarvon for two days at Highclere Castle, Berkshire, Prince William telephoned his grandmother at Windsor and told her that he and Kate were splitting up. The Queen was apparently surprised and a little upset. 'The Queen felt for them both and is sad because she knows there was bound to be some hurt,' a senior courtier revealed.

Following this, Kate and her parents must have looked back on the officers' passing-out parade at Sandhurst four months before and asked why they had been invited. After all, there was no question that the Sovereign's Parade was a family day. Moreover, on 15 December 2006, when William graduated as a young subaltern, his family had been out in force. It was no wonder that as far as the bookmakers were concerned all bets on the likelihood of a future engagement were off.

The fact is that on that passing-out day at Sandhurst, when the Middletons gazed on with heart-stopping expectations of their daughter becoming Queen, William was already having doubts. He did not let on to Kate about this, however. In fact, William had been vacillating about Kate for months, particularly since completing his Sandhurst training had led to his discovering a completely new social life among fully fledged army officers where fun young women seemed to circulate.

Royal biographer Christopher Wilson described it at the time as a 'historic act of folly and supreme egotism on the part of the prince.' The historian Andrew Roberts said the Royal Family had missed a great opportunity in letting Kate slip through their fingers.

It is fair to say that Kate's only mistake, like Diana before her, was to expect too much of her man. William was increasingly surrounded by yes men, sycophants who seemed bent on indulging his every whim. And, in the fallout of the break-up, it emerged that among William's friends it was deemed endlessly amusing to mock Kate's mother's past career as an cabin crew – shouting 'doors to manual' at Kate's approach and asking when the trolley service would be coming through. Even if this is untrue, it is an image that did the prince few favours it made him look like the kingpin of a set peopled by crashing snobs who snigger like schoolchildren at those they deem not the 'right sort.' William, perhaps unfairly, risked being tarred with the same brush, while some feared his decision augured badly for his future and that of the monarchy. In Kate Middleton, undoubtedly he had found one of the most grounded young women to set foot in a royal court. He seemed to have found such promised happiness, and the monarchy stood to gain a vital infusion of new blood and fresh, more modern thinking.

The break-up of William and Kate was given global media

attention. Of course, it was sad but both knew the pain would pass with time. There is no doubt from the courtiers I spoke to that many believed Kate was well received. But the talk of her family not being grand enough and too middle-class did more damage to the reputation of William and the Royal Family than that of Kate and her family. The Queen's aides were determined to dismiss claims of snobbery about Kate's mother in particular in the wake of the split. 'I can assure you Her Majesty had never even met Mrs Middleton and certainly had not made any such derogatory remark,' one senior adviser told me.

The damage was already done. Talk of the Queen and her aides disapproving of Carole Middleton on class grounds was damaging stuff. Whether reports that the royals and the household were upset that Carole did not introduce herself properly or used the wrong vocabulary were true or the work of mischief makers did not matter, they remain in the public consciousness. Meanwhile, Kate got on with the business of moving on and dusting herself down. Whether she felt like it or not, she presented the sort of positive face to the world that underlined what the vast majority of the public had already concluded: when it came to sheer dignity, Kate's innate class more than made up for any shortage of points on the *Burke's Peerage* scale. She smiled through her pain. She posed for the paparazzi when she was photographed buying a tennis racket before being driven away by brother James. In a few days, she was back to her best, embracing her single life without a prince.

In a figure-hugging minidress and a smile to match her mood, Kate emerged from Mahiki at 2.30 a.m. on the Friday after the split, looking fabulous. Her broad smile signalled she was back to her best. The headline in the *Standard* the next day mirrored the picture. WHO NEEDS WILLIAM? the splash headline screamed, sending out a clear message to her ex-boyfriend. Clearly, from the look on her face, she did not. 'She was dancing in the middle of a group of about five guys, who all seemed a lot more drunk than her,' said one partygoer. Alex Shirley-Smith told how he caught Kate's eye: 'The James Brown song "Sex Machine" came on and she flicked her hair and looked over her shoulder at me. The next thing I knew she had twirled backwards towards me so her back was up against me. She started doing some very sexy moves and she was gorgeous. She was a great dancer. I thought she looked the bee's knees but I didn't know who she was, so I asked her name and she said, "Kate." She had fantastic legs and, when my friend told me who she was, I thought she looked much prettier and thinner than she does in the papers. Then she was snatched away by a really drunk guy who I think was one of her friends.'

A few days later in the same club, to mark Prince Harry's scheduled departure with his regiment to Iraq, William arrived alone at 11.30 p.m. ready to party. Harry had invited Kate, but at the last minute she decided not to show. It was just as well, for William did not seem too worried by the prospect of seeing his brother disappear, and celebrated his newfound single status by partying until 3.30 a.m. – running up a £5,000 drinks bill in the process. According to one partygoer at the Mahiki club, William 'was clearly on a mission to get as drunk as possible' with his friends, including Sir Richard Branson's daughter, Holly. 'It was a case of complete role reversal,' said another partygoer. 'Harry was on his very best behaviour. He and Chelsy were not really drinking. It was quite clear Harry had other things on his mind. But William didn't care at all about getting drunk.' He even ended the evening passionately kissing a mystery blonde.

Perhaps this is the shape of things to come. The Windsors are historically a lusty lot and it was predicted that it would not take much effort for the prince to catch up on the past five years and sow his wild oats. What impact would that have on the institution he was born to serve? Lurid headlines about another playboy prince would not be welcome at the palace. Commentators speculated that William would now select a new posse of aristocratic girls with double- and triple-barrelled names, or models who would throw themselves at him. They may have looked good through the booze-fuelled nightclub haze or in magazines and newspapers, but I for one doubted that William would be able to form the same sort of relationship with them as he enjoyed with Kate.

In the immediate aftermath of the split, there was one woman whose lofty name and frame were linked romantically with the William – a woman whose attentions Kate apparently simply could not bear in the past. However, the actor, aristocrat, socialite and flawless beauty Isabella Anstruther-Gough-Calthorpe, who was dating tycoon Sir Richard Branson's son Sam, has always dismissed claims of any romance with William. This did not stop the rumours circulating. It is true that she struck up a close friendship with William. Their friendship was first seen in public in 2005, when they were spotted deep in conversation at a black-tie ball. It reportedly infuriated Kate so much that she stormed out of the ball. Isabella, the daughter of banking heir Lady Mary Gaye Curzon, and heir to a fortune in her own right, is one of the few women to have rejected his advances. It was something he probably realised he would have to get used to, as, having seen what Kate had had to endure, some may have begun to see him as not such a great catch, heir to the throne or not. Two of William's ex-girlfriends remained close to him throughout his relationship with Kate: Jecca Craig and Arabella Musgrave. William was linked to Holly Branson, Richard Branson's beautiful blonde daughter, who had been friendly with Kate, too.

It would have been foolhardy for the prince, so desperate for freedom, to charge headlong into another long-term relationship. He, after all, knew better than anyone that the consequences of such a decision could be dire. Being William's permanent girlfriend was not just about being pretty and posh. To stand a chance of one day becoming Queen at his side, any future girlfriend would need attributes that were rare enough for anyone. That was not on his mind, though. He had loved and lost the greatest love of his life. If Kate had been guilty of anything, or so it seemed, it was being the right girl at the wrong time.

CHAPTER 17

BACK FOR GOOD

'Prince William and Prince Harry, you have put on one heck
of a show. Congratulations. If you ever get tired of running this
country, you can come and work for me producing TV shows.'
MUSIC MOGUL SIMON COWELL, ON WILLIAM AND HARRY'S
WEMBLEY CONCERT IN MEMORY OF THEIR MOTHER

Kate sat alongside her sister Pippa in the Royal Box two rows behind William. He took a place on the front row next to his brother Prince Harry and his long-time pal Thomas van Straubenzee. Officially, Kate and William were still apart but there was a buzz in the press box at the new Wembley Stadium that she was there for the charity fundraiser concert arranged by William and Harry to honour their mother Princess Diana. Therefore, when pop group Take That's songwriter Gary Barlow started singing his hit song 'Back for Good', when William and his former lover swayed along to the melody, when Kate was picked up on the TV monitor singing the words, the journalists had their intros.

Clarence House officials went out of their way to play down talk of reconciliation and the significance of Kate's invitation to the event. 'Look, they're friends. We said at the time of the split that it was amicable and they'd remain good friends,' one said to me. I was not convinced and my instincts were correct. After all, earlier that day, 1 July 2007, the tenth anniversary of Diana's death, I had received a tip-off that on the eve of the concert Kate had spent the night with William at his apartment in Clarence House. It was confirmed when her car was spotted arriving at his place and being waved through by the police guard at 1.45 a.m., reinforcing reports that the romance was definitely back on for good.

Rumours to that effect had been circulating for weeks. In fact, some wrongly suggested that the split had just been a rouse to calm down the media interest in Kate. It was true that a few weeks earlier, on 9 June, William had invited Kate to a decadent 'Freaky-Naughty'-themed party at his army barracks. Kate wore a nurse's uniform. He could not take his eyes off her. They were seen kissing on the dance floor at around midnight. Afterwards, eyewitnesses said they sloped off to his private quarters at his barracks at Bovington, Dorset. However, it was still early days – the first tentative steps towards reconciliation. They were both still emotionally raw from the split and did not want to expose themselves to more pain. If they were going to get back together, they first wanted to be sure, as they knew the press interest would be relentless. Kate undoubtedly enjoyed his company, but she made it clear that she would not become involved with William again unless he made a firm commitment to a future together. Even then, she was unsure whether it is what she wanted.

At Wembley in public, Kate and William kept their distance. After all, William was there to 'work'. He appeared relaxed, and all his pre-concert nerves vanished when he and brother Harry took to the stage. The duo had no trouble getting into the groove once it kicked off – at one point joining in a Mexican wave and showing off their dance moves. As they stepped onto the stage in front of the 63,000-strong crowd to open the musical extravaganza, they received a standing ovation that Harry responded to with a typical rock-star greeting, calling out 'Hello, Wembley!' The princes had previously said the event, which coincided with what should have been their mother's 46th birthday, had to be the best birthday present their mother ever had. Moreover, there was no doubting they achieved their aim. 'This event is about all that our mother loved in life, her music, her dancing, her charities and her family and friends,' said William. Elton John opened the six-hour-long evening with 'Your Song', taking to the piano in front of a huge image of Diana by famed photographer Mario Testino. There followed Rod Stewart,

Status Quo, Nelly Furtado and P Diddy – who reprised his hit track 'I'll Be Missing You' in honour of the princess.

It was a night to remember. There were words of praise from music mogul Simon Cowell who said, 'Prince William and Prince Harry, you have put on one heck of a show. Congratulations. If you ever get tired of running this country, you can come and work for me producing TV shows.' However, behind the scenes it was a significant night in the Kate-and-William story. Bookmaker William Hill said it had turned away punters looking to place bets on Prince William and Kate Middleton getting back together. 'The fact that Kate and William were not sitting next to each other has not fooled anyone. We are confident that they are back together and it's now a question of wedding bells or not,' said a spokesperson. The bookmaker announced that it was prepared to offer 5–1 that the couple would announce their engagement before the end of 2008 and 12–1 about a 2007 announcement.

William and Kate had not been seen in public together since their split in April. They may have still been working things through slowly but now the cat was out of the bag. After the Diana concert, the couple danced the night away at the after-show party; when they weren't dancing, they were locked in intimate conversation at a private candlelit table. Then both jumped to their feet and hit the dance floor when the Bodyrockers hit 'I Like The Way You Move' came on. They went wild, as it used to be their song. Kate danced provocatively in front of William. The chemistry was just oozing off them.

It may not have been a conscious bid to win back her prince. Nevertheless, Kate had undoubtedly played her hand brilliantly. She knew that by giving him time and space she could probably get him back, and she did so by being very clever, stepping out at his favourite clubs, looking glamorous and fabulous, and making him realise what he was missing. In reality, the 'split' lasted only a few weeks. I discovered that their reunion was sealed when they were invited to Upton Viva, the 17th-century mansion and home of Sam Waley-Cohen, son of racehorse breeder and trainer Robert Waley-Cohen, a favourite of the Royal Family. At that time the couple were officially apart, but that night changed everything. Sam and his brother Marcus, who had their own wing at Upton Viva and often entertained there, gave the party. Marcus, then 30, is an Old Etonian who co-founded a successful health-drinks company, Firefly. His Wake Up drink was promoted as a herbal cure for hangovers, not least by Prince Harry; he was photographed swigging it from the bottle before a polo match. Sam, 25, a talented jockey and member of William and Harry's inner circle, played host. Nobody was surprised to see William at the party. Some, however, were taken aback when they arrived and Kate was there.

She too was a friend of Sam and his great chum Holly Branson, daughter of Virgin tycoon Richard Branson. The word among this set during most of the summer was that, although Kate and William had been seen together, they were no longer an item. Indeed, it was not clear to guests at the party, at the beginning of August, whether they had arrived together or just met up by chance. However, it soon became apparent as the evening at Upton Viva gathered pace, that they were very much together again.

'The body language said it all,' a guest confided. 'You got the impression that if we had not been there they would have been all over each other. You could practically hear the chemistry fizzing.' At one point, the couple sat together on a sofa, deep in conversation. According to a well-placed source it was at Upton Viva that William and Kate decided to take a holiday together to see if they could, after all, make their relationship last. It transpired that the holiday, two weeks later, was to become a turning point. They returned to London with a new understanding. They made an agreement that could underpin their future together.

Both knew they had to find a way to manage two serious threats to their happiness: William's predilection for lads' nights out with his friends, and the paparazzi. So when they decided on a holiday, the priority was to find somewhere they could be alone, without their usual posse of friends and beyond the reach of photographers. When money is no object, it was not that hard to do.

William decided on Desroches in the Seychelles to woo back the woman he loved, a private island resort where the local police and military made sure they were not disturbed. This meant setting up an exclusion zone, patrolled by the Seychelles navy. It proved highly effective. At one point three ambitious photographers, including one linked to a British tabloid, were detained as they piloted a small boat towards a beach where William and Kate were sunbathing. The Seychelles holiday was significant because it opened the way for a new phase in the couple's life together.

The story that they were an item again was, of course, out, no matter how secretively they tried to conduct their relationship and no matter how hard spin doctor Paddy Harverson tried to keep a lid on it. In November, Kate apologised to Jigsaw boss Belle Robinson and said she needed to leave her job there. She needed some space. The couple sneaked away on holidays when they could. On one occasion, Prince Charles was photographed teaching Kate how to shoot; unlike Diana, Kate seemed to enjoy outdoor life.

She was seated prominently when William graduated in April 2008 from RAF Cranwell, just as she would be at the Garter ceremony in June – and at the weddings of Peter Phillips and, later, Lady Rose Windsor. Her fashion sense had changed: she had taken the advice of fashion consultant Leesa Whisker and was often seen in the label Issa; the clothes were more sophisticated than the high-street chain-store outfits she used to wear, but not as expensive as couture labels. Increasingly, she was looking more effortlessly regal. In September, Clarence House reorganised public-relations staffing so that Princes William and Harry would have their own press secretary, the diligent former Ministry of Defence high flyer Miguel Head. Some saw his appointment as 'confirmation' that the relationship was about to go to the next stage; why else would William need a full-time press secretary?

One of Head's first duties was to reveal William's new career plans. The prince would begin his training in January, with a view to joining RAF Search and Rescue. It was quite a shock to many royal observers. It meant he would have to spend eighteen months in training, and it was wrongly reported that this would be followed by a compulsory seven years of service. Miguel Head quickly corrected this: 'That is nonsense. Most officers spend around 30 to 36 months in the Search and Rescue division once they have completed their training,' he said.

Quick to write the couple off, some feared that this might spell the end for William and Kate's relationship, but in truth it was precisely what both of them needed. One thing was clear: William's decision to spend five years as a full-time RAF search-and-rescue helicopter pilot meant that he and Kate were in no rush to marry. This was not to say, friends cautioned me, that he did not 'love' her. They all thought he absolutely did. The question was simply: was William's chronic fear of being locked too soon into the straitjacket of royal ribbon cutting so great that he was prepared to risk the relationship to avoid it? His decision – and according to aides, it was his decision alone – would inevitably mean lengthy periods of weeks and even months when he and Kate would be hundreds of miles apart.

His decision did not seem to faze Kate. Her response – as the economy shook in the country in September 2008 – was to be pictured in disco sequins and tiny shorts and capering about in roller skates, laughingly falling over with her long legs stretched out on the dance floor at a charity fundraiser. Her efforts were not in vain. Hundreds of people turned out to the event in Vauxhall, London, to help raise £100,000 for a new surgical ward at Oxford Children's Hospital, set up in memory of Thomas Waley-Cohen, who had died from bone cancer in 2004 when he was just 20. She had gone to school with Waley-Cohen, who also became friendly with William and Harry.

Was there a hidden reason for such a public appearance? Whatever the reasons, her message was clear: ignore me at your peril. Whether she was wise to disport herself in this inelegant manner is another matter. The Queen, reportedly, was unsure of such publicity-seeking behaviour. Apparently, Buckingham Palace courtiers were 'appalled' at what they saw as a 'most unladylike display' at the roller-skate charity evening. Never have the pitfalls of being a royal girlfriend been more cruelly exposed. 'What do they want her to do – sit at home every evening watching television just because her prince is away?' complained one of her oldest chums. 'Kate's in an impossible position. She hates that awful phrase "Waity Katy" and it makes her mother quite upset. It's why she's asked all her friends to call her "Catherine".'

Cynics started suggested that William's decision, at the age of 26, to become a regular in the RAF, which would take him away for long periods, was, at the very least, convenient in terms of his relationship with Kate. In addition, something of a peacock, he was said to be 'in love' with the RAF dress uniform. His decision provided her with the perfect opportunity to walk away – if she wanted. Of course, it would test their relationship; but it had survived previous separations, so why not this? Without any defined role or any proper guidance from Clarence House of what was expected of her while William was away, Kate was left to make her own decisions about how best to fill her days. Her new job at the time was helping compile and edit catalogues for her parents' Party Pieces business. Kate's uncertainty concerning her position even spread to the Royal Protection Squad. Her lack of official status meant they could not look after her when she was not with William, because she remained simply his girlfriend, and feared they would 'cop it' if anything untoward were to happen to her.

By 2008, officers did watch over her when she was with William, though. For example, when she and William flew to Salzburg in Austria in September for the wedding of the sister of a friend from their St Andrews University days, an experienced officer was assigned specifically to protect her. When they got home, however, she was alone again as William returned to his military duties, and the protection officer disappeared.

Earlier in 2008 – in April – William had dropped a huge PR clanger when he landed a £10 million RAF helicopter in Kate's back garden to impress her with his pilot skills. Her parents Michael and Carole watched from their million-pound home as the prince practised a series of landings and take-offs. His macho display backfired when the *News of the World* got wind of his jaunt. News of the two-hour £30,000 flight sparked furious criticism, especially as it came days after it was revealed that he had flown himself and Harry to cousin Peter Phillips's stag do on the Isle of Wight in another Chinook – with an RAF pilot on board to fly it back. At a time when the armed forces were desperately short of money and there was a lack of kit in Afghanistan and Iraq, it was rightly seen as a total waste of taxpayers' money.

Aviation analyst and RAF-trained pilot Jon Lake slammed the flight as 'ridiculous and inappropriate'. He said, 'This is an absolute waste of training hours on the Chinook helicopter that the military are hard-pressed to afford. No other pilot at Prince William's stage of training would be allowed anywhere near the left-hand seat of a Chinook. It's like a learner driver being given the keys to a Formula One car just because his father owns the racing team.'

Politicians waded in, too. Nick Harvey, Lib Dem defence spokesman, said, 'The prince will look back on this and realise it was a PR own goal. It's going to leave a lot of people wondering where the sense of priority lies if very serious helicopters are being made available for this sort of thing at a time when they are in such extreme need.' Moreover, Matthew Elliot, boss of the Taxpayers Alliance, said, 'When the military can't afford kit for our boys serving abroad and those at home have to put up with awful housing conditions the money could definitely have been put to better use.'

William had flown out of RAF Odiham, Hants, first travelling 16 miles to Kate's house under the instruction of his tutors. William came up with the idea himself, claiming a shortage of landing spots in Hampshire. He asked permission from Kate's family and flew one circuit of the field before landing and then heading back to Odiham for further tuition.

The RAF had no choice but to defend the 'legitimate' decision for the 250-mile flight, claiming that the necessity of flying over London and across water completed William's training. William made matters worse when it emerged that he had even had the cheek to give brother Harry a lift, picking him up at Woolwich barracks in southeast London. The Ministry of Defence spokesperson defended the decision for the Chinook to land in the Middletons' field. 'Battlefield helicopter crews routinely practise landing in fields and confined spaces away from their airfields as a vital part of their training for operations. These highly honed skills are used daily in conflict zones such as Iraq and Afghanistan.

The sortie on April 3 was fully authorised and planned and was an agreed part of Prince William's attachment to the RAF,' he said. It didn't wash with the public or the press.

A month later, it was Kate's turn to come in for criticism. She was forced to pull out of her cross-Channel rowing team known as the Sisterhood – after the Queen and William intervened. The message was blunt. The fuss surrounding her early-morning training sessions on Thames had got of hand. She also faced pressure from lawyers who feared that posed magazine pictures of her with the rest of the 21-woman Sisterhood crew could prompt charges of hypocrisy over complaints about paparazzi intrusion. The Sisterhood went on to pose for a raunchy calendar, raising more than £100,000 for charity posing as different athletes in the 12 pictures, with their sporting costumes painted directly onto their naked bodies. Perhaps, on reflection Kate's decision was a wise one.

In April Kate joined Prince William as his father presented him with his RAF pilot's wings. She was accompanied by Princess Diana's sister, Lady Sarah McCorquodale, at the ceremony at RAF Cranwell, a sign of Kate's growing closeness and confidence among William's family. It was the first time she had appeared at an official engagement with William since the Wembley Concert for Diana. Charles made the presentation to his son and 25 other graduates at the Lincolnshire air base in his role as Air Chief Marshal. Kate had not been expected at the ceremony, also attended by Camilla, due to fears over media speculation. The key moment came as she left with William. She wore white as the two posed happily together. The smiling shot – taken by my friend, the award-winning photographer Michael Dunlea – was reminiscent of past royal 'engagement' portraits of the Queen and Prince Philip. Again, it fuelled speculation that a marriage announcement would follow. The headline in the *Standard* said it all: KATE IN WHITE. Perhaps next time it would be for real.

In fact, William did walk Kate down the aisle the same year, on 6 September. Again, it was not their wedding but that of a friend. What was significant, however, was the strength of the security afforded to her. He asked that his father's bodyguard, SAS-trained

Dominic Ryan, be Kate's for the day. The couple happily posed for photos at the friend's big day in Austria - the first wedding they had attended as a couple for nearly three years.

William's girlfriend had attended two royal weddings alone in the same you - that of her boyfriend's cousin Peter Phillips and Autumn Kelly and that of Lady Rose Windsor, daughter of the Queen's cousin the Duke of Gloucester. On both occasions, she had represented William and mingled freely with his close relatives.

CHAPTER 18

MR AND MRS SMITH

'You'll be next.'
ARMY CAPTAIN NICHOLAS VAN CUTSEM
TO HIS FRIEND PRINCE WILLIAM AT THE FORMER'S
WEDDING IN AUGUST 2009

They emerged arm in arm from a country pub, the Potting Shed in the village of Crudwell, Wiltshire, on Saturday night. As they stood in the car park, Kate pulled her man close. What followed – their first public kiss for more than two years – surprised even him. The reason for the couple's uncharacteristic openness, as a photographer recorded the moment for posterity, was soon apparent. She knew what was coming hours before the story appeared. The *News of the World* had informed Gary Goldsmith, Kate's uncle, that they had carried out an undercover operation run by Mazher Mahmood, the legendary investigation editor of the paper known as the 'Fake Sheikh', before publication in accordance with Press Complaints Commission guidelines. Kate decided to break the news to William when they went out the evening before. Never had that old truism about being able to choose your friends while being stuck with your family and relatives been more appropriate. Over the years, William had learned to live with it. Now, by association with the Royal Family, it was Kate's turn. The newspaper exposed Goldsmith's darker side, showing him to be a cocaine-proffering millionaire who spent much of his life idling around Ibiza. It was only a matter to time before this particular time bomb would go off right under Kate, and with it, some thought, her chances of becoming a royal bride.

The reporters had filmed him with his belly hanging over the kitchen table, as he cut a line of cocaine to snort through a bank note. It was an enduring image of the black sheep of the Middleton family plastered across the front page. He was caught red-handed telling undercover reporters on a secret camera, 'I can get cocaine delivered to your door.' He bragged about his friendship with William and claimed his niece and the prince were weeks from announcing their engagement. He also boasted that William and Kate were due to revisit his crudely named La Maison de Bang Bang – or House of Sex – for a romantic break that summer, even joking that he would give the bride way.

'Yeah, so they all turn up with their MI6 to guard them. My first words to Prince William were, "Oi . . . Did you break my glass pyramids?" ' he unwittingly blurted to male and female undercover reporters. He went on, 'He and a pal had been throwing balls around and broke all these ornamental pyramids I had – loads of them. We got people stopping, camping outside our house. My friends were here teaching William how to mix [music on DJ decks]. Yeah, it was brilliant. And they told him he needs a shout, "The King's in da house!" He's a very friendly guy.'

Chatting about his unfortunate niece's pending nuptials did not bother him either. 'They're talking about an announcement later this year.' Then he joked, 'I'll be giving her away. I'll be the Duke of Slough . . . I'm going to be upfront. I want a speaking part.'

Clearly, for Mr Goldsmith discretion was not the better part of valour. For Kate and her mother Carole, Goldsmith's older sister, it was an intimidating disaster. The devil was in the detail and the hapless Goldsmith gave plenty of detail. Prince Charles, ever supportive, sent her a message of support urging Kate to put it out of her mind. Royals are well versed in handling family crises. The method is to say nothing and wait for it to pass. Kate had taken a lot of dissension, with snobbery, perhaps, at the root of much of it. Most was aimed unfairly at her mother Carole. Kate remained cool, while Carole, 'spitting blood' at the *News of the World*'s exposé, called a family meeting urging them not to let the side down. As ever, Charles was right: with time, the moment and the embarrassment passed. Kate knew she would have to toughen up if she was to be a royal bride.

If there was any doubt that Kate's place was in jeopardy due to her family's unsavoury behaviour, her safety was soon apparent. She had already twice represented William at royal weddings: at the first, the wedding of Peter Phillips and Autumn Kelly, she met the Queen.. On both occasions, Kate freely mingled with her boyfriend's close relatives. This time, however, full of smiles at the Salzburg wedding of friend Chiara Hunt, sister of Olivia Hunt, who went to St Andrew's University with them, Kate had her man.

And on 14 August 2009 it looked like the entrance of a fully fledged princess. Kate, tanned and relaxed from her recent holiday in the Caribbean and looking stunning in a white dress under a blue silk coat, emerged from a silver people carrier flanked by four of William's Scotland Yard Protection Officers. Most guests had walked into the Wellington Barracks near Buckingham Palace for the ceremony, but not Kate: she was chauffeur-driven inside the compound along with three of William's friends. The prince and his brother Harry, both ushers, had arrived an hour early with the groom at the barracks' Guards Chapel. William had just walked Kate down the aisle after van Cutsem had tied the knot. He went to shake the groom's hand and to congratulate his bride, Alice Hadden-Paton, when Nicholas saw the opportunity to tease his friend. 'You'll be next,' he said.

It must have dawned on William that he had been with Kate far longer than most of his close pals – and more and more of them were already married. Van Cutsem's comment was meant only as a joke – but it must have touched a nerve. The princes have known van Cutsem, whose father Hugh is a close friend of Prince Charles, all their lives. Nicholas, like Harry an officer in the Household Cavalry, was about to head out to Afghanistan and was joined by fellow soldiers at his wedding reception. Even Prince Harry was joking about it. When pressed about when his brother was going to put everyone out of their misery while on a charity trip to Barbados in January 2010 he shrugged his shoulders and joked that, if the date leaked out, his brother would probably change all the plans.

A few weeks before the van Cutsem wedding William and Kate had checked into a holiday home as a married couple, the woefully unoriginal Mr and Mrs Smith. This was a treat for William's 27th birthday, but any hopes the famously shy couple had of a private break were dashed when William's brother Harry and a bunch of friends tagged along too. The ordinariness of the couple's made-up names mirrored that of the ones Charles and Camilla famously used to refer to themselves in code: Fred and Gladys. Soon, Kate's surname would be Wales not Smith; and as a royal duchess, which she should become on her marriage, she would not have to worry about making bookings herself: she would have a coterie of staff to do that for her.

That said, the couple's royal future would be different from the lives of other Princes and Princesses of Wales. After all, William has made it clear that he will not be limited to a walk-on part in the British monarchy. At a meeting of the Princes' Charities Forum in 2009, which was set up three years earlier, he said he would gradually increase his number of engagements but develop his 'own way' of doing things. 'You could turn up and open things. However, it is about bringing some other things into it as well. There's a time and place for being an ornament, shaking hands and showing support, but I think there is a lot more [to be done] by actually doing stuff' he said.

He put this into good effect on his first official visit to New Zealand and a private one to Australia in January 2010. I accompanied the prince on the trip as one of the accredited correspondents. What struck me was his poise and natural nobility. The trip for me, somebody who had watched at first hand as his mother had wowed the crowds around the world on official foreign forays, evoked memories of the past. His performance mirrored Diana's popular foreign walkabouts and his father's campaigning work for the environment. However, there was something more about him. As we chatted in a bar in Wellington, he was relaxed and at ease among the media, just as his mother had been. If he had been a little nervous when he delivered his first speech representing his grandmother the Queen as he opened the Supreme Court in New Zealand's capital, he did not show it.

Outside, before his arrival, a group of republican supporters had gathered. They had been shouting for about an hour, but, as soon as his car swept into view and he stepped out, the shouting stopped. Even the republicans seemed fascinated by this new-generation royal. Afterwards, despite the protestors, he came out and worked the crowd for around 45 minutes. It was a brilliant performance. In Australia, the coverage was just as breathless, much to the annoyance of the local republicans. When William saw at first hand the devastation caused in the Black Saturday bushfires in Victoria that killed 173 people in February 2009, they were unimpressed despite his rapturous welcome. The Victorian convener of the Australian Republican Movement, Simon Bateman, said William's visit had generated a lot of breathless media coverage.

'It seems to be lots more a cult of celebrity than anything else,' Bateman said. 'I mean we had a lot of media when Paris Hilton was here too, so I'm not sure what it [the trip] means. It doesn't really mean much in terms of how we live and are as Australians.'

Mr Bateman's comments were not representative of the warmth he had received by both supporters and opponents of the institution of monarchy; the Australian peoples' monarchy As Diana's son, as far as the Australians were concerned he had a special dispensation. Any punches thrown at William he rode like a pro. He had a little help too, for the Queen had called in a team of top Royal mandarins dubbed the 'Three Wise Men' to watch over the future King to make sure he didn't put a foot wrong. Career diplomat Sir David Manning, her brilliant former private secretary Lord Janvrin and her new top aide Christopher Geidt were all drafted in to sharpen up her grandson's public performance. By 2010, things had moved up a notch or two. Sir David was there to teach him about diplomacy and world affairs, Lord Janvrin to cover his charity role, and Christopher will assist on strategy and overview. It was a delicate balancing act and all were conscious that, while promoting William they had to be careful not to eclipse his father Prince Charles. That was difficult. 'We've never had a monarch, an heir to the throne and the second in line to the throne all competing before,' one senior courtier explained to me.

When William came to make his keynote speech in Melbourne at the end of his tour of Australia, he thanked Australian girls for continuing the tradition of kissing members of the Royal Family. He made a light-hearted reference to an infamous kiss for his father, the Prince of Wales, from a model named Jane Priest on a Perth beach in 1979 – though he wrongly believed, the incident had taken place on Sydney's Bondi beach. At Government House, and in the build-up to Australia Day, he told 1,000 guests: 'Being in Australia is the realisation of a dream. As far back as I can remember, I have heard from my family about the wonders of Australia, and the hospitality and friendship of the Australian people. 'My father had such a great time here at school – and is still misty-eyed about an immortal moment on Bondi, when an Australian beauty planted a smacker on his cheek. It's good to see this tradition is continuing!

'I also remember my mother coming back from her time here in 1996, telling me what a profound impression this country had made on her, and how much she loved Australia. Three days here and now I know why.'

Prince William, who was ending his first foreign trip there as an adult, also made an affectionate reference to Prince Harry: 'And, of course, there's that other guy with the ginger hair – who just never ever stops banging on about you, and how I haven't lived because I haven't been to Australia. Because of this, and because of the respect the world has for your unique way of life, for your vibrancy, your straightforward ways, your classic sense of humour, I have been longing to return. The last time I was here I was nine months old and seeing the world from a very low level – certainly not one from which to appreciate this awesome place.

'What has struck me during this visit to the southern hemisphere is what "shared heritage" actually means. It really is about core values and our way of life. It really is about humour and decency. It is about courage and an ability to face down adversity.'

He went on, 'What an exciting place Australia is! This truly is a country for the 21st century . . . I only wish I had a little longer to see a bit more of Melbourne, this legendary city of sport and culture. But, if I may, I'll be back!'

Keynote speeches are important, but for me one moment that I witnessed personally captured the essence of this man, a genuinely caring soul of whom his mother and father would and should be proud. Away from the cameras in the fire-ravaged mountains he went to meet a woman whose home had been ravaged by the devastating forest fires in Victoria. She was a genuine, proud Australian. Like so many people from that wonderful country she had no airs and graces, but was still conscious of William's royal status. Modern royalty, even the Queen, do not expect people to curtsey to them. They are relaxed about it. It is only the media that get overexcited if someone touches the Queen, as a former Australian prime minister, Paul Keating, found to his cost and was dubbed 'The Lizard of Oz' by the 'Pom' press. In the excitement this woman forgot to use William's title 'Prince' as she shook his hand. She instantly realised the error of her ways, and apologised profusely, flushing scarlet with embarrassment. William, with a warm a smile, reassuringly touched her arm and whispered, 'William is fine, don't worry.' He reminded me of his mother at that moment; and, away from the cheering fans, staged protests, the overhyped headlines and barbed criticism from desperate republicans determined finally to get their way and jettison the monarchy from their shores, it was *the* moment of the tour. I for one was proud that he was my sovereign prince. The Royal Family, after all, have made it clear that if the Australian people want an elected head of state instead of a king or queen, they are more than happy for them to have their way. That, of course, does not mean they will give up without a fight, not for them, but for the people of that country who like things just as they are and don't want to change.

Undoubtedly, there will be those who now see the dynamic new double act of William and Kate as a stellar royal couple who can save the monarchy Down Under at a stroke. One tour, a lot of smiling and cute quips and photo-ops and, hey presto!, all will be well and the Australians will be hooked. In the fallout from the engagement – and even in the preceding months – Channel 7's flagship programmes *The Morning Show* and *Sunrise* called me in the early hours London time to discuss the royal story. They could not get enough of Kate and William, nor too, it seemed, could the Australian people, according to the feedback.

The palace and indeed William himself want one of his and Kate's first overseas tours as a married couple to be of Australia and New Zealand. Canada would follow soon afterwards. It will probably dampen republican fever there for a while, but in my view the chances of William and Kate ever becoming the King and Queen of Australia are at this moment in time slim. Even if palace and government officials are keen to capitalise on the popularity of the new generation and wow the crowds there, it is debatable their influence will be able to turn the inevitable tide. Time will tell. In the preceding summer, Australia's government indicated that the country should drop the British monarchy after Queen Elizabeth. Welsh-born Australian Prime Minster Julia Gillard of the centre-left Labour Party said, 'What I would like to see as Prime Minister is that we work our way through to an agreement on a model for the republic. The appropriate time for this is when we see the monarch change. Obviously I'm hoping for Queen Elizabeth that she lives a long and happy life and having watched her mother I think there's every chance she will.'

That said, the Queen was rightly delighted with the way the five-day tour had gone. William had taken another important step forward in his apprenticeship as future King. In the words of Jamie Lowther-Pinkerton, his private secretary and wisest counsel, it has enabled him to 'learn the ropes'. It was important that the prince should have a chance to learn the ropes before his marriage to Kate. It was important too that he would take the lead. After all, then, and only then, could he be ready to prepare his young wife for what to expect when they stepped out together on the world stage.

When William returned in triumph from Australia and New Zealand he seemed more confident. His relief was palpable. He was more relaxed in public, and the prospect of his future life as the lead player in the royal goldfish bowl perhaps seemed a little less daunting. But, just when the world's media could not get enough of their new star, the apparatchiks at the palace decided it was best to put the genie back in the bottle. He had, after all, still to finish his course as an RAF search-and-rescue pilot. He passed out in September 2010; he was at last ready for his day job. It had been 'challenging' but it was something he just had to do; another box ticked on his wish list of what he wanted to achieve as a single man. Now he is ready for the next stage in his preparation as husband, working prince and eventually King.

The announcement of the royal engagement may have been a traditional affair, but inherently Kate and William are a thoroughly modern royal couple. Like so many young couples, they lived together at first, setting up home, in their case, for the previous eight months in Anglesey, where William, as Flight Lieutenant Wales, serves as a helicopter pilot at the nearby Royal Air Force Base Valley flying search-and-rescue missions. In fact, within 48 hours of the announcement he was back at the controls of his helicopter, involved in a mission to save a stricken man. Gym worker Greg Watkins was stuck up Mount Snowdon, the highest peak in Wales, in stormy conditions after suffering a suspected heart attack. The 28-year-old prince was part of a four-man crew. 'If it wasn't for him and the rest of his crew, I'd be dead,' Watkins revealed later. 'Hearing his helicopter getting nearer and nearer was the best sound I've ever heard. He and his crew saved my life.'

Hero lifesaver as well as Prince Charming! The palace could not have wished for better headlines than if they had written them themselves

William's life was one of contrasts: the excitement of his day job, the expectations of his title and royal position and the peace of his private life with Kate. Far away from the media glare in this isolated and windswept part of North Wales, they made their first home in a secluded whitewashed farmhouse. There they tried to lead a normal life, shopping at the local supermarket, picking up takeout dinner, and having an occasional drink at the pub. I had revealed that the couple had moved in together in the *News of the World* under the headline WILLS AND KATE'S LOVE NEST. It had caused quite a stir at the time with the palace asking the media not to specify where their rented farmhouse was situated, for security reasons. Of course, in these dangerous times of international terrorism it made sense, even though everyone knows where the Queen, Prince Charles and other senior royals live, including Camilla, who has a second home, Ray Mill House, which costs the taxpayer millions to protect. To me it was a clear sign that the wedding announcement would follow. He could have taken officer's quarters at his RAF base, but wanted instead to enjoy domestic bliss with Kate when off duty. They are expected to live there for the foreseeable future. I wrote in the same article, 'We have also been told the couple have "an understanding" that their eight-year relationship *will* end in marriage – but probably not until 2011 at the earliest.' It was spot on.

Kate, like a previous much-loved Queen Consort, Queen Alexandra – William's great-great-great grandmother and wife of the philandering but respected Edward VII – is a keen photographer. She would while away her days photographing the spectacular landscape when William was on duty or she was not working at her family firm in Berkshire. On clear days the landscape is spectacular, with white sandy beaches overlooked only by the grazing cattle and sheep. Around every winding lane the skies alter and the light changes – a wildlife and photographer's paradise. Here the seabirds embrace the wind, solitary couples walk undisturbed and almost everyone has a dog. It is a coastline of lighthouses and rainbows, ancient churches and small villages, where life has changed little for decades, and a world away from Buckingham Palace, the Mall and Westminster Abbey. Dewi Davies, North Wales's tourism director, said, 'It's a great place to live, it's a great place to holiday. And, of course, it's fantastic scenery you can see all around.'

Holyhead is the main town on the tip of Anglesey, where ferries come and go from and to Ireland. The entertainment centre is at the Empire Arena, a bedraggled building where paint peels and has long since disappeared from the green lettering at the front of the building. Staff talk of their pride in having William and Kate living in their midst like any ordinary couple. Across the road a rundown shop advertises 'tutus and tiaras', dresses and evening wear, but Kate is unlikely to shop there. However, the couple often shop at the local Tesco on a trading estate on the edge of town like so many other ordinary people.

Anglesey's great charm lies off the beaten track in its glorious beaches, well maintained forests and wealth of seabirds and wildlife. Rhosneigr is a small town where many of the personnel from RAF Valley live in married quarters. The distinctive yellow Sea Kings no longer attract attention but the roar of the training jets is unmistakeable. Locals speak of William and his fellow pilots frequenting Sullivan's. The owner of the local gift shop has wedding planners for sale and would be delighted to welcome William and Kate. She speaks of William's reputation for politeness and how he is 'just as his mother would have wanted'.

At the nearby village of Rhoscolyn is the reasonably priced, modern and tastefully renovated White Eagle. A meal for two with wine costs just £45. A short walk from the pub, packed in summer and weekends, are the dunes and wild sea. The couple's preferred mode of transport is his Ducati motorbike with his lady Kate on the back. With their helmets on they are anonymous, and that is how they like it. But their determination to continue this lifestyle could prove difficult. They both know it will be different now.

Kate will have to get used to being guarded 24 hours a day by elite officers from Scotland Yard's armed SO14 Royal Protection Department. They will keep her safe, whereas Mr Mohammed Al Fayed's bodyguards failed Princess Diana. William has got used to having them around. He has good relationships with the men and women who are there as his last line of defence. In their care I have no doubt our new princess will be safe from harm. Ken Wharfe served as an inspector in Scotland Yard's elite Royalty and Diplomatic Protection Department from 1986 to 2002, guarding Diana and her sons as well as training a new generation of SO14 officers before he left. He says Kate will have to get used to life without freedom. To stay safe she must be compliant; it is the only way.

'Those chosen to guard Kate will be working off the Diana template of compliance, where the exchange of information, trust and honesty is two-way. William is a veteran in receipt of protection – he has clearly briefed Kate on the high and low points of personal security, and indications are that this transition will be relatively painless for her.' Wise words.

The engagement announcement led to a wave of good publicity for the Royal Family. But it was not all good reading, particularly for Prince Charles. An ICM poll in the *News of the World* signalled that the people of Britain wanted change – they sent a resounding signal that William and Kate are the people's choice to be the next King and Queen. The poll, published on 21 November 2010, revealed that 64 per cent of people want the newly engaged royal couple in the top job after the Queen. Just 19 per cent – under one in five – wanted the crown to pass to Charles and Camilla. It must have been a blow to the dutiful and longest-serving heir to the British throne in history. He had worked tirelessly to win back the favour of his people since his popularity hit an all-time low after the divorce from Diana in 1996, and her subsequent death a year later. It could, too, prove a point of tension in the loving relationship with his son and heir as they vie for the role of 'shadow King' in the Queen's dotage. The findings came just after the Charles admitted for the first time – in an interview with Brian Williams of the US's leading network NBC – that his wife Camilla could be Queen. Until that moment, the palace had fudged the issue, insisting she would never be crowned and would be called 'Princess Consort' when Charles ascended the throne. They even issued a statement to that effect. This was, of course, nonsense. If Charles becomes King, it is Camilla's right, with more than 400 years of precedence already establishing that fact.

But royalty is on ever-changing sand. Nothing, despite its appearance of stability and tradition, is ever set in stone. Most people said they would prefer the crown to bypass Charles. It was a stunning reversal in the popularity of the Royal Family under Wills and Kate, with 72 per cent believing the young couple's marriage will strengthen the monarchy.

Meanwhile, the Prime Minister, the Right Honourable David Cameron, when asked about the issue, told Sky News in November 2010 that he was 'a big Camilla fan'. He felt that the country was getting to know her and seeing that she is a 'warm-hearted person with a big sense of humour and a big heart'.

Using words that bring to mind Tony Blair's 1997 description of William's mother as the 'people's princess', Cameron added that Camilla would like to be 'a queen of people's hearts', adding, 'But it's too early to talk about these things and I'm sure that it will all be discussed and debated.'

Diana famously said that Charles was not suited for the 'top job' in her devastating BBC *Panorama* interview with Martin Bashir. Since that rapier thrust – watched by millions – Charles has worked tirelessly to rebuild his public image and popularity. But despite palace statements that Camilla would not be Queen he has been secretly plotting to make her so for years with or without the Queen's approval, as I revealed in September 2008, under the headline CHARLES: I WANT CAMILLA AS QUEEN. He has always believed that it would be an 'affront' to him when he is King if his wife is not bestowed what he sees as her proper title.

His U-turn on what he officially announced when he married his divorced long-term lover five years ago will infuriate those who believe Camilla should never be Queen. Opponents say it is wrong because Camilla's relationship with Charles caused the breakdown of his marriage to Diana.

Constitutional experts say it is possible for Charles to give up the right to the throne in favour of his son – but it would prove difficult. He would have to sign an Act of Renunciation once he had government backing, in the realms too. Of course, William would have to want to ascend the throne, which he does not. He more than anyone understands the need for continuity, the need for him and his new bride to learn the job, first as Prince and Princess of Wales and then the top job.

By demonstrating serious social concern, just like his mother and father before him, and by choosing a bride who shares these concerns, William has shown himself to be a prince of the people. When he does become heir to the throne as Prince of Wales he will inherit too its royal crest consisting of three white feathers emerging from a gold coronet. The ribbon below the coronet bears the motto 'Ich dien', German for 'I serve'. William, I have no doubt, will live up to expectation and not take his position for granted. It is not in his nature to fail. Taking the easy course is not an option; it is not in Kate's nature, either. He knows that he and his new bride will have to work hard to win over the hearts and minds of a new generation, a generation raised to be less deferential, particularly when it comes to monarchy. He will, I am sure, continue the Windsor dynasty's knack of moulding itself to the times through which it lives. He has made it clear he wants to make a difference with action and not just words. Now, with Kate at his side, they can show that monarchy is not only a 21st-century institution that matters, but one that has real strength and purpose too.